STATE FORMATION, AGRARIAN GROWTH AND SOCIAL CHANGE IN FEUDAL SOUTH INDIA

c. AD 600-1200

State Formation, Agrarian Growth and Social Change in Feudal South India

c. AD 600-1200

RAMENDRA NATH NANDI

MANOHAR
2026

First published 2000
Reprinted 2026

ISBN 978-81-7304-290-4

Published by
Ajay Kumar Jain *for*
Manohar Publishers & Distributors
4753/23 Ansari Road, Daryaganj
New Delhi 110 002

Printed and bound in India

Contents

Abbreviations

ABORI	*Annals of the Bhandarkar Oriental Research Institute*
Ak.	*Arsikere*
ARMAD	*Annual Report of the Mysore Archaeological Department*
ARSIE	*Annual Report on South Indian Epigraphy*
Bl.	Belur
Bp.	Bowringpet
Cd.	Chitradurga
Cg.	Coorg
Ch.	Chamarajnagar
CII	*Corpus Inscriptionum Indicarum*
Cl.	Challakere
Cm.	Chikmaglur
Cn.	Channarayapatna
Cp.	Chennapatna
Ct.	Chintamani
Dg.	Davangere
EC	*Epigraphia Carnatica*
EI	*Epigraphia Indica*
Gu.	Gubbi
Gn.	Gundlupet
Hg.	Heggadadevankote
Hk.	Holalkere
Hn.	Hasan
Hs.	Humsur
Ht.	Hoskote
IA	*Indian Antiquary*
IHQ	*Indian Historical Quarterly*
JAHRS	*Journal of the Andhra Historical Research Society*

JBBRAS	*Journal of the Bombay Branch of the Royal Asiatic Society*
JBORS	*Journal of the Bihar and Orissa Research Society*
Jl.	Jagalur
JRASB	*Journal of the Royal Asiatic Society of Bengal*
KI	*Karnataka Inscriptions*
Kl.	Kolar
Kp.	Koppa
Ma.	Magadi
MAR	*Mysore Archeological Report*
Mb.	Mulbagal
Md.	Mandya
Mg.	Mudgere
Mj.	Manjarabad
Mk.	Molakamuru
Mr.	Malur
Ng.	Nagamangala
Nj.	Nanjangud
Nr.	Nagar
Sb.	Sorab
SBE	*Sacred Books of the East*
Sd.	Sidlaghatta
Sh.	Shimoga
Si.	Sira
SII	*South Indian Inscriptions*
Sk.	Shikarpur
Sn.	Srinivasapur
T. Narsipur	Tirumakadal Narsipur
Tl.	Tirthahalli
Tm.	Tumkur
Tp.	Tiptur
Yl.	Yelandur

Note on Transliteration

a	अ	ā	आ	i	इ	ī	ई		
u	उ	ū	ऊ	ṛ	ऋ	e	ए		
ai	ऐ	o	ओ	au	औ				
k	क्	kh	ख्	g	ग्	gh	घ्	ṅ	ङ्
c	च्	ch	छ्	j	ज्	jh	झ्	ñ	ञ्
ṭ	ट्	th	ठ्	ḍ	ड्	ḍh	ढ्	ṇ	ण्
t	त्	th	थ्	d	द्	dh	ध्	n	न्
p	प्	ph	फ्	b	ब्	bh	भ्	m	म्
y	य्	r	र्	l	ल्	v	व्	ś	श्
ṣ	ष्	s	स्	h	ह्				

anusvāra	ं	ṃ
visarga	:	ḥ

Introduction

The centuries which intervened between the rise of imperial Pallavas and the decline of the Cola empire have long been a focal period of research in early south Indian history. The use of the term 'early medieval' in respect of this period underlined its distinction from the preceding ancient phase as well as from the succeeding Turko-Afghan period. In recent times there has been some attempt to define and explain this distinction in social, political, economic and religious terms. All these studies put together outline the substantial nature of transformation which the society was undergoing about this time. However, it would be naive to think that such transition could take place without difinitive changes in the mode of production. This awareness seems to have led some scholars to apply the model of feudal social formation to India, notwithstanding persistant formulations to the contrary in both Western and Eastern writings.

The wide divergance of opinion on the nature of early medieval social formation springs mainly from the articulation of social immutability in traditional commentary on Asian history and society. In the Indian context, the chief marker of an unchanging social order is the Hindu caste organization. On the political front such immutability is said to be represented by the inevitability of despotic rule. An economic dimension was added to it when Marx developed the hypothesis of an unchanging Asiatic Mode of Production. The effect of all this was to infect intellectual minds in both Asia and Europe with the image of 'indolent peoples' and 'sluggish societies'.

The idea of an inferior and habitually subservient East, first surfaced in the writings of ancient Greek philosophers. But, during the late middle ages it developed into an ideological ploy for commercial exploitation and political intervention in Asia by the colonial powers of Europe. Understandably, the most important aspect of this ideology was the concept of oriental despotism which derived strength from the supposed inherent incapacities of eastern peoples. Some of these incapacities related to the qualities of body and mind while others related to material conditions of life such as absence of towns, self sufficiency of autarchic villages, absence of private property in land and absence of private enterprise in irrigation. The idea of self-sufficient villages, which was first suggested by Hegel and was structured on the 'political indifference of common Hindus' would appear to stress, as 'indolence of body and mind' does in the writings of Montesquieu, the psychological basis of oriental despotism.

The influence of these traditional ideas on the writings of Karl Marx and Frederick Engels is evident from the Marx's repeated assertions about the 'stagnation and immutability of the oriental world'. The hypothesis of Asiatic Mode of Production which replaces a psychological explanation of oriental despotism by a 'reasoned' economic explanation would thus appear to put the image of 'unchanging east' on firmer ground and deny all possibilities of social development to Asian peoples. However the two writers show little firmness of views either in regard to the various components of thier construct or the relative significance of these components. This is besides the fact that in a 'conceptual slippage' the Asiatic Mode of Production was applied to non-Asian American societies of Mexico and Peru.[1] Attention has also been drawn to hesitant views of Marx on the absence of private property in land, the 'real key' to the understanding of oriental society and one of the main constituents of the Asiatic Mode of Production.[2] In recent years the Marxian formulation has received renewed exposure to anthropological[3] and archaeological[4] data resulting in considerable marginalization of the concept.

Despite this and other criticisms of the immutability idea the overall Western perception of pre-modern societies remains un-affected. This is evident from persistent attempts to stereotype political formations in pre-capitalist societies. For instance, it is argued that in traditional societies state formation was a continuing process and state itself was a system of tribute extraction.[5] The feudal state is said to be no exception to this. This seems a little heavily weighed in favour of a determined political class, simulating the 'oriental despot' engaged in the extraction of tribute and taxes. In certain cases, however, the political class itself may be the product of challenges in the economic sector. The military and juridical aspects of the feudal political system are also no less important. Perhaps the problem of feudal state needs to be consider in the wider perspective of feudal social formation.

The understanding of a feudal social formation has been deeply influenced by personal interpretations about the nature of feudalism and what constitutes its most important factor. To a large extent these divergent views are products of differing research areas undertaken by each group of scholars. In every case a particular aspect of feudal development has been the focus of incisive investigation enriched by intense recovery of related data. In certain cases these diverse models may reflect regional peculiarities of the feudal experience though none may have any universal application.

For the British historians of late nineteenth century, the most important feature of feudalism was its military basis.[6] The preference for a military perspective is often said to be the hang over of imperialist pride. Compared to this, the French historians consider feudalism in terms of economic change and perceived attitudes. Accordingly, a subject peasantry, widespread use of fiefs or service tenements, supremacy of a class of specialized warriors and relationship of aid and protection are identified as the most important determinants of a feudal development.[7] Arguing in the same Marxist vein,[8] Wickham underlines the mode of production as the crucial feature of feudalism. For him, alteration of surplus, augmented by coercive force, characterized the transition from slavery to serfdom. The institution of feudal lordship has also been widely commented by scholars. For instance, Ganshoff's[9] interpretation of feudal lordship lays stress on legal ties associated with the land which supported feudalism,but Duby[10] who stipulates three feudal ages in place of two proposed by Bloch and Ganshoff, however draws a distinction between lordship over land and lordship over rights. Opinions also differ on the primary function of lordship. For some it is the lord's role in local government. For others it is control of resources.[11]

Emphasising the military aspect of feudalism, an English historian of the Norman period has argued that the role of castle was an essential part of feudal society.[12] The 'defensive earthwork' is stated to be the symbol of a feudal society, a base for the military activity which was the *raison d'être* of feudal lordship. Subsequent research however seems to relegate the military and administrative functions of castle or rampart to the economic motivations of lordship. At many places the defences of a site are said to be secondary to the site's prime function as an economic estate centre.[13] Moreover, the 'defensible sites' do not represent all aspects of defensive behaviour. For instance, soldiers can be deployed defensively away from any defensible sites. In the Indian situation, the mobile army camps might well represent such defensive deployment of troops although very little has been done to understand these issues in the light of archaeological record. Since lordships could exist without forts and ramparts, attention must also converge on differential pottery scatters and finds of prestige goods in important village sites with recorded history suggesting status and seigneurial centres. In the peninsular region of India such centres may not be difficult to identify on the basis of epigraphic data.

Although the idea of feudal mode of production is an integral part of the Marxian concept of historical materialism it need not be exclusive to either the Marxian model of social development or to European history which Marx used to refurbish his idea. As such, the feudal phase may appear and disappear irrespective of two nodal points conceived by Marx namely slavery and capitalism. In other words the feudal mode of production may surface in any part of the world and under very different compulsions. However, it must fulfil certain essentials of feudal polity and economy, if not in form at least in substance. And, where the model is feudal Europe one must not shy away from the determinants of European experience. Sometimes the feudal experience may be widely varied within the same country as can be seen from the European experience itself. Clearly, the task needs to rule out any kind of generalization or simplification. A handful of scholars who derived their inspiration from the Marxian formulations of history however could not fall in line with the traditional European perception of an unchanging social order in India and the Marxian construct of Asiatic Mode of Production which too strengthened such a perception. But the methodology needed to question such presumption and situate a feudal social formation on the basis of gross unflinching data seems to be missing from most articulations on the subject. No wonder, perceptions of a possible feudal development in India have been of a bizarre nature ranging from the idea of a paramount ruler with tax-paying autonomous chiefs to that of a class of priestly feudatories called Brahman-Sāmantas.

Methodologically speaking, there is little evidence of a rigorous concept which can be tested on the basis of quantifiable data. In the absence of a determinable model of feudal development articulations on the subject seldom go beyond the realm of conjectures and notional constructs. As regards data recovery scholars generally rely on inscriptional and literary data of a disparate nature and uneven merit. The uneven value of inscriptional evidence might be a good marker of the uneven nature of feudal development itself. Excavation of early medieval sides, with or without mound formation may also confirm this. But there is no awareness yet of any archaeological reconstruction of lordship centres either in terms of defensive earthwork or on the basis of resource control so well suggested by the construction of irrigation tanks, subjugation of rural crafts and the foundation of towns and trading marts.

A word needs to be said about the much articulated idea of a class of Brahmana-Sāmantas supposedly resulting from the creation of Brahmana freeholdings.[14] A situation in which priestly functionaries offering sacrifices to fire or worshipping idols in temples have to stand up and pose as armed feudatories would be a precarious one for the growth of political feudalism. Sāmanta or feudatory is an armed person bound to his immediate lord by contractual relations of political interdependence. A Brahmana priest on the other hand was neither an armed person nor bound by any military or administrative obligations. Further, the fiefs or service tenements were an essential feature of feudal polity whereas a Brahmana freeholding was a form of religious charity which could exist irrespective of feudal polity. Similarly, the fief-holders or the holders of service tenements formed the essence of a political class whereas the Brahmana freeholders were no more than adjuncts of such a class.

Some degree of precision is also necessary in determining the various essentials of feudal polity. This is imperative in view of simplifications attempted by some scholars to implant Sāmanta feudatories and lord-vassal relations on the Śaka-Kuṣāṇa polity of India.[15] Perhaps, a superior-subordinate relationship of political nature can not automatically pass for lord-vassal relationship. In other words the provincial and district level governors of the Śaka-Kuṣāṇa rulers were not feudatories in the strict sense of the term. Nor the areas ruled by these subordinates were, like the fief, constituted domains of private military authority. One should also distinguish between the administrative divisions of a kingdom and fiefs held on the condition of mounted mail service. Similarly, the grant of a piece of land to a political subordinate may not by itself constitute a fief. The person so benefited may simply be entitled to the usufruct from the land without any right to free disposal, adjudication or estate honours.

Some amount of rethinking is also necessary in regard to the problem of origins. Scholars have frequently turned attention to political decentralization and decay of towns as the chief causes of a feudal development although both of these await their own convincing explanations. In traditional India, where an empire or kingdom has largely been an aggregate of autonomous areas of political and economic authority without any organic cohesion and held together by conquest and coercion, political decentralization would be a recurrent feature but not feudalism. Perhaps the focus should be on political insecurity of an intense nature which would drive two or more armed persons of uneven strength into contractual relations of aid and protection and develop a hierarchical networking of political interdependence. Widespread insecurity could be as much the result of weak monarchical authority as it could be of conflicting local ambitions. The leaders of powerful kin-communities who were emboldened by the king's weaknesses could well be trying to gain more land and resources at the expense of others.

As regards decay of towns, the archaeological record of urban sites between the fourth and sixth centuries seems quite obliging though it would call for considerable space of time to give rise, if at all, to a feudal political order. This is hardly likely when scholars trace the growth of feudalism from the fourth century itself and even before.

Any serious study of feudal social formation must also distinguish between a largely subsistence-based agrarian economy of big villages and petty administrative headquarters which followed the decay of towns and a feudal political economy which, depending on conditions other than these, may have surfaced in certain parts of the country. In other words, there is no direct causal connection between the decline of a market economy of towns and the emergence of a feudal polity and economy. The decline of a market economy of towns itself was far from a uniform development. For, parts of peninsular India are known to have experience long distance commercial exchange and the use of minted money till at least the middle of the eighth century. The early Gupta phase which is said to coincide with the beginnings of urban decay also witnessed extension of India's trading activities to South-East Asia.

The expressions such as 'closed economy', 'natural economy' or 'subsistence economy' which are freely used to denote the post-urban economic order and symptomise a feudal milieu are also highly imprecise. It would be naive to think that the decay of towns automatically led to subsistence production or that such production was entirely bereft of exchange processes. Perhaps it is more appropriate to characterize the development as the relapse of a market economy of towns into a low surplus economy of peasant localities and petty administrative headquarters. The surplus was low not because of any actual shortfall in the existing level of production but because the hinterland had to take on a larger number of surplus appropriators with various types of chartered entitlement. These people were turning to the countryside because inter-regional circulation of goods which kept the urban places throbbing was fast dwindling in the absence of good roads, lack of security, failure of administrative coordination and scarcity of an acceptable medium of commodity exchange.

Administrative failure which resulted from inherent corruption and inefficiency may have been further accentuated by king's weakness, dynastic infighting, court intrigues and usurpation of power. This must have been aggravated by unstable conditions in the agricultural and commercial sectors. Agricultural production may have suffered on account of low technology, floods, draughts and pillage by marching armies. Commercial exchanges on the other hand suffered from rising incidence of highway brigandage, absence of communicable roads and low returns.

Trade and urbanism was also affected by changes in the brahmanical social organization and the emerging norms of behaviour. A society which, on grounds of purity and pollution, consistently theorised against towns and urban vocations, extra territorial travel, lending money on interest, certain conspicuous consumptions and fattered the trading and artisan castes with social disabilities could not but constrain large-scale commodity production. Such theorising is often part of a religious ideology which aspiring elites and interest groups utilized to establish, challenge or change a specific social order and to transform the 'arbitrary' into 'necessary'. Understandably, the internal compulsions of social development in India would need much greater focussing than the percussion effects of some external event.

In the ultimate analysis these would be a much grater handicap to commercial activities than a supposed absence of minted money. Indeed, the relative absence of the actual finds of minted money between the seventh and tenth centuries need to address itself to the limitations of field archaeology in India. The urban places which centered round garrisons and petty administrative headquarters during the early medieval centuries are yet to be properly excavated. Many of these places grew up in the countryside and kept on shifting leaving little scope for mound formation. The three capitals from which the Cālukyas of Badami ruled during the short span of less than three hundred years would be a case in point. It is also important to remember that in an age of diminishing money circulation the metallic value of minted coins may have fetched handsome returns to any one offering these to prospective buyers.

The constitution of fiefdoms and service tenements also depended on the military and administrative expediency. In small and relatively docile areas a small band of itinerant officers may still be useful in gathering revenues and maintaining law and order with the help of local people. The epigraphic records of the period frequently refer to these officers and the goods and services requisitioned by them from villagers. Compared to this, fiefs and service tenements would be a normal feature in areas torm by perpetual insecurity.

With polity undergoing a feudal development the economic order could not remain unaffected. However, the study of feudal economy relates not so much to either manorial system or serfdom as to the dynamic of agrarian growth. The manorial system which preceded feudal social formation remain confined to certain parts of feudal Europe.[16] In this sense the manor or the manorial system cannot be considered a universal determinant of feudal economy. As regards serfdom, it may not be difficult to identify increasing presence of a servile labour force often bound to the master's estate. Although the servility was more a result of prevailing conditions of peasant production than of any legal or contractual stipulation it nevertheless represented conditions similar to serfdom. It may also be pertinent to mention that the feudal mode of production never existed in a pure state anywhere in medieval Europe. Probably, the feudal formation can be better understood as a composite system in which other modes of production survived and intertwined with feudalism proper.

The quest of serfdom or a pure feudal mode of production need not however detain us since the principal concern here is to understand the process of agrarian growth and determine the compulsions which motored it at different points of time. Considering these compulsions one might observe three distinct stages of feudal economy between the seventh and twelfth centuries. The incipient stage which roughly covered the seventh and eighth centuries witnessed the networking of the domains of surplus appropriation in fiefs, service tenements, Brahmana freeholdings and the temple *devadāna* holdings enjoying varying degrees of autonomy. As demands increased in the wake of rising non-peasant population in these areas, need was felt to raise production through extension of the arable, new drainage devices, adoption of new crops and labour servility. All these developments are very well documented in the epigraphic records of ninth and tenth centuries which may be characterised as the incubation time. The effects of these developments began to manifest during the ultimate breakthrough stage (eleventh-twelfth centuries) which witnessed large-scale commodity production, recirculation of minted money and revival of urban places.

All these developments could not have been unaccompanied by necessary innovations in the field of technology. Given the mode of production, the extension of the arable, new drainage devices, adoption of new crops and increasing labour servility would suffice to ensure a hike in peasant surpluses. Greater application of rotary motion in certain areas of agro-industrial production would also appear significant in this connection. In view of all this there does not appear to be much substance in the idea of 'constant factor' in technology[17] which is nearly an euphemism for technological stagnation and which tends to refurbish the traditional European thoughts on an unchanging social order in India.

Another familiar refrain in Western writings on Indian history relates to the relegation of the material needs of life to spiritual aspirations. Resounding this notion one scholar observes that irrigation was considered a work of religious merit with the result that during all the known history of southern India we notice inscriptions detailing construction of tanks, dams etc.[18] A close view of the inscriptional corpus of southern India would however reveal that enterprise in irrigation works was most brisk during the eighth-thirteenth centuries when the urge to increase local production of peasant goods was most intense. The instances we have examined do not also oblige the contention that the construction of an irrigation system was beyond the labour resources of a single household. Most of these examples relate to private holdings, but collaboration among individual landholders is also witnessed. Incidentally, the absence of private enterprise in drainage activity and the absence of private ownership of land are said to be the two important determinants of the Asiatic Mode of Production.

The understanding of feudal social formation may remain in complete without some perception of its social religious and economic consequences. One of the important social consequences relates to violent conflicts, between erstwhile collaborators of social production in fiefs, freeholdings and free peasant holdings. Considering a similar situation in feudal Europe some scholars have focussed attention on the plurality of peasant exploitation which in a social world dominated by overlapping claims and powers created latent interstices and discrepancies.[19] The attempt to explain away such discrepancies or conflicts in terms of changing social alliances in a harmonious and assimilative social evolution in India may however appear to be simplistic.[20]

The instances of violence examined in this work involved Brahmana freeholders, feudal lords and peasants. The first to constituted a class of surplus appropriators but never hesitated to fight among themselves. The peasants, on the other hand, were a class of surplus producers whose rights and interests were frequently violated by the Brahmanas and feudal lords leading the peasant to rise in arms. It is the latter type of violence which might be characterized as some kind of class conflict. As for the Indian peasant who lived in habitual subservience to brahmanical norms of social discrimination, resorting to violence for redress of grievances could not however be a matter of choice. He was thus incapable of combining into a common action across distant localities; he was still less capable of any thought of changing the old order. Necessarily, the sporadic incidents of peasant protest remained isolated attempts to counter abuses of landlord.

Compared to these passing episodes of rural unrest, the formation of new subcastes from within the old social order could appear to be more enduring and significant. Gleaning through the history of caste in India one might notice that the period between the eighth and thirteenth centuries was marked by a large number of subcastes which formed as a result of hereditary performance of government offices and hereditary enjoyment of land as salary by certain enterprising families. Unlike the freeholding, most of these families were non-Brahmanas and included farmers, local traders and officers. Together they constituted a large intermediate class between the orthodox Brahmanas and the Adi-Dravidas or their counterparts. The three-tier division of society which today dominates most parts of peninsular India would thus appear to have sharpened and intensified in the wake of early feudal development. Alongside of this one may also notice the emergence of new subcastes of Brahmana functionaries in temple institutions and *agrahāras* or *brahmadeyas*. Many of these can be located today in the same localities.

In the religious sector, particular attention may be drawn to the mushrooming of large masonry temples in the countryside which hoarded social surpluses by mutiplying the number of rituals and priestly officiants. Most of these temples were surfacing in feudal domains and very often enclosed within the fortified area. For the lord, temple tax-holdings were both a means to legitimize lordship rights and economic gains. The nexus between lords and temple priests may have led to considerable disentitlement of land rights in the lower rungs of peasantry besides heightening social distancing on the basis of purity and pollution. A part of the peasant goods was also cornered by Brahmanas in the form of free-feeding centres, which attracted Brahmana destitutes from outside. The religious ethos created by the sanctimonious presence of temples and Brahnanas lent a measure of sanctity to the concerned localities many of which were now being projected as pilgrim destinations or *tīrthas*.

The trends and perspectives of a feudal development outlined above would apply to a broad sub-region of peninsular India comprising eastern Andhra Pradesh or Venginadu of ancient times, the *maidān* tracts of southern Karnataka and the *malnād* areas of north-western Karnataka which furnish the main chunk of data used for the present work. In certain cases, however, the sources belonging to adjoining Maharashtra and Tamil Nadu have been used to facilitate a full view of related developments. The periodization of early feudal age suggested here also emerges from this documentary evidence.

NOTES AND REFERENCES

1. Perry Anderson, *Lineages of the Absolutist State*, London, 1977.
2. R.A.H.L. Gunawardana, 'The Analysis of Pre-Colonial Social Formations in Asia in the Writings of Karl Marx', *The Indian Historical Review*, vol. 2, no. 23, January 1976, pp. 372-3.
3. P. William Mitchell, 'The Hydraulic Hypothesis—A Reappraisal', *Current Anthropology*, XIV, December 1973.
4. P. Hirst and B. Hindess, *Pre-Capitalist Modes of Production*, London, 1975.
5. T.C. Patterson and C.W. Gailey, 'State Formation and Uneven Development', in John Gledhill, Barbara Bender and Mogens Trolle Larsen, eds., *State and Society*, London, 1988.
6. E. Freeman, *The History of the Norman Conquest*, Oxford, Clarendon Press, 1877-9; J. Round, *Feudal England: Historical Studies on the Eleventh and Twelfth Centuries*, London, 1895.
7. Marc Bloch, *Feudal Society*, London, 1961.
8. C. Wickham, 'The other Transition: From Ancient World to Feudalism', *Past and Present*, Vol. 103, 1984.
9. F. Ganshoff, *Quest-Cequela Feodalite*, Brussels; Neuchatel, cited in John Gledhill, Barbara Bender and Mogens Trolle Larsen, eds., *State and Society*, London, 1988.
10. Georges Duby, *The Early Growth of European Economy*, London, 1979 (tr. from French).
11. C.J. Harfield, 'Control of Resources in the Medieval Period', in J. Gledhill, B. Bender and M.T. Larsen, eds., *State and Society*, London, 1988.
12. R. Brown, *English Castles*, London, 1976.
13. J. Decaens, 'Residence Seigneuriale' *Archaeologie Medievale*, vol. 2, 1981, pp. 167-201.
14. R.S. Sharma, *Indian Feudalism (A.D. 300-1200)*, Calcutta, 1965.
15. B.N.S. Yadava, *Society and Culture in Northern India in the Twelfth Century*, Allahabad, 1973.
16. Marc Bloch, *Feudal Society*, London, 1961.
17. Burton Stein, *Peasant, State and Society in Medieval South India (c. 800-1300)*, Delhi, 1980.
18. L.B. Alayev, 'The Systems of Agricultural Production, South India', in Tapan Raychaudhuri and Irfan Habib, eds., *The Cambridge Economic History of India*, vol. 1, Delhi, 1984 (rpt.).
19. Perry Anderson, *Passages from Antiquity to Feudalism*, London, 1974, p. 149.
20. Burton Stein, *Peasant State and Society in Medieval South India (c. 800-1300)*, Delhi, 1980.

PART I

The Growth of a Feudal Polity

1

Towards a System of Private Government

Arguments have been put forward against the use of the term feudalism in the context of early medieval south Indian history. Burton Stein,[1] for example, observes that the fief 'as a constituted political sub-region of a private military authority was largely absent from medieval south India', thereby conceding the existence of the fief system in south India, albeit on a small scale. Second, Stein argues that those binding ties of allegiance which characterize the lord-vassal relationship of feudal Europe and Japan are missing from medieval south India. Stein's principal criticism seems to be the lack of sufficient evidence to support the development of a feudal politico-administrative structure. While a full-length study of the growth of feudalism in south India is outside the scope of the present study, much that follows will show that in its more general aspects, the concept can be fruitfully used for an understanding of medieval society of southern India.

The development of a system of private government based on inseparable association of landholdership with the powers of government can be studied on the basis of inscriptions that record the delegation of fiscal and administrative rights to a host of chiefs and officers capable of rendering armed service. The executive order which brought about such a change at the provincial, district and village levels had the effect of creating autonomous units which seem to correspond to what Stein describes as the constituted political sub-region of a warrior's private authority. The generic term for those who administered larger territories was Sāmanta though in the inscriptions of Karnataka the terms *maṇḍaleśvara, mahāmaṇḍaleśvara, mahāsāmantādhipati* and *mahāsāmanta* are also frequently used in the sense of a feudal lord and as representing different rungs in the hierarchy. There were others who served the territorial administration in different official capacities but none the less had acquired the position of a Sāmanta with chartered lordship over a village or group of villages. Going by the inscriptional evidence it would appear that any officer of the state with proven loyalty could be the nucleus of a private governmental jurisdiction no matter whether he was a keeper of revenue records (*heggaḍe*), a district headman (*nāḍgāvuṇḍa*), a headman of the village (*gāvuṇḍa*), a minister for war and peace (*sandhivigrahika*), a secretary (*amātya*) or an officer in the armed forces (*daṇḍanāyaka*).

Delegation of administrative and fiscal rights seems to have been warranted by the increasing inability of ruling houses to centrally control and administer large territorial states with the help of salaried ministers and officers. This is as much evident from the payment of salaries in land and land revenue as from the ceremonial delegation of the state's coercive power to armed private persons or groups of persons exercising local, private authority. The decline in the coercive power of the state, in turn, encouraged local political ambition which caused dynastic infighting and further parcellization of sovereignty.

The Domains of Private Government

If the inseparable association of landlord and government is considered the chief trait of the feudal state, the growth of a feudal polity in medieval south India can scarcely be doubted. In many cases the acquisition of governmental powers by local land-owners was an outright seizure of royal functions along with the income pertaining to them. In other cases the inability of kings to set up or control an efficient administration obliged them to resort to the next best expedient of entrusting political rights to private individuals. In still other cases the need for some kind of assumption of political authority arose locally in the demand for protection against outside attack. It would thus appear that, whether by usurpation or by a formal gift from the crown, monarchy as a type of centralized royal government was increasingly being replaced by innumerable local governments.

The inscriptional sources would bear out that the acquisition of political rights by private landowners followed as much as a result of usurpation as from formal transfers of such authority by the crown. The usurpation of political rights by ambitious warriors was invariably followed by the ceremonial act of vassalization amounting to legitimation. A warrior prince of the western Ganga family styles himself as one who brought various kings under his control by means of the sword and the *paṭṭa*.[2] Similarly, the Hoysala Viṣṇuvardhana (twelfth century) is described as one who made, by his fierce valour, the whole of Gangavāḍi-96000, as far as Lokkiguṇḍi, obedient to him. He is further praised as one to whom the kings of various directions gave up their possessions; trembling with fear they always served under him.[3] The countries and peoples subdued by this prince included the hill-fort of Ucchāṅgi, the capital of Pombuccapura, the Kongas and the Ṭuluvas.

The usurpation of sovereign political rights by ambitious chiefs does not seem to require many illustrations in the case of medieval south India. Many of the dynasties were founded by usurpers. The examples of Dantidurga, Āditya Cola and Taila, who came to acquire sovereign rights by ousting their overlords, are too wellknown to be mentioned. At the lower echelons of political power also the process of acquiring political rights by usurpation is frequently noticed.

However, the instances in which political rights were acquired by means of a formal gift by the overlord would appear to be far more numerous; the gift formed the basis for the extension of private domains of political power. Such gifts were generally made to trusted battlemates and warriors who held official positions. In either case the act of vassalization was prefaced by an approving declaration of the distinguished military service rendered by the warriors concerned. A few examples may be cited here. The *seṭṭi* warrior of a village is said to have been awarded certain lands in recognition of the victory he had won in a battle. The lands were constituted into a *sarvanamasya* holding with absolute rights of possession and powers of private justice.[4]

The political authority which the *seṭṭi* was now entitled to exercise was symbolized by the gifts of an umbrella, a palanquin and a throne. Another warrior of a *mahāmaṇḍaleśvara* chief, who already held the position of a petty locality officer, was similarly elevated to the status of an underlord after he had 'extirpated' the enemies of his lord in a battle. The vassal-rights which the warrior acquired is evident from the fact that, on his elevation to the position of a vassal, the lord invested him with the three powers of government.

The domains of private authority were also created in favour of Brahmanas, temple institutions,[5] and mercantile associations, the last one being the consequence of commercial revival from the close of the tenth century. A distinction may, however, be made between the professional autonomy of merchants and their private governmental authority over specified localities. In the former case the merchant corporations were under no obligation to render military service to the state although they maintained their private armies and possessed rights of private justice. The main concern of merchant associations was promotion and protection of their professional interests; the rights conceded to them by the territorial chiefs, who had begun to appreciate the benefits of commercial revival, were also directed towards this precise purpose. In an inscription of AD 1000 it is reported that the trading corporation called the 500 *svāmīs* of Ayyavole and its affiliated bodies maintained its own militia and courts of law and a seal of authority. The record refers to the practice of tying the badge of honour on warriors who served in the merchants' armies and distinguished themselves by showing exemplary courage in protecting merchants and merchandise.

Grants for Military Service

The custom of military service in return for a grant of land, which formed the basis of political relationship in feudal south India, is mentioned fairly widely in the inscriptional sources. In Europe, where the practice was already well established in the eighth century, the depredations caused by Mongolian nomads and the Saracenic cavalry rendered service on horseback indispensable.

Mounted service became an indispensable ingredient of the new military system and for obtaining well-equipped horsemen, fiefs had to be assigned.

In medieval south India, however, there was no such external stimulus for mounted service, even though the inscriptions would suggest that horses and horsemen were dominant factors in battle. The mounted mail, it appears, had developed into a prized symbol of aristocratic military status. Frequent references to warriors shooting horses and bringing down horsemen, gifts of horses to loyal followers and the lifting of horses from the enemy's camp are not wholly without significance. A Hoskote inscription of AD 75 refers to the ceremonial vassalization of a warrior who was presented lands, bent-bow, servants and horses.[6] A Kanakanhalli record of 1190 tells us that during a fight between two Sāmantas 50 horses of the camp of one of the chiefs were carried off by the soldiers of the other.[7] Another record of the same taluka praises a warrior who died after shooting at numerous horses and horsemen of the enemy's army.[8] Surveying the overall inscriptional evidence it would appear that although cavalry had become essential to medieval warfare, there was no marked preference for horsemen in the matter of granting land for military service as in Europe from the eighth century onwards.

The practice of military service in return for a grant of land can be traced back to the fifth century on the basis of early Pallava inscriptions, though the development was clearly uneven in different sub-regions. The pace and rhythm of feudalization appears to have been determined by the extent of peasantization and by political exigency. For example, there were large areas in present day Andhra Pradesh and Karnataka where peasant settlements were extremely sparse. In such areas there was little scope for alienation of governmental powers in favour of private landholders. The Telangana region and certain parts of north-eastern Karnataka came under such political 'rainshadow'. But in the basins of Krishna and Godavari rivers, the southern districts of Karnataka and also north-western Karnataka, where physical conditions were highly conducive to an extensive growth of peasant settlements, the politico-administrative arrangements were necessarily far more complex. It is precisely in such areas that private domains of government were carved out by different ruling families. The problem of strategic defence was also acute in these regions. Most of the inscriptions that we have examined in connection with the growth of feudal polity in the Andhra-Karnataka region also come from either Gangavāḍi, which covers almost the whole of southern Karnataka or from Veṅgi, which covers fertile tracts in the lower reaches of the Krishna and Godavari. Towards the far south, Toṇḍaimaṇḍalam and Cola-maṇḍalam were two important sub-regions which witnessed large-scale peasant and political activity around the beginning of the sixth century.

The records of the eastern Cālukyas would suggest that in the Veṅgi area in eastern Andhra, particularly its southern part, political instability was fairly acute owing evidently to rival political ambitions. It appears that to ward off the imminent danger of outright disintegration, alienation of the rights of government in favour of military hangers-on was found expedient. The process seems to have been accelerated with the foundation of the eastern Cālukya dynasty by Kubja Viṣṇuvardhana. An order issued by the king read that the Paścimagiri province, which consisted of 73 villages, was henceforth to be administered by Buddhavarman, who was an 'ornament' of the fourth caste and the shield of his overlord on the battlefield.[9]

In the reign of Cālukya Bhīma I, several military officers gravitated to the powerful army of the king. One of them was Paṇḍaraṅga who, during a Rāṣṭrakūṭa attack, captured twelve strongholds from one Vāso Boya, probably a Rāṣṭrakūṭa partisan; he also captured the hill forts of Veṅgināḍu.[10] Following the conquests of Paṇḍaraṅga, the king bestowed upon his brave general the governorship of conquered areas. Paṇḍaraṅga is stated to have made Kandukur in the Nellore district as famous as Bezwada, the capital of the eastern Cālukya kings. He also founded the new township of Paṇḍaraṅgam and built a temple of Śiva to which he donated land sowable with 80 candies of paddy.[11] He made the grant without any reference to his overlord. In the army of Cālukya Bhīma I, Mahākāla was another brave warrior whose military exploits are extolled and who is stated to have gone ahead of his master and fought and annihilated more than one enemy army.[12] To him was granted the village of Druzzuru which was exempted from all taxes. Similarly, Vemarāja, a distinguished general in the army of Ammā I, is stated to have been raised to the position of a *grāmaṇi* by the king, who placed the village of Umkili under his sole control. As *grāmaṇi* of Umkili Vemarāja was required to pay 8 *gadyāṇas* as annual tribute to the king, but he was granted exemption from other taxes.[13] Vemarāja was also authorized to receive certain revenues including the income of Saveram 10 *kandus*, 17 *tumus* measured by the measure of 24 full *puttis* as well as 1 *tumu* of *tammulam.*

Several other examples can be cited to show that vassalization of warriors was a typical political necessity of the medieval state. The eastern Cālukya king Badapa granted a village to a general named Gaṇḍanārāyaṇa.[14] Two other villages in the vicinity were granted to general Kuppanayya by Taila II.[15] The three villages ruled by armed feudatories served as an effective buffer against a possible offensive from the south. They lay in the Repalle taluk on the south bank of the Krishna near the coast. The Addanki Stone Inscription shows that the region of Repalle was a bulwark against southern aggression with the river Krishna as the second line of defence; it was under the control of the hostile Boyā chieftains during the reign of Cālukya Bhīma I. It was Paṇḍaraṅga, the general of Cālukya Bhīma I, who freed the region from the control of the Boyā tribesmen. Another strong feudal pocket was Kolanur, near lake Kolleru in West Godavari district.

In the reign of Ammā II two chiefs, Bhīma and Naravāhana II received various symbols of feudal status including the *śrīdvāra* (gate symbolizing prosperity), *chatra* (parasol), *cāmara* (flywhisk), peacock's tail, water-jars, horses, and musical instruments such as the *kāhala.*[16] The chiefs are described as skilled in the use of various weapons. Their grandfather also appears to have been a feudatory of the eastern Cālukyas, for he is stated to have enjoyed the privilege of sitting on the lion-throne like a crowned prince.[17]

Vassalization of fugitive princes and their placement in strategic areas is noticed in several inscriptions of the eastern Cālukyas. Kuppanayya, who received two villages from Vijayāditya IV is, for instance, described as a member of the Pallavamalla family,[18] apparently a scion of the imperial Pallava dynasty of Kāñcī. He seems to have fled the country following the overthrow of the Pallavas by Āditya Cola in 893. Indaparāja, who received a village from Ammā I, is referred to as the grandson of Indaparāja of the *Mahāraṭṭavaṁśa*, the lord of the city of Mānyakheṭa.[19] The prince probably took shelter in the court of Ammā I following the overthrow of his father Amoghavarṣa II by Govinda IV in 927.[20]

If inscriptional evidence is any indication, the custom of military service in return for a grant of land would appear to have been much more widespread in Karnataka than in the neighbouring regions. Evidence for this is found engraved in hundreds of stone inscriptions in different parts of the state. A warrior could serve his lord as a camp-follower by responding to the lord's summons from a distant country home as part of official duties like the numerous Gāvuṇḍa chiefs and Heggaḍe revenue officers are reported to have done. In cases where a death occurred, the family of the deceased warrior was favoured with additional grants of land and revenues. In cases where the warrior survived a battle, the overlord either granted him land with state honour and elevated him, if he was already an underlord, to a higher rank. We have examined several examples in which such an elevation took place as a result of notable military service.

Although the overwhelming majority of inscriptions suggest that most land transfers were made in favour of individual warriors, on certain occasions plots of land were granted to groups of warriors. A Gundlupet taluka inscription of the eighth century praises the seventy soldiers of the village of Upagolla for having broken the ranks of the enemy army. The Ganga overlord responded to their feat of valour by granting certain paddy fields as a rent free holding.[21]

North-western Karnataka, which was another important political region, furnishes several early instances of the monarchical states alienating sovereign rights to create domains of private governmental authority. In an inscription of Pulakeśin II, a warrior named Pṛthivī Duvarāja is praised as an expert in seizing neighbouring territories on behalf of his master and as one who showed exemplary courage on the battlefield. The record mentions that Pṛthivī Duvarāja was rewarded with the lordship of a large territory by the king.[22] Another trusted general, Āluka Mahārāja, was similarly granted the lordship of the Kallura province by the king.[23]

However, the inscriptions from the south Karnataka districts are more numerous and significant for studying the operational aspects of an emerging feudal state apparatus. The Bangalore taluka provides an interesting example of a chief responding to the overlord's call for military service. The inscription, which bears the date 890, states that a chief named Nagattara, on receiving orders from his Ganga overlord, mobilized his own vassals and rushed out against the invading armies, but died in action. On hearing this, the Ganga overlord undertook to renew to the vassalage by binding the badge of chiefship held by Nagattara (*nagattara-paṭṭam*) on the forehead of one Iruga, who appears to have been the main successor in the family of the deceased warrior. The conferment of chieftaincy vacated as a result of the death of its holder was accompanied by the grant of Bempur-12 district as *kalnāḍ*[24] or military service holding to the new chief. Unobstructed enjoyment of the *kalnāḍ* was guaranteed by means of a stone charter or *śāsana*, which seems to amount to a written contract of vassal service. The 12 villages which constituted the Bempur-12 territory are all named in the inscription. Bempur which is included in the list was evidently the headquarters of the ceded locality.

On the question of the renewal of vassalage the above-mentioned record may be compared with another inscription coming from the Nanjangud taluk of Mysore district and dated to the tenth century.[25] This inscription states that an underlord of the Ganga king named Racheya lost his life in a battle against the Nolamba chief fought in the fort of Uttarillage. The Ganga over-lord rewarded the family of the deceased by creating a *kalnāḍ* in its favour. The record then stipulated that if the family of the deceased suffered an absence of warriors, the wives and children of the deceased hero would enjoy the *kalnāḍ* free of taxes. It is evident that *kalnāḍ* tenure was not necessarily a freeholding and that taxes had to be paid by the grantees. It also signifies that the wives and children could enjoy a *kalnāḍ* as a tax-free holding only so long as no son had grown to be a warrior to make the vassalage operative. Thus the *kalnāḍ* was a fief given for military service.

In several instances, warriors-turned-landholders are described as running to the rescue of an endangered overlord. A Kankanhalli inscription of the twelfth century refers to one Mannayan, who is described as a landholder of Nāḍusolan in the Kilālanāḍ district, rushing to the rescue of his master, the lord of the Kilālanāḍ district, who was fighting enemies in the plains of Pondan.[26] Anka Nāyaka, the landholder of Taṇḍalapāḍi, is similarly praised for having joined his overlord in a battle in which he shot horses and horsemen before himself falling.[27] Evidently, all these warriors held plots of land on the condition that in times of necessity they would rally round the chief who gave them the non-cultivating occupancy right over the concerned lands. Other examples of planting warriors as landholders are also available. A Mysore inscription of the eighth century refers to the swordsman (*balāla*) of a chief as governing the Kudalur territory.[28]

Governmental rights were often alienated in favour of the chiefs of occupation armies as a short-term measure. In such instances the transactions involved temporary transfers of revenue from land, and not the land itself to chosen warriors. A Cola record of 1050 refers to a *senādhipati* of the Cola army that had defeated the Cālukya army led by Āhavamalla, as receiving grants of several revenues on the lands of Sannaināḍu to be enjoyed by the *senādhipati* during his lifetime.[29] The revenue included half the produce of Sannainadu lands, one part of the government's share and one and a half parts of the cultivators' share on wet lands, one part of the government's share and three parts of the cultivator's share on forest tracts and ploughed fields and the gross produce of the land on which *kumārī* cultivation was carried. The details of revenue transfer, which are mentioned in other records also, though infrequently, convey some idea of the extension of private jurisdiction over the fiscal rights of the government. The favour granted to the Cola *senādhipati* was evidently a reward for his success against the Cālukyas of Karnataka.

The grants in lieu of military service seem to suggest that

during the early medieval centuries the character of the nobility was essentially rural. However, from the close of the tenth century, when evidence of a commercial revival and growth of towns begins to surface, the activities of the noblemen also centred round urban localities. The revival of commercial activities brought into prominence a new class of traders whose activities did not remain confined to trade. They received prominence in the spheres of administration. We would like, however, to emphasize that from the beginning of eleventh century onwards professional merchants were also covered by the network of lord-vassal relations. The charter contained in a Bangalore taluka inscription dated in the year 1105 illustrates this point. The document mentions Māro Seṭṭi, the chief merchant (*vaḍḍa-vyavahārī*) of the Cālukyas and a resident of the Hadahalli village (*mulika-hadahalli-grāma*), as the principal *Gangavāḍikāra*. The last term probably refers to the invaluable service rendered by the Seṭṭi to the Cālukyas in the conquest of Ganga territory. The record then proceeds to state that Māro Seṭṭi, proceeding from the army encampment at the village Henjeru, fought one Kilva Rāya and brought him down.[30] Rural garrisons, such as the one in the Henjerugrāma are frequently mentioned in inscriptions, suggesting thereby a predominantly rural setting for feudal warfare which was also the nobleman's chief source of wealth and power.

The concluding portion of the inscription furnishes details relating to the vassalization of the Seṭṭi by his Cālukya patron. The record states that, impressed by the exemplary service rendered by the Seṭṭi, the king granted him lands with full powers of possession and the right to impose and collect fines. The state honour conferred upon the new vassal included an umbrella, a palanquin, a throne and a staff, and bodyguards.[31] The terms *sarvanamasya* and *aṣṭabhoga-teja-sāmyasahita* clearly show that the territory granted to the Seṭṭi was for all practical purposes a domain of private government under a warrior.

In settling competent warriors as landholders the most common ceremony appears to have been to bind a badge of honour on the forehead of the concerned warrior thereby validating his vassal-status. The practice appears to have been most widespread in

Karnataka in the tenth-thirteenth centuries, but can be noticed in earlier times also. For example, in 720 the Ganga king Śrīpuruṣa is stated to have tied a badge of honour on the forehead of a warrior named Ganga Mahā Naiga and given him land. At the same time he tied a badge of honour on another soldier named Śrīpuruṣa Naiga and gave him land. The ceremonial act of knighting the soldiers becomes evident from the use of the term *paṭṭam gaṭṭi* or tying the badge of honour in both the cases.[32] Another early record, dated in 750, mentions that an overlord called Singavallarasa gave a warrior named Perbba land, horses, bent-bow, servants and house. The gift of horse, bent-bow and servants would appear to have constituted a state honour which ritualized the knighting of the warrior.[33]

Hereditary Nature of Vassal Service

The inseparable association of a landlord with the powers of government gradually took on a hereditary character. With a particular piece of land went a particular official position and the two were handed down together as family inheritance. The process is fairly evident from the inscriptional sources.

Several records speak of official positions as hereditary. In an inscription of the tenth century,[34] a person who held the office of revenue officer is described as the hereditary *perggaḍe* (*kramāgatada perggaḍe*) of Chattaratehalli. The use of the term *abhyantara-siddhi* in respect of the *heggaḍe* is clearly suggestive of the private jurisdiction of the officer over civil matters in the Chattaratehali holding in the district of Edenād. Some other examples show that an official position in medieval southern India was mostly in the nature of a family inheritance. In one case the wife of a district headman succeeded her deceased husband to office, and when she became old and infirm her daughter Pittabbe became her successor.[35] Succession was matrilineal and the hereditary nature of the office of district head is amply clear. Hereditary succession also appears in village headships. An inscription[36] states that the headmanship (*grāma kūṭatva*) of a village was conferred on a certain Kusumāyudha. The headmanship is stated to have been conferred in perpetuity.

These inscriptions seem to emphasize not only the invariable association of landholding with an official position but even suggest that in most cases grants were based on the condition of military service which evidently formed part of a person's official obligations. Unlike Europe and northern India the patriarchal element did not dominate the millitary service rendered to the overlord. When the occasion demanded even women took up arms on behalf of their overlords.[37] This is evidently on account of the survivals of strong matrilineal traditions.

Two important inscriptions[38] from the Sagar taluka of Shimoga district introduce two different families of loyal officers who served their chiefs on a hereditary basis. One of these was issued in 1089 and the other in 1096. The two inscriptions mention several instances in which different members of the two families were granted lordship over a particular plot together with control of the concerned revenues. In all these cases the acts of vassalization followed outstanding military service rendered by persons who held the offices of *amātya* (minister), *gāvunda* (headman) and *perggaḍe* (keeper of revenue records). Terms such as *samaradhurandhara* (adepts in warfare) and *rāya-ankakāra* (warriors of the king) which are used in relation to these officers suggest that such men performed military functions for and on behalf of the feudal overlord.

In the earlier document Sirivarmma Gauda is introduced as dweller at the lotuș feet of Rāya Sāntara Deva and Rāya Tailapa Deva, the two *mahāmaṇḍaleśvaras* of the Cālukya Mahārājādhirāja Tribhuvanamalla, who together ruled the Santalige-1000 province. His grandson Biravarma is then introduced as worshipper at the lotus feet of the kings of the Sāntara *kula* (dynasty). Biravarma's son was Perggaḍe Nāgavarma, and Perggaḍe Nagavarma's son was Kannaya who held the office of *amātya* (minister) under the two Sāntara chiefs.

The record then turns to Kannaya and describes him as the warrior of Tailapa Deva (*tailapa-deva-ankakāra*). On instructions from Tailapa Deva his warrior-minister extirpated the mighty hostile enemy of the Sāntaras and earned the epithet *billankakāra* meaning warrior of the bow. The remaining part of the inscription describes Kannaya as a powerful underlord possessing the threefold powers of government;[39] he was entrusted with the responsibility of administering the whole kingdom.[40] This is clearly a position of eminence with title to vassal authority coming as a result of military service rendered by Kannaya, who, in the earlier portion of the inscription, is described as an *amātya* and an *ankakāra.* In addition to this personal elevation to the position of a vassal, the family of Kannaya received further benefactions. The concluding part of the inscription adds that the son of Kannaya (referred to as the son of the wife of Kannaya) and four others received Kolur, a hamlet of Basavur, with three kinds of enjoyment. The use of the terms *tribhoga* and *abhyantara-siddhi* suggests that Kannaya was entitled to enjoy not only various types of income from the transferred holding but also perpetual private jurisdiction over it.

The growing tendency of the ruling chiefs to create more and more areas of private governmental jurisdiction by providing armed officers with holdings of varying size is further brought out by the second record, which enumerates four generations of loyal officers who distinguished themselves by exemplary military service and were consequently raised to the position of vassal. The record begins with Singa Gāvuṇḍa who is described as dwelling at the lotus feet of Rāya Sāntara Deva and governing an area within the Santalige-1000 province. Singa Gāvuṇḍa's habitual allegiance to the overlord is further publicized by the expression which calls him a wishing-gem among the servants dwelling at the lotus feet of Rāya Sāntara Deva.[41] Singa Gāvuṇḍa appears to have been succeeded by his son Arjuna Gāvuṇḍa, who is described as proficient in the enjoyment of holdings[42] and as a wishing tree to those who take shelter under him.

The inscription then introduces Padavala Ereyamma, the son of Arjuna Gāvuṇḍa. Ereyamma described as the master warrior (*samaradhurandhara*), an expert in the use of the long spear (*bhalla*) and adept in the science of archery (*dhanurvidyā-śāstra-pravīṇam*), who worshipped the feet of Rāya Tailapa Deva (*pādārādhakam*). The valiant Ereyamma is then described as having overcome a certain *perggaḍe* chief in a fight. Impressed by this act of bravery Rāya Tailapa bound the badge of honour (*paṭṭam gaṭṭi*) on the forehead of Ereyamma and gave him

200 *gadyāṇas* of gold currency from the royal treasury together with control over the petty taxes of 4 Śivane of Belguli and the Kurukula dues. The Rāya also honoured this minion of valour with the title 'supporter of the kingdom' (*rājya-samuddhārana*), which was inscribed on a plate of gold and presented to Padavala.

The inscription then adverts to Padavala Singana, the son of Padavala Ereyamma. The son received from his father the control of 3 Śivane which the father had earlier obtained from Rāya Sāntara Deva. It is evident that Padavala Ereyamma had received 3 Śivane from Rāya Sāntara Deva and, again, 4 Śivane from Rāya Tailapa Deva together with state honour and control over various types of revenue. The second benefaction was made in recognition of the military service rendered by the warrior-officer. All this passed as family inheritance to his son Padavala Singana, who delegated the control of 3 Śivane to a temple he had constructed. That Padavala Singana was a hereditary holder of a landed estate is evident from the use of the same qualifying epithets as were applied to his father after his vassalization by Rāya Tailapa Deva. Like his father, Padavala Singana was 'entrusted with the responsibility of administering the whole kingdom', 'holding the office of a chief minister' and 'possessed of the threefold qualities of government'.[43]

The eastern Cālukya records also show that vassalization of warriors and officers on a hereditary basis continued unabated giving rise to powerful feudal families. Durggarāja, great grandson of Paṇḍaranga, is described as ruling as an autonomous chief of Ammā II. Durggarāja requested his overlord to make the grant of a village to his own minister, Musiya.[44] The family of Makariyarāja served the eastern Cālukya kings as military officers and feudatories on a hereditary basis. Makariyarāja is stated to have lost his life in the service of his master, king Taila II.[45] His son Kuppanayya also served the king as a general. He is stated to have successfully stood the tests of loyalty, courage and disinterestedness. He was granted two villages, Śrīpundi and Adur, which lay between a stream and a river forming a delta. Gaṇḍanārāyaṇa and his father Nṛpakāma also served the eastern Cālukya kings as military officers and local chiefs.

Gaṇḍanārāyaṇa, who received a freehold grant from king Bādapa, appears to have been a general in the army of the king. He is described as a famous archer and was known as Kārmukārjuna or Arjuna. The father of Gaṇḍanārāyaṇa was ruling as a trusted deputy of the king in the Godavari district; he gave his daughter to king Ammā II in marriage.[46]

NOTES

1. Burton Stein (ed.), *Essays on South India*, Delhi, Vikas, 1976, p. 85ff.
2. *EC*, 4, no. 354, p. 707, new series.
3. *EC*, 2, no. 176, AD 1123.
4. *EC*, 9, Bn. 143.
5. See Ch. 3 below.
6. *EC*, 9, Hoskote 83.
7. *EC*, 9, Kanakanhalli 26.
8. *EC*, 9, Kanakanhalli 44.
9. See K. Satyanārāyaṇa, *A Study of the History and Culture of the Andhras*, vol. 1, New Delhi: PPH, 1975, p. 276.
10. R.C. Majumdar (ed.), *The Age of Imperial Unity*, Bombay: Bharatiya Vidya Bhavan, 1960, p. 136ff.
11. G. Yazdani, *Early History of the Deccan*, p. 476ff, London, 1960.
12. *EI*, 5, p. 131ff.
13. *EI*, 27, no. 10, p. 41ff.
14. *EI*, 19, no. 24 A, p. 137ff.
15. Ibid., no. 24 B, p. 148ff.
16. *EI*, 24, no. 38, p. 268ff.
17. *EI*, 24, no. 38.
18. Ibid., 19, no. 24 A, p. 137.
19. R.C. Majumdar (ed.), *The Age of Imperial Unity*, op. cit., p. 137.
20. Ibid.
21. *EC*, 8, Gn. 207.
22. *ABORI*, 4, p. 53.
23. *Andhra Pradesh Government Museum Copper Plate Inscriptions*, Hyderabad, 1962, p. 12.
24. *EC*, 9, Bn. 83.
25. *EC*, 5, Nj. 207.
26. *EC*, 9, Kankanhalli 84 A.
27. *EC*, 9, Kankanhalli 44.
28. *EC*, 5, My. 192, new series.
29. *EC*, 9, Devanahalli 76 (Old Series).
30. *EC*, 9, Bn. 142.

31. *Chatra-sukhāsana-bala-gaddi-anka-daṇḍa khandane-etabhogateja-samya-sahita.*
32. *EC,* 9, Hoskote 86, AD 720 (Old Series).
33. *EC,* 9, Hoskote 86, AD 750 (Old Series).
34. *EC,* 8, Sorab 70, AD 938.
35. *EC,* 7, Sk. 219.
36. *EC,* 7, no. 25.
37. *EC,* 8, Sk. 13.
38. *EC,* 8, Sagar 103, AD 1089; *EC,* 8, Sagar 80, AD 1096.
39. *prabhū-mantr-otsāha-śakti-sampanna.*
40. *samasta-rājya-bhāra-nirūpitam.*
41. *tat-pāda-padmopajīvi-bhṛtya-cintāmaṇi.*
42. *bhoga-dhūrandhara.*
43. *samasta-rājya-bhāra-nirupitam-mahāmātya-pādāri-virājamāna-prabhū-mantr-otsāha-śakti-sampanna.*
44. *EI,* 18, p. 233ff.
45. *EI,* 19, no. 24 B, p. 148ff.
46. Ibid., no. 24 A, p. 137ff.

2

The Gradations of Rank and Power

Although vassals were all men of military calling and shared a certain mode of life, they did not belong to an egalitarian order. There existed profound differences of wealth and power which led gradually to the formation of a hierarchy among them. The distinctions which separated different grades of Sāmanta hierarchy can be perceived on the basis of inscriptions. The sources also indicate that the vassal of a lower order could attain a higher Sāmanta status depending on his professional skill and how it was assessed by his overlord. The three important conditions which determined the status of a vassal in the hierarchy were wealth, share of authority and bearing of arms. Any material change in these variables altered the hierarchical position of a vassal. We have seen that the principal locality officers, lords or private warriors of outstanding skill and courage, were raised to the position of higher vassals by their superiors. Such elevation invariably followed some notable display of military might and subsequently augmented the warrior's wealth and authority.

An analysis of the descriptions of the vassals in different feudal charters suggests three main rungs in the hierarchy of the Sāmanta.

The Three-tier Hierarchy

At the top of the hierarchy were great territorial feudatories who were directly under the king. The middle ranks were filled by the numerous locality officers who administered the villages and districts on behalf of these territorial chiefs. The third level consisted of ordinary country-based soldiers who were granted plots of land. Broadly speaking, such an arrangement not only shows hierarchy but also subinfeudation. The large number of petty warriors who are called by such generic terms as *balāla*, 'swordsman', *ankakāra*, 'warrior' and *besavagal*, 'bond servants' constituted the bottom level of the Sāmanta hierarchy. The *rāya-ankakāra*, 'warrior of the king' and the *bill-ankakāra*, 'warrior of the bow' also occur in a few records. The popular ceremony by which these country-based warriors were appointed is characteristically described as the tying of a badge of honour (*paṭṭaṃ gaṭṭi*) on the forehead of the concerned person. The ceremony was invariably accompanied by the assignment of plots of land.

The ritual of badge tying could be performed either by the sovereign or his vassals. It calls to mind the contemporary European practice of dubbing a warrior in which the girding on of the sword, followed immediately by a heavy blow with the flat of the hand of the lord on the neck or cheek of the warrior. But the ceremony of giving the blow is not found in inscriptions. The *paṭṭa* did not represent the sword but it did emphasize a formal contract based on the mandatory performance of military service in lieu of a grant of land. In certain cases the ceremony was symbolized by the delivery of arms by the overlord. A Hoskote inscription of 750 refers to a warrior who received from his lord a bent-bow and horses besides plots of land, servants and a house.[1]

A higher category of vassals comprised petty country officers who represented the lowest rungs of territorial government in villages and at the district headquarters. Some were *gāvuṇḍa* headmen of villages and districts and others *beggaḍe* revenue officers. Though the *gāvuṇḍa* and *perggaḍe* were not the exact parallels of the French *ministeriales*, in terms of hierarchical gradation they occupied the same intermediate position as the latter. The hereditary and personal subjection of many of these functionaries is well attested in inscriptions and emphasizes the special vassal service which they were expected to perform in a feudal structure. Appointed officers, all men of proven military merit, rendered military service in addition to performing normal administrative tasks comprising fiscal and executive work. Numerous instances of the vassalization of *gāvuṇḍa* or *perggaḍe* officers show that the conferment of the estate and state honour followed mostly in recognition of some outstanding military service. A *perggaḍe* officer, holding charge of revenue officer in a portion of his lord's territory, is entrusted with the entire burden of administration (*samasta-rājya-bhāra-nirupitam*), invested with the three powers of government (*prabhū-mantrotsāha-saktisampannam*) and decorated with the title of a great minister (*mahāmātya-padavi-virājamāna*).[2] Investing a revenue officer with three powers of government amounted to nothing short of creating a private domain of governmental authority within the lord's territory. The vassal authority of the *perggaḍe* is amply borne out by the three expressions and the obligations arising out of vassal service are stressed by such expressions as call the *perggaḍe* the dweller at the lotus feet of his lord or the rutting elephant of his lord. In one inscription of the tenth century, the *perggaḍe* officer of a territorial lord is described as the protector of the lord's territories.[3] The *perggaḍe* earned this distinction after he had, on orders issued by his chief, defeated a mighty enemy. The conferment of vassal status was symbolized by the tying of a badge of honour on the forehead of the *perggaḍe* warrior and the grant of certain revenues. Vassal status is indicated by several terms which emphasize the habitual servility of the vassalized officer. For example the new underlord is described as a skilful Garuḍa in carrying out the command of his master or a Hanumāna in devotion to his lord.

Variable Estate Honour

Although the vassal authority of enfeoffed officers is unimistakable, several terms which connote the formal status of a Sāmanta are not applied to them. Nor are the five great musical instruments, parasol, flag, pleasure-grove or throne ever conceded to a *perggaḍe* or *gāvuṇḍa* vassal. Inscriptions indicate that a *perggaḍe* ruling a district could not be called a Sāmanta though a professional warrior who lorded over only two or three villages or even a still smaller territory would invariably be described as a Sāmanta. Probably a distinction was made between great professional warriors who constituted the battlemates of the sovereign monarch and possessed a higher social origin than the petty locality officers who were generally recruited from among the peasantry and for whom military service was only a part of their usual official duties.

Occasionally, however, a *perggaḍe* officer could rise very high in the Sāmanta gradations and attain the status of a great territorial chief. An inscription of 924 refers to Heggaḍe Yogeśvaradeva who held the office of the minister for peace and war in the Kannada country. A *mahāmaṇḍaleśvara* chief, who ordinarily occupied the position next only to the sovereign, is described here as the underlord of Heggaḍe Yogeśvaradeva.

The formal status of a Sāmanta would then appear to have been a prerogative of the military campaigners whose support was basic to the survival of great territorial chiefs. These battle-mates of kings, who are termed variously as *daṇḍanāyaka*, *daṇḍanātha*, *senādhipati*, formed a separate order within the hierarchy, quite distinct, in both wealth and power, from the great body of ordinary warriors and the various rural officers enfeoffed on account of the special needs of the territorial lords. The position of eminence which these men carved out for themselves in a feudal society is at once brought out by the ostentatious decorations of a Sāmanta lord; the most important of which was the gift of five great musical instruments or *pañcamahāśabda*.

The gift of the *pañcamahāśabda* signified the virtual alienation of sovereign political rights in favour of the great warriors who fought the main battles for the monarch and who received in reward portions of the sovereign's territory as the domains of their private authority. On their appointment, the military generals claimed or were accorded the status of Sāmanta. The newly acquired status was proclaimed by the gift of the five great musical sounds. The warriors who were honoured with this comprehensive symbol of territorial authority are almost invariably referred to as *mahāmaṇḍaleśvara*, *mahāsāmantādhipati* and *mahāsāmanta*, as indeed is shown by the numerious feudal charters. But in cases where all these grades figure in the same charter, the honour is always associated with those vassals who ranked next to the sovereign or *mahārājādhirāja*. Usually this position is occupied by a *mahāmaṇḍaleśvara* or a *mahāsāmantādhipati*.

Other standard decorations of these high lords were the umbrella or *chatra*, the crest or *lāñchana*, the banner or *dhvaja* and the pleasure-garden or *nandana-vana*. Of these, the crest and the banner of different feudatories bore different symbols, probably as a mark of distinction between lords belonging to rival dynasties. Though the umbrella, crest, banner and pleasure-grove constituted, together with the *pañcamahāśabda*, the standard decorations of a great Sāmanta, other symbols and decorations are also mentioned in inscriptions. For example, an eastern Cālukya record mentions the *śrīdvāra, cāmara*, water-jars, peacock-tail and horses. In yet another case a vassal was decorated with a throne and palanquin besides umbrella and bodyguards.

In certain cases none of the formal decorations was mentioned. Instead a completely different set of gifts, could be made. In a Coorg inscription of 1095 a *mahāmaṇḍaleśvara* is stated to have received from his overlord 15 horses, 50 male servants, 250 soldiers, 45 retainers of good family, bodyguards, landed proprietors and numerous subjects.[4]

It is tempting to compare such descriptions with those in European sources. Bertrand de Born, a medieval poet, highlights the motives of economic gain which bound the vassal to his lord. The poet is quoted as saying that there is no pleasure in peace because a rich man is much more noble, generous and affable in war than in peace. Barons make much of poets . . . and if they want them to remain with them, they will give them trumpets, drums, flags, pennons, standards and horses.[5] The Sāmantas' acquistion of crest, flags, parasol, palanquins, musical instruments besides horses and other equipment of war is no less vividly described in inscriptions though these are hardly as explicit as the one quoted above on the mutual relationship between the lords and the vassals.

Within the order of great territorial feudatories there also existed differences of rank and power, as can be inferred from a large number of feudal designations. The more important of these terms are *mahāmaṇḍaleśvara, maṇḍaleśvara, mahāsāmantādhipati, mahāsāmanta, mahāmāṇḍalika* and *Sāmanta*. Put together, they would represent different levels in the Sāmanta hierarchy. For example, a *mahāmaṇḍaleśvara* or a *maṇḍaleśvara* would always take precedence over a *mahāsāmantādhipati* or a *mahāsāmanta*. This did not bear any relation to the size of the territory ruled. Sizes of the houses and also territory are indicated in the *Aparājitapṛcchā*.[6] Depending on the territorial authority of the sovereign monarch the warriors holding different Sāmanta ranks could administer either large or small areas. For instance the *mahāmaṇḍaleśvara* under a petty dynasty, would rule a much smaller area than the Sāmanta of a powerful dynasty although in terms of rank and power the Sāmanta would be always inferior to the *mahāmaṇḍaleśvara* and a *mahāsāmanta*.

High Sāmanta status could be gained by a show of superior military skill, in which case it was a reward from above. But the status could be also acquired by overthrowing an overlord's dynasty, which even substantially extended the territorial authority of all the vassals of the ousted overlord who may have been a direct feudatory of the king. We find that the Ganga, the Bāṇa, the Vaidumba, and Hoysala and the Kadamba feudatories of the Cālukyas and Rāṣṭrakūṭas overthrew the authority of the overlords and called themselves sovereign monarchs or *mahārājādhirāja* in place of *mahāmaṇḍaleśvara*.

Lord-Vassal Interdependence

Depending largely on the extent of disposed political authority and prevailing insecure conditions in different places, territorial chiefs and their armed entourage entered into a network of mutual relationships whereby the vassal surrendered to the lord and threw himself on his protection. The most important obligation of the vassal consisted in rendering certain services and making payment of certain dues. The lord, on his part was expected to give protection to the person and properties of the vassal.

Although the mutual obligations of lords and vassals are not mentioned specifically, some idea of these can be formed on the basis of the available sources. According to an inscription of 991 a *sāmantādhipati* granted the revenues from all those fields in which *rāgi* was cultivated to the eldest son of a district headman. The record stipulated that if the cultivators of the *rāgi* crop failed to raise the apportioned revenues, all the *nāḍgāvuṇḍas* (district headmen) who were collectively responsible for the administration of the district would be subject to fines and punishments. Apparently the district headmen compelled the cultivators to produce the specified cereals in such quantities as would meet the demands of the state or of its beneficiaries. If the district headmen failed in their duties, they were visited with fines and punishments which may have been transfered to the peasants. In this particular case fines and punishments were to be inflicted on headmen, presumably by the new chief who was given coercive powers over the holding (*sadaṇḍadoṣa*).[7] The contractual nature of the whole transaction becomes clear from two passages which emphasize the mutual obligations of the lord and the vassal. The holder of the benefice was supposed to render military service whenever needed. The relevant passage states that one who turns away from the battlefield loses whatever respect he enjoyed previously and that king Śāntivarma (the overlord) would cast a spell if by chance he sees a warrior doing this. This is followed by a passage which reads that king Śāntivarma should not, even in his dream, think of violating the word he had uttered in proclaiming the grant.

The lord-vassal relationship is brought into prominent relief by tendentious eulogistic passages in inscriptions. In those of the eleventh-thirteenth centuries these descriptions account for more than three-fourths of the text, giving the impression that praise of the overlord and homage to him are the theme, not the grant for which the record was issued. An expression which typifies the personal bond between the lord and the vassal is *tat-pāda-padmopajīvi* or dwelling at the lotus feet of the overlord. The term occurs very frequently and virtually means a declaration of surrender. Everybody seemed to be a dweller at the lotus feet of a superior person. The village headman (*gāvuṇḍa*) says this in respect of his *mahāsāmanta* overlord, the *mahāsāmanta* says this in respect of his *mahāmaṇḍaleśvara* overlord and the *mahāmaṇḍaleśvara* says this in respect of his *mahārājādhirāja* overlord. Interestingly enough, all this swearing in by different grades of feudatories, of what appears to be a oath of allegiance, figures in the same inscriptions suggesting thereby that from one level of the hierarchy to another the vassal was irrevocably bound to a personal lord who gave protection and patronage.

Ordinarily, *tat-pāda-padmopajīvi* was considered a sufficient vindication of absolute dependence. But similar expressions supplement it frequently in a record of the eleventh century in which an underlord is described as a bee at the lotus feet of his master, a worshipper of the feet of his overlord (*pādārādhakam*), a monkey-god (Anjaneya) in devotion to his lord, a divine eagle (Garuḍa) in carrying out the orders of his master and a wishing gem among the servants of his overlord (*bhṛtya-cintāmaṇi*).[8] Elsewhere a vassal is described as the servant who always pleases the lord (*svāmīsantoṣam*), the dweller at his lotus feet and the worshipper of the feet of his overlord (*svāmī-pādārādhakam*).[9]

The terms describing the lord as *svāmī* and the vassal as servant *bhṛtya* remind us of the bondsmanship which characterized lord-vassal ties in classical feudalism. In certain Kannada inscriptions the term bond-servant itself is mentioned in relation to warriors who served Brahmana freeholders and Sāmanta lords. A Sorab taluka inscription of 1141 refers to the *besa-vagal* of village Neralige who were fighting a violent boundary dispute with the neighbouring Kuppatur *agrahāra*. We learn from a hero stone that a Seṭṭi warrior of the *agrahāra* attacked the bond-servants of Neralige and died.[10] Another Sorab taluk inscription of 1158 mentions a bond-servant of the thousand Brahmanas of Kuppatur *agrahāra* who fought bravely on behalf of a feudatory against the latter's enemy, a *mahāsāmanta*.[11] Evidently the chief with whom the *besa-vagal* of Kuppatur *agrahāra* sided was the lord of the territory within which Kuppatur was included. A record of 1218 laments the death of this chief, Bomma, who is stated to have been unjustly killed at Kuppatur by an officer of Kalacuri Bijjala.[12]

Bond Homage and Bondsmanship

In view of the prevailing brahmanical norms of courtesy and obedience, the practice of saluting by prostrating oneself or kneeling in homage or standing with hands folded in supplication (*añjali*) can be said to represent homage to a lord. An inscription of AD 819 refers to a Ganga king whose pair of lotus feet was radiant with the rays emanating from the jewels set in the crown of prostrate kings.[13] Another charter of 550 states that the Punnāṭa king Rāṣṭravarma was borne like a garland of flowers by those kings whose arrogance had been destroyed and who did constant homage by bearing *añjali* on the heads.[14] All this would underline the significance attached to court service by the vassals in times of peace. Easily available in the courts of their lords, they could run to their rescue in times of war. Several instances have been discussed in the foregoing sections, and make this aspect of the relationship fairly clear. Constant military service is indicated by the description of vassals as armour for their lords on the battlefield, or lions and rutting elephants of their masters.

The servile nature of the relationship seems to be highlighted by feudal epigraphic records which describe a person as the servant of another man. Whoever was a subordinate was a 'servant' for this epithet alone connoted habitual surrender. As such the term was used irrespective of rank or power of a vassal or subordinate. For example, a direct feudatory of the Kalyani Cālukyas, who is described by as longish and eulogistic a name as Tribhūvanamalla Vīra Ganga Hoysala Pratāpa Narasimha Deva and who was ruling as large a territory as Gangavāḍi-96000, was after all the 'servant' of his Cālukya sovereign. Similarly, Sāmanta Biṭṭideva, who ruled Huligere *vṛtti*, is described as a servant of his Cālukya sovereign.[15] In several Channapatna inscriptions, a scribal officer repeatedly appears as the *kanmi* or servant of a Gāvuṇḍa lord.[16] In emphasizing servile status the term *kanmi* falls in line with the term *besa-vagal*; the same is true of expressions in which a subordinate describes himself as a lion, a rutting elephant, a Hanumāna or a Garuḍa of his lord. The element of personal bond is also stressed by the characteristic description of vassals as the 'men' of their lord. In Sanskrit charters the term *tat* (that) symbolizes personal relationship. Kannada and Tamil records also contain corresponding terms. We have cited several examples which refer to a landholder, warrior or Sāmanta of such and such a person. All such expressions become meaningful in the context of personal bonds existing in a feudal society.

The extent to which the obligations of bondsmanship were performed in feudal south India can be made out from inscriptions which mention instances of self-immolation in fulfilment of bond-service or as a mark of loyalty. Persons were ready to die if some obvious good could be done to the lord. A Sorab taluka inscription of 965 refers to a person who had taken vow in the name of goddess Kālī to immolate himself if his lord who did not have a son was blessed with a son. The person died by jumping from the top of temple when his wish was granted.[17] In both feudal Europe and Japan it was customary for a feudatory not to survive the overlord. This practice was also fairly popular in different parts of feudal south India. A Honnali taluk inscription of the eleventh century states that the younger brother of a *māṇḍalika* chief accompanied the Cālukya overlord to heaven in fulfilment of his 'time-vow' (*samaya-jola*).[18] A Davangere taluk inscription of 930 praises one Alliga as the servant of the shining feet (*belaradica*) of his master. Alliga, who followed his master in death, was buried under the grave of his master (*kilgunṭhe*).[19] Bhogi, another faithful follower of a chief, commited self-immolation on the death of his master, Muddaka[20] and the inscription was engraved in the year 973. Yet another inscription from the Pulināḍu region of Andhra Pradesh mentions a similar instance in which a vassal burnt himself to death as a mark of loyalty to his overlord, the Bāṇa King.[21]

The reciprocal protective functions of the overlord are stresssed in inscriptions. The sources frequently refer to the promises of protection and also to the actual acts of protection against all kinds of danger. Upholding of law and morality constituted an important aspect of a lord's protective values in a feudal society. Benevolence to subordinates, which complemented the protective functions of the lord, is also mentioned. The Hoysala King Vinayāditya is described in one of his records as a celestial tree to men who reached for help and asylum.[22] The same record represents Hoysala Viṣṇuvardhana as the sole promoter of the prosperity of his kingdom, an adamantine cage to refugees and a non-slayer of the frightened. The brave and benevolent lord was, however, not merely a protector of peoples and their properties.

As an embodiment of virtue and right conduct, the medieval lord upheld the prevailing moral order. A charter of the sixth century emphatically states that the great Punnāṭa king was forthright in upholding traditional laws. He is praised for having eliminated the evils of the *kaliyuga* and put justice and morality on the right path.[23] An upholder of *dharma*, the king set up numerous temples and *basadis* (Jain monasteries). He established districts and villages and settled subjects in them. Another king of the same family is styled as one who never swerved from the path of justice. Pṛthivīpati, also of the same family, is described as one whose right hand was always busy bestowing gifts to the poor, helpless, depressed, friends, guests, learned men, gods, servants and relatives.

Plural Homage in Joint Holdings

In feudal Europe, the prospects of wealth and influence often prompted a vassal to be 'the man of several men'.[24] But in the inscriptional records of southern India the plurality of homage is not so much in evidence, though in joint Sāmanta holdings such a custom became unavoidable. This point may be discussed on the basis of two Sagar taluka inscriptions, which were issued in 1039 and 1096 respectively.[25] The two Sāmanta lords, who are introduced as Rāya Tailapa Deva and Rāya Sāntara Deva were jointly ruling a territory called Santalige-1000 from its capital Sāntarapura. Both chiefs were *mahāmaṇḍaleśvara* and both obtained the five great musical instruments (*pañcamahāśabda*) from their overlord the Cālukya king Tribhūvanamalla.

Although the two chiefs are described as equals, the details mentioned in the two records suggest that one of them, Rāya Sāntara Deva was the senior, with greater access to the Cālukya overlord. The two inscriptions taken together not only highlight the relationship between Rāya Sāntara Deva and the Cālukya sovereign but also that between Rāya Tailapa Deva and his *perggaḍe* or *gavuṇḍa* subordinates. For instance, Rāya Sāntara Deva is described as a *vinatānandana* in carrying out the orders of his master Parmmadi Deva. He is also credited with the performance of the *tulāpuruṣa* (a great gift) and the *aśvamedha* sacrifice. Rāya Tailapa Deva is not credited with such distinction. Instead, his authority over his *perggaḍe* vassals is emphasized. A *perggaḍe* called Kannaya is called the warrior of Rāya Tailapa, a Garuda skillful in carrying out his commands and an Anjaneya in devotion. At the bidding of Rāya Tailapa he fought and defeated an enemy and was consequently decorated with estate honour besides a gift of gold and lands.

Whatever be the position of the two lords in relation to the Cālukya overlord, the *perggaḍe* or *gāvuṇḍa* performed homage to both. Perggaḍe Kannaya, who is explicitly characterized as the warrior of Tailapa Deva in one inscription is also described as the rutting elephant of Rāya Sāntara Deva. Similarly, in another passage a *gāvuṇḍa* hereditary officer is described as dwelling at the lotus feet of the two chiefs and as a wishing gem among the servants of the two chiefs.[26] Several gifts of land, gold coins and estate honour were made to the subordinates by the two Sāmantas as reward for military service.

Certain inferences can reasonably be drawn from the analysis attempted above. It appears that a large part of taxes due to the state was collected as rent by the vassals from the peasants and only a portion was passed on to the state. The burden of rent on the peasants would inevitably have increased on account of increasing subinfeudation. Taxes may also have been collected directly by state officials, but the overlapping areas of this collection need to be precisely ascertained. Similarly the number of professional soldiers maintained by the state may have been drastically reduced, changing the military organization of the feudal state. The reduction was caused not only by the fall in state revenues but also by the supply of military service from the vassals. The vassals also performed those routine administrative functions which under the Sātavāhanas had been the direct charge of regular state officials. What is further significant, the vassals enjoyed the right of private justice in civil and criminal matters. Judicial matters being an indispensable element of the state apparatus, its partial control by the vassals was a new phenomenon.

NOTES

1. *EC*, 9, Hoskote 83.
2. *EC*, 8, Sagar 80.
3. *EC*, 8, Sb. 477.
4. *EC*, 1, no. 62 (1972).
5. Quoted in Marc Bloch, *Feudal Society*, London, 1961, p. 296.
6. See R.S. Sharma, *Social Changes in Early Medieval India (c. AD 500-1200)*, Delhi, 1969.
7. *EC*, 8, Sorab 477.
8. *EC*, 8, Sagar 80 and 103.
9. *EC*, 6, Kd. 34, AD 1148.
10. *EC*, 8, Sb. 253.
11. *EC*, 8, Sb. 255.
12. *EC*, 8, Sb. 256.
13. *EC*, 5, Kr. 49; *EC*, 4, Ch. 347, seventh-eighth centuries.
14. *EC*, 4, Yl. 167.
15. *EC*, 16, Chikkanayakahalli 98, 1169 (supplementary inscriptions in the Tumkur district).
16. *EC*, 9, Channapatna, 127, 129, 130, 132A.
17. *EC*, 8, Sb. 479.
18. *EC*, 7, Hn. 47.
19. *EC*, 11, Dg. 119.
20. *EC*, 10, Mulbagal 66.
21. *SII*, 9, pt. 1, no. 9.
22. *EC*, 2, no. 176, AD 1128.
23. *EC*, 4, Yl. 167.
24. Marc Bloch, op. cit., p. 211.
25. *EC*, 8, Sagar 80 (AD 1096) and Sagar 103 (AD 1089).
26. *EC*, 8, Sagar 80.

PART II

Agrarian Expansion and Market Development

3

The Nuclei of Agrarian Growth

A major consequence of the decay of towns was the dispersal of a section of urban population and the rise of a surplus appropriating class in the hinterland.[1] In our opinion this was the principal factor in initiating a whole series of developments—the growth of private farming and a servile labour force,[2] improvements in the technique of agriculture[3] and increase in crop-production[4] and the cumulative effect of all this on the ultimate growth of a market-economy of towns during the eleventh century.[5] The number of fiefholders and freeholders who were the chief architects of this transition may have been small in the beginning, but this could hardly prevent these powerful and demanding people from developing their exclusive domains as the focal points of agricultural expansion.

Expansion of Fiefdom

The decline of monarchical centralization that encouraged feudal development in India is already noticeable in the large measure of autonomy conceded by the Sātavāhanas to their provincial governors, whom Nilakantha Sastri describes as feudatories under the control of central officers.[6] A distinction may however be made between provincial autonomy under a weak central authority and a system of government based on inseparable association of landholding with the powers of government and the numerous hierarchically structured private domains of governmental jurisdiction. It is in this sense that we refer to feudalization of the state in India.

In the peninsular region feudalization of the state can be traced from the close of the sixth and the beginning of the seventh century[7] though the early instances of ceremonial vassalization relate to higher officers of the state. Subinfeudation at the lower rungs of administration followed soon afterwards, from the first quarter of the eighth century.[8] With the planting of warriors as landholders and the creation of service tenements the various characteristics of the feudal development began to manifest itself.

The appearance of a large number of *viragals* registering the names and heroic deeds of folk-heros and warrior underlords[9] from the middle of the eighth century would also suggest the rising pace of subinfeudation from this period. In many cases the *viragals* are a recognition of the fulfilment of contractual obligations by a subordinate in responding to the chief's summons for armed service and by the overlord in extending protection and reward to the families of concerned warriors, fallen or alive. The contract itself was symbolized by the ceremonial tying of the badge of honour (*paṭṭamgaṭṭi*) on the forehead of the subordinate by his lord-superior in the case of low-ranking fiefholders. In the case of high officers and commanders the contract was symbolized by gifts of estate honour and the usual insignia of feudal authority as also horses, servants and an agricultural tract commensurate with the status of the enfeoffed lord. Variations in the grant of seigneurial rights appear to have been determined by the size of the fief and the rank of the fiefholder in the hierarchical gradations of rank and power. A four-tier feudal hierarchy is also fully in evidence by the close of the tenth century.[10]

The breakthrough achieved by fiefholders and Brahmana freeholders in the commodity production of peasant goods does not appear before the close of the tenth century. But the preparatory stage in this development could not have been any less significant. The two prerequisites for fiefholders to play an effective role in the existing system of production were exclusive control over agricultural land and control of servile labour to work on these lands. That this was achieved by the beginning of the eighth century will be shown below.[11] Control of agricultural land and a servile labour force probably sufficed for the production of cereals required by the household. But surely enough the feudal landholders were looking for much more than subsistence, for reasons of luxurious life and an expanding feudal entourage. The desired increase in production of foodcrops and other agricultural goods could not, however, be achieved in the absence of technological improvements, of which drainage was the most important. We will show below that from the eighth century the state's initiative in construction and maintenance of irrigation works was fast receding with a corresponding increase in the private management of irrigation.[12] The increasing presence of a surplus-appropriating class, which initiated the process of agricultural expansion, may have strained labour resources and made labour-saving technological improvements an imperative. During the seventh century and probably the greater part of the eighth production in feudal estates was dependent on the exploitation of existing resources. The pressure for increasing production was however felt from ninth century when instances of drainage works begin to surface.[13] Production was also sought to be raised through establishment of new villages and extension of the cultivable land in existing villages. A Sorab taluka inscription of 903 refers to the subordinate of a *mahāsāmanta* chief who founded a village, excavated a tank and laid out groves in it.[14] The village appears to have been established in the forested Malnad region of the taluka. Feudal chiefs making new paddy fields on the riverside of a village to provide service tenements to underlords would also become meaningful in the present context.[15] A Chintamani taluka inscription of 1047 mentions a chief who was rewarded by grants of land for his good work in constructing a tank and reclaiming fresh land by levelling the surrounding ground.[16] The transfer was granted by his superior who held the rank of a *daṇḍanāyaka*.

During the eleventh century, however, there are frequent references to fiefholder's initiative in the development of irrigation works in concerned localities. A Tiptur taluka inscription of 1107 mentions a Sāmanta who widened a village tank and granted permanent sowing rights (*bittuvatta*) for the maintenance of the tank.[17] This new tank was a stone construction, to judge from the praise of the stone worker who carried out the job. Subinfeudation was often an incentive to the expansion of irrigation. A Sira taluka inscription of 1072 shows that a warrior who was vassalized by his territorial lord who tied a *paṭṭa* (badge) on his forehead, undertook to construct as many as five irrigation tanks in his new domain.[18] In another instance, the *gauḍa* landlord of a village is said to have built a stone tank with a stone sluice in his village.[19]

The effects of agricultural expansion can be measured both in terms of the enrichment of petty rural lords and the large productions of cereal crops, fruit, and vines in feudal holdings. We have an instance to show that production on the fief was increased by successive generations of a petty country lord through construction of a series of irrigation tanks the total number of which was in double figures and which ultimately enabled a member of the fifth generation to construct a hill fort of stone masonry and an impressive temple within its precincts.[20] The contribution of large irrigation works in increasing production of cereal crops and garden crops can be seen from the descriptions of advanced peasant localities. In one such account a *naḍ* or district is said to have been distinguished by 'rows of rice-fields from town to town, with channels running from place to place with darkly shaded gardens of betel leaf, plantains and sugarcane, with groves of areca-nut, coconut, jackfruit, mango and rose-apple and flower-gardens filled with the fragrance of areca, *punnāga*, *nāga*, *campaka*, jasmine, screw-pine, white rose and sandal.[21] Similar descriptions also figure in connection with the *agrahāra* holdings which too were experiencing the effects of agricultural expansion. In one example the expanding *agrahāra* (*vistṛta saratarāgrahāra*) which was replete with livestock and labour force and inhabited by almost all categories of craftsmen and service castes, is compared with the wealth giving breasts of lady earth (*samasta-dharā-ramaṇī-stanabhog*).[22] In another contemporary record the three criteria of a prosperous *agrahāra* are said to be large number of Brahmanas, rows of temples and huge stocks of grain.[23]

Multiplicity of the Freeholdings

In point of time Brahmana freeholdings appeared on the rural scene much earlier than fiefs. On epigraphic grounds the earliest Brahmana freeholding in Karnataka goes back to the middle of the second century. But it was not before the seventh century, by which time the chartered Brahmana villages had infiltrated a larger area of peasant production and assumed the characteristics of the private domains of governmental jurisdiction, that these units of advanced agriculture were able to exercise some influence on the modes of surplus production.

The developments which characterized the growth of rural economy in and around these focal points of agricultural expansion can be summed up as (1) attempts to increase the production of food crops by reclaiming new lands, converting old dry land into wet rice fields through consolidation of drainage facilities,[24] (2) development of new modes of surplus collection by means of the free feeding places (*satra*) and sanctification of the village as rural place of pilgrimage (*tīrtha*) and (3) introduction of the brahmanical temple institution. Each of these forces was the product of internal contradictions which distinguished different stages in the history of Brahmana freeholdings. It is highly unlikely however that in traditional India a leisured class of surplus-appropriators would strain itself to raise production of food surpluses unless compelled to do so by a rising population and increasing adoption of temple institutions to fortify the ritual basis of peasant subordination.

The Population Factor

Although precise data on the growth of population in India is as difficult to come by as in medieval Europe,[25] the inscriptions do sometimes throw light on this rather obscure subject. The appearance of the *sabhā*[26] in the eighth century is probably the first indication of a sizeable Brahmana population whose interests had become too complex and exclusive to be looked after by the common village assembly. We may also mention here that small-sized *sabhās* are a characteristic feature of the earlier period; but from the same areas larger bodies numbering 300, 500, 1,000, 2,000, 3,000 and 12,000 are frequently reported in later inscriptions. This coincides significantly with the rise in the number of collective landgrants[27] in different parts of the country. In many cases the shares of each of these families are specified as in the Pithapuram Inscription of Vīra Coḍa[28] which mentions the shares of 528 families which had settled down in a cluster of three adjacent villages forming a *caturvedīmangalam*.

In many areas however such large groups had a small beginning. For example the Gautama Agrahāra of the Shikarpur taluka had a *sabhā* of 1,000 chiefs in the year 890 but its total Brahmana population rose to 32,000 in 1027. Whether 1,000 Brahmanas could swell into 32,000 in the course of 137 years can be debated.[29] The gap would however narrow down if we recall that 1,000 was the size of the Brahmana assembly whereas 32,000 refers to the entire population of Brahmanas. Since the former consisted of family chiefs and a Brahmana family would have at least four members including the chief, the total Brahmana population of Gautama *agrahāra* in 890 may be placed at four thousand. Also considering that every twenty to twenty-five years there would have been at least two additional members in a family and with average longevity of 70 to 75 years the village could easily acquire a population of eight to ten thousand after three generations. This increase was more likely because all marriages could take place within the village where exogamous families would not be difficult to find. At this rate a population in the vicinity of 32,000 after a century and a half may not be unrealistic. The importance of such widely variable estimates of population lies not in the exactness of demographic data but in the unmistakable impression of a slowly rising Brahmana population in the villages.

The growing density of Brahmana population in a locality can also be evidenced from the increasing number of Brahmana settlements in that area. For an illustration, in the Shikarpur taluka which lay in the heartland of Taradavadi and which was in the full focus of feudal development, the history of Brahmana settlement began with just one family of freeholders[30] in the second century. A hundred years later another twelve villages, nucleated around Sahalatavi, were donated to a descendant of the earlier recipient.[31] By the close of the ninth century, however, the taluka had no less than sixteen Brahmana villages,[32] some of which were administered by 3,000 Brahmana chiefs and some by 1,000 members. A century later many of these *agrahāras* were teeming with thousands of Brahmanas and in one specific instance the population is given as 32,000 of which 12,000 were Agnihotris (orthodox fire ritualists).[33]

Pilgrims on Rural Tracks

From the ninth century onwards the appropriation of food surpluses was meant not only for the resident Brahmanas but also for those Brahmanas and non-Brahmanas who had started frequenting villages in quest of food[34] and in many places were giving rise to prebendary sects. We have shown elsewhere that the formation of monastic orders in the peninsular region can be traced only from the first quarter of the ninth century.[35] In the beginning, the free boarding places (*satra*) which catered to the requirements of roving bands were established independently of temple institutions but from the tenth century, free boarding houses were becoming an integral part of the emergent temple institutions. Apart from accelerating the process of social inter-dependence across peasant localities the choultry and the temple brought added sanctification to some villages which were soon proclaimed rural centres of pilgrimage.

The interconnection between legitimation and surplus appropriation can be illustrated by case studies of single villages. One such settlement was the Begur *agrahāra*, first mentioned in a Shikarpur taluka inscription of 1032[36] in connection with the repair of a temple. By 1066,[37] the village had developed into a pilgrim destination for the locality, as reflected in its description as Begur *sthāna*. In this year an army chief of the Vaiśya descent constructed several tanks in the village to increase crop production. Between 1032 and 1066 the village became the centre of a prebendary order[38] and by the close of the century it acquired a large Vaiṣṇava temple complex.[39] The additional surplus appropriation is indicated by the fact that of the nine Begur village inscriptions as many as four refer to the establishment of free boarding houses. In one case the specified purpose was to feed local Brahmanas as well as those who came from outside.[40] In another case the choultry was to offer food to students and ascetics of the newly constituted monastic sect of this place.[41] Grants of rice fields and the construction of new tanks to help irrigation in the locality, which accompanied the opening of a free boarding house, would appear to be particularly significant in the context of our arguments.[42]

The inseparable association of temple and choultry with

improvements in irrigation and reclamation of land emphasize the view that improvements in existing technology could not alone ensure a surplus; technological advance had to be supported by an appropriate ideology to 'persuade' the peasantry to produce and relinquish more and more of the surplus.[43] In the context of early feudal India, this ideology is characterized by attempts to mobilize habitual obedience[44] and increasing peasant support to new groups of political and religious leaders. That the ideology was bearing fruit is as much evident from the charity network in villages as from proclamations of country lords that wealth was meant not for burying in the ground but for expenditure on Brahmanas and temples,[45] that not even a single coin was to be spent except on Brahmanas and temples. The coercion necessary to sustain the ideology is already manifest in the growth of servile labour,[46] arbitrary taxation and forcible collection of taxes, tributes and rents.[47]

The Temple Factor

The origin of the temple-based cults of Brahmanical deities goes back to the early Christian centuries, but it was only in the early middle ages that the temple emerged as a legitimizer of political power and an instrument of peasant subordination and surplus accumulation. At the outset, temples were located in urban places of political importance such as Kanchipuram and Mahabalipuram in Tamil Nadu and Pattadakal, Aihole and Badami in Karnataka, all of which witnessed great development of temple architecture. From the eighth century, temples also began to invade the rural world, hitherto dominated by folk deities and folk rituals and unassociated with permanent architecture. The ruralization of the Brahmanical temple institutions, which began on a low key during the eighth century but took on the character of a widespread enterprise during the tenth and eleventh centuries, seems to be related to the progressive feudalization of the state structure.

As the domains of private jurisdiction began to expand, the temple's legistimizing role became more and more relevant. The apportionment of *agrahāra* land to some Brahmanical deity, first noticed in the charters of the eighth century and the feudal patronage extended to temples by petty country lords from the ninth century in their villages appears to be convincing testimony to this development. A ninth century Sira taluka inscription refers to a *mahāmaṇḍaleśvara* who established his army camp in a chosen village, constructed a brick temple of Śiva, offered his 'palace' to the god and donated a whole village for maintaining offerings to the deity, temple repairs and for running a free boarding house.[48] There is no dearth of evidence to show that between the ninth and eleventh centuries, vassalization was a major incentive behind the patronage of temple institutions by feudatories of widely varying rank and power.

A major compulsion behind the growth of a rural network of temples seems to have been a desired direct access to peasant goods. The constantly shifting feudal garrisons and modest *pura/durga* settlements of the period that had grown out of rural settlements, also helped the process considerably. However, the vulnerability of these places to total destruction as a result of wars was a constant deterrent. The destruction of towns would mean complete snapping of administrative links between town and country, on which alone the priests could depend. This was the plight of many temples which came up at important urban places during the seventh century. We hear of nearly seventy temples built at the Cālukya capital of Aihole and many others at Pattadakal and Badami. But hardly any of these remained in active service after the overthrow of the Cālukyas in the mid-eighth century.[49] A similar fate befell Mahabalipuram after the fall of Pallava dynasty, even though Kanchipuram, the Pallava capital, continued to receive royal patronage during the succeeding Cola period. This is not to suggest, however, that the ruralization of Brahmanical temples protected them from the effects of feudal warfare and dynastic changes. But the temple was now a landlord and in full control of the means of production and could easily overcome a political or military calamity.

A comparison of the Brahmanical temples with Jain *basadis* (which entered the rural world at a much earlier date) shows that the impact created by the former on the mechanism of surplus production was unmatched in the religious sector. For one thing the largest of the *basadis* were still much smaller than an average

Brahmanical temple in the medieval period. This is evidently because of the fact that the structural growth of the temple was integrally related to an inflating ritual, a large pantheon and a wide functional base. The sanctum, vestibule, assembly hall, dancing hall and circumambulatory are all related to the ritual requirements of a deity in addition to numerous smaller shrines for relatives and attendants of the principal deity. Wherever resources permitted, temples achieved this imposing stature. But given the resources, the Jain *basadi* was unlikely to attain similar proportions. Apart from other considerations, these ran contrary to the Jain ideal of simplicity and humility.

We have offered some explanation of great structural activity during the eleventh century, but more compelling reasons may have prevailed, political and religious. During the eleventh century the state was trying to reassert its authority and for that reason needed to increase its rental income. The existence of numerous freeholdings would thus appear to be a major fiscal constraint on the growth of political authority. This might explain the growing patronage of temple institutions and a corresponding decline in the patronage of *brahmadeyas* and *agrahāras* during the opening centuries of the second millenium. Unlike the freeholdings, the temples replenished the revenues of the state besides providing a stronger basis of legitimization. The decline in the patronage of *brahmadeyas* in the Tamil region after the time of Kulottunga I has been noticed by some scholars.[50] From Tamil Nadu we also get several instances of the conversion of *brahmadeyas* into *vellanvāgai* to be transferred to temples,[51] besides the torture and humiliation of freeholders unable or unwilling to pay rent.[52]

The brahmanical thinking also underwent changes. In view of large-scale commodity-production of peasant and artisanal goods Brahmanas needed enduring masonry structures for accumulating large quantities of these goods, not possible in their modest village homes. Such a necessity was far greater during the opening centuries of the second millennium, when Brahmana freeholdings were being subjected to forcible rent collections, cattle-lifting and crop-looting besides destruction of rural fortifications and wanton killings.[53] The fortified temple structures assured a fair degree of security to the priestly community in addition to offering considerable storage facility within the temple precincts. The inviolable character of a south Indian temple can be judged from the fact that despite frequent attacks against *agrahāras* and *brahmadeyas* there is not one example of a temple being attacked or destroyed. One would also notice that during the eleventh century there is a significant coincidence between the large-scale construction of masonry temples in important Brahmana villages and the increasing armed attacks against some others in the same locality. It may also be mentioned that besides providing security and legitimation to the new centres of political and social power in the *agrahāra* and the *skandhāvāra,* the temple facilitated the integration of a large non-functional population in the existing structure of village community by offering different types of job in the temple. It would thus appear that during the tenth-eleventh centuries the new interests of the state and the Brahmana class were different and even contradictory, but both had their own reasons to encourage the growth of temple institutions.

The country-based expansion of temple network during the eleventh century can be illustrated by single village studies of inscriptions and temple structures. Turning to one such village, Periya Malavur in the Channapatna taluka of Bangalore district one would notice that the earliest inscriptional reference to the village or its shrine is dated 1000. In this year a commander of the Cola armies built the present Isvaram stone temple and purchased certain lands from the *sabhā* of Malavur to provide for offerings to the deity and food to the priests.[54] It seems clear that although the Malavur *agrahāra* was already in existence, it did not have any important temple institutions before this date. This is confirmed by the architectural dating of temples at the village.[55] The construction of the Isvaram temple marked the beginnings of a long drawn structural activity and in less than 15 years' time three major temple establishments, all characterized by extensive stone constructions and giving full representation to the important Brahmanical sects appeared at the village.[56] The constructions and endowments continued till the days of the Vijayanagar empire, but the evidence relating to the beginnings of this process in the first quarter of the eleventh century would suffice for our present formulation. As the expansion of temple network in the village continued, need was felt to develop new lands for cultivation by constructing tanks and channels. An early instance (Channapatna-88) shows that endowments for the Durga temple of the village consisted of land reclaimed by the concerned donor through the construction of tank.

Although the chief centres of structural activity were the Brahmana villages and feudal headquarters the peasant villages in the neighbourhood could not remain unaffected. In most cases, however, the initiative came from a Brahmana village as shown by several Channapatna taluka inscriptions of the eleventh century. In one example, the *sabhā* assemblies of four neighbouring *agrahāras* held separate meetings in the premises of a Viṣṇu temple which had been built in the adjoining peasant village of Manalur and issued four separate stone charters constituting a number of *devadāna* holdings in different villages including the *agrahāras.* At Belgami, which lay outside the Cola influence and which became the headquarters of a *mahāmaṇḍaleśvara* lord about the beginning of the eleventh century and where the first ever temple charity was registered in 1019 grew fast into a repository of large masonry temples belonging to all brahmanical and non-Brahmanical sects. By the end of the century there were no less than eighteen temple establishments besides a large number of monastic institutions.[57] The temper of the age seems to be reflected by inscriptions which highlight the deep faith of feudal lords in promoting temple institutions by spending whatever wealth they earned.[58] It is also significant that much of the hidden treasure was coming overground and finding way in the construction of tanks and temples.[59]

NOTES

1. While most of the Brahmanas left their urban homes in quest of a secure livelihood, those who remained tried to revive the values of gift-exchange by proclaiming decaying towns as places of pilgrimage and formulating a

whole series of gift-sharing rituals (R.N. Nandi, 'Client, Ritual and Conflict in Early Brahmanical Order', *IHR*, vol. 6). The epic and puranic descriptions of the Kali age, which bear witness to widespread political anarchy and social destablization between the third and sixth centuries would appear to be significant in this context, see R.S. Sharma, 'The Kali Age: A Period of Social Crisis', in S.N. Mukherjee, ed., *History and Society* (Essays in Honour of Professor A.L. Basham), Calcutta, 1982, pp. 186-203 and B.N.S. Yadava, 'The Accounts of the Kali Age and the Social Transition from Antiquity to the Middle Ages', *The Indian Historical Review*, vol. 5, nos. 1 and 2, pp. 31-63. It would also appear that while the epics and early puranic records lay stress on the disintegration of the social economy the middle and late puranic sources are preoccupied with the consolidation of a subsistence-based agrarian economy. The rural orientation of the gift-sharing rituals and, in conformity with this, the gripping concern of puranic authors for the preservation and multiplication of agricultural inputs—fields, livestock and irrigational networks is also characteristic of the growing ruralization of a surplus-demanding class. The puranic prescriptions for mandatory gifts of cultivable land, farm cattle, ploughs and sources of irrigation also fall in line with the more dependable epigraphical data on the subject.

2. See Ch. 4, Private Farms and Servile Labour of this volume.
3. See Ch. 5, The Technique of Agriculture of this volume.
4. See Ch. 6, Increase in Crop-Production of this volume.
5. See Ch. 7, The Growth of a Market Economy of this volume.
6. K.A.N. Sastri, *A History of South India*, London, 1956, p. 92.
7. R.N. Nandi, 'Feudalization of the State in Medieval South India', *Social Science Probings*, vol. 1, no. 1, March 1984, pp. 33-59.
8. Ibid, pp. 41-3.
9. *Memorial Stones*, S. Settar and Gunther D. Sontheimer, eds., Dharwar, 1982, pp. 311-12.
10. R.N. Nandi, 'Feudalization of the State in Medieval South India', op. cit. Variant categories of seigneurial rights accompanying grants of land to different categories of people were widely known in Western European feudal development particularly in France, Marc Bloch, *Slavery and Serfdom in Middle Ages*, London, 1975, p. 100.
11. See Ch. 4, Private Farms and Servile Labour of this volume.
12. See Ch. 5, The Technique of Agriculture of this volume.
13. *Annual Report of the Mysore Archaeological Department*, 1932, p. 242.
14. *EC*, 8, Sorab, 216.
15. *Archaeological Survey of Mysore*, 1929, p. 269.
16. *EC*, 10, Chintamani 30.
17. *EC*, 12, Tiptur 105.
18. *EC*, 12, Sira 9.
19. *EC*, 12, Tiptur 57, AD 1091.
20. *EC*, 10, Chintamani 9, AD 1100.
21. *EC*, 8, Sorab 135, AD 1145.

22. *EC*, 12, Kunigal 1, AD 1157.
23. *EC*, 8, Sorab 179, AD 1189.
24. See Ch. 5, The Technique of Agriculture of this volume.
25. Georges Duby, *The Early Growth of European Economy*, London, 1979 (English trans.), p. 181, Duby views population growth as an undercurrent which is impossible to observe. This is because of the nature of documentary evidence, which precludes any attempt to measure the scale of population growth except in England where statistical data of exceptional value is available during the 'last third of the eleventh century'.
26. C. Minakshi, *Administration and Social Life under the Pallavas*, Madras, 1938, pp. 120-4. The earliest epigraphic references to *sabhā*, *ur* and *nāḍu* are found in the inscriptions of Nandīvarman Pallavamalla (731-795).
27. B.P. Mazumdar, 'Collective Landgrants in Early Medieval Inscriptions (*c*. 606-1206 AD)', *Journal of the Asiatic Society of Bengal*, vol. 10, 1968, pp. 1-17. The Study shows that of the 29 collective grants 6 belonged to the seventh century and 20 to the eleventh-twelfth centuries probably coinciding with the preparatory and breakthrough stages respectively in the growth of rural economy.
28. *EI*, 5, no. 10.
29. Compare *EC*, 7, Shikarpur 45 (B) and 47.
30. *EC*, 7, Shikarpur 263. From the name Sahalaṭavī the donated village appears to have been carved out of a forest (*aṭavī*) tract in the Malnad region of the district before it was constituted into a freeholding.
31. *EC*, 7, Shikarpur 264; *EC*, 7, Shikarpur 20 of AD 400 mentions 20 *nivartanas* of land donated by a sub-king to his *guru* or preceptor.
32. *EC*, 7, Shikarpur 45(B). Several of these villages were managed by large-sized Brahmana assemblies consisting of 1000 members on an average.
33. *EC*, 7, Shikarpur 47.
34. A Bowringpet taluka inscription of 944 refers to the Brahmanas of a freehold village who undertook to feed all those people who had no one to support them, *EC*, 10, Bowringpet 2. An earlier record from the same area refers to Brahmanas of a locality as binding themselves to feed 20 persons who arrived separately every month in search of food, *EC*, 10, Bowringpet 1, AD 900.
35. R.N. Nandi, 'Origin and Nature of Śaivite Monasticism', in R.S. Sharma and V. Jha, eds., *Indian Society: Historical Probings*, New Delhi, 1974.
36. *EC*, 7, Shikarpur 20 A.
37. Ibid. Shikarpur 9.
38. Ibid. Shikarpur 20 B.
39. Ibid. Shikarpur 19.
40. Ibid. Shikarpur 15, AD 1089.
41. Ibid. Shikarpur 14, AD 1089.
42. An earlier instance of this type relates to the initiative of a *sāmanta* lord who established his camp at the village Baragur, built a brick temple, offered his 'place' to the god and transferred a whole village for maintaining offerings to the god, repairs to the temple and for running a free feeding establishment.

Nearly forty years later the place is described as Baragur *sthāna*, cf. *EC*, 12, Sira 38 of AD 878 and Sira 39 of AD 920.

43. Gideon Sjoberg, *The Preindustrial City: Past and Present*, New York, 1960, pp. 119-20.
44. For the *bhakti* idea and its social context see D.D. Kosambi, 'Social and Economic Aspects of the *Bhagavad Gītā*,' *Journal of the Economic and Social History of the Orient*, vol. 4, pt. 2, 1961, pp. 198-224; Suvira Jaiswal, *The Origin and Development of Vaisnavism in India*, Delhi, 1967, pp. 110-15; R.N. Nandi, 'Some Social Aspects of the *Nālayira Prabandham*', *Proceedings of the Indian History Congress*, 37th Indian History Congress, Calicut, 1976.
45. *EC*, 5, Hassan 72 and 76.
46. See Ch. 4, Private Farms and Servile Labour of this volume.
47. See Ch. 8, From Collaboration to Conflict of this volume.
48. *EC*, 12, Sira 38, AD 878.
49. That a temple complex could not by itself sustain urban life is evident also from later instances like Halebidu in south Karnataka. Halebidu, once a propsperous Hoyasala capital was reduced to an obscure village after the decline of the Hoyasalas despite its imposing network of stone masonry temples. If at some places the towns did continue in a reduced form after the withdrawal of political patronage it could not have been solely because of religious activities, as has been supposed by some scholars, see R. Champaklakshmi, 'Growth of Urban Centres in South India: Kudamukku and Palaiyarai, the Twin City of the Colas', *Studies in History*, vol. 1, no. 1, pp. 1-29. Probably the whole problem awaits a classificatory study of medieval towns to judge which towns depended on subsistence production and which ones on commodity production of crops and accordingly which functional groups dominated these places, See Ch. 8, under 'The Emerging Towns'.
50. Burton Stein, *Peasant State and Society c. 800-1300*, Delhi, 1980, p. 243.
51. K.A.N. Sastri, *Cholavaṃśa* (Hindi), Delhi, 1979, pp. 442-3.
52. Ibid, p. 415.
53. See Ch. 8.
54. *EC*, 9, Channapatna 92.
55. *Annual Report of the Mysore Archaeological Department*, 1935, pp. 12-14.
56. *EC*, 9, Channapatna 88, AD 1014; these three new temples were the Śrīkailāsam Śiva temple, the Apprameya Svāmī Viṣṇu temple and the Dūrgā temple.
57. *EC*, 7, Shikarpur 87-169; nearly 90 per cent of these inscriptions belong to the eleventh and twelfth centuries and all are temple endowments. Many of the temples reported in these inscriptions can still be traced.
58. *EC*, 5, Hassan 72.
59. *EC*, 5, Hassan 76; *EC*, 5, Hassan 65, AD 1149, refers to a Hoysala palace guard who built nine Viṣṇu temples in nine different villages of which one was an *agrahāra*.

4

Private Farms and Servile Labour

Private Farms

An important consequence of the expansion of private farming during the early middle ages was the growth of private property in land. In the context of the supposed absence of private property in land it may be pertinent to examine epigraphic data on the alienation of land through gifts and sale and also identify the parties involved in such transactions. We find that the evidence for the sale of land is more positive during the eleventh-thirteenth centuries. Though this need not suggest the absence of such transaction in the earlier period, it certainly indicates a fair demand for cultivable land about this time. Again, although communal holdings were freely transferred to Brahmana free-holders, military and other officers and temple *devadāna* holders, individual holdings could not possibly be taken away with as much impunity or without a price being paid.

To illustrate individual ownership of land we may discuss some early eleventh-century epigraphic sources from Karnataka. A Mysore district inscription of 1027 refers to a *gāvuṇḍa* landowner who sold, in return for an unspecified amount of money, certain plots of land to a co-villager.[1] The sale deed was registered by a revenue officer (*heggaḍe*) of the locality at the request of seven peasant elders who were witnesses to the sale and who belonged to as many neighbouring villages: Purchase of land from individual peasant owners was also made by kings and the Brahmana *sabhās*. A Coorg inscription of 1070 mentions the purchase of 10 *kandugas* of land by the king from a landlord, Naraka Gāvuṇḍa.[2] The land was acquired for constituting a *devadāna* holding. In another land sale transaction the purchaser was the *sabhā* of an *agrahāra* and the sellers were a woman and her relatives. But the price of the land and the size of the plot remain unstated.[3] The same assembly purchased on the same date another piece of land from an individual landowner. In this case the price of the land is specified as 9 *kalañju* of gold, but no indication of the size of the plot is given. During the eleventh-twelfth centuries the fiefs granted to officers or subordinate chiefs also appear in the land market. In one such instance we observe that a plot originally granted to a *gāvuṇḍa* village headman as *vṛtti* or maintenance fee was subsequently sold to an enterprising merchant for an unspecified amount of money. However the transaction was contested at a later stage by a grandchild of the family on grounds of fraud and nonpayment of the agreed amount. Surprisingly, however, the merchant who lost the suit and 'hung his head in shame' continued as the owner of the Elamballi fief.[4]

Individual property in land was also growing on *devadāna* lands during the tenth-thirteenth centuries. The development appears to have been facilitated by the ruralization of temple institutions from the ninth century and the consequent growth of vested hereditary rights on the plots earmarked for the maintenance of the families of priests and ecclesiastics. The fields appear to have been worked by attached persons characterized as the servants of the priests, or farmers of the monasteries.[5] Later instances of individual *devadāna* holdings are, however, characterized as alienable. A Bangalore taluka inscription of 1294[6] mentions 28 men of a village who received grants of certain plots of land with the absolute right of disposal through gift and sale (*dāna-vikraya-yogyam*). These 28 men were to act as the *sthānapatis* of the local temple establishment and look after its charities. The land evidently was remuneration for the work these 28 men would do in their capacity as *sthānapatis*. A Devanahalli taluka inscription of 1283[7] refers to the grant of certain specified plots to 32 Brahmanas with the right to make additions through purchases and to alienate through gifts and sale (*kraya-vikraya-dānayogyam*). This again was payment of salary in land converted into private property for a service to be rendered on hereditary basis. In this case the 32 Brahmanas were asked to recite the Vedas in the local temple on specified days. Bequest of individual holdings along with the cattle, agricultural labour, agricultural inputs, crop, and houses would indicate that cultivable land was as much a family inheritance as farm cattle or dwelling houses.[8] References to individual holdings and private pastures in boundary descriptions of villages and fields donated to Brahmanas or temples are equally significant indications of private property in land.[9] A Managoli inscription of 1161 from the Bijapur district mentions the agricultural land of an individual named Cenna Gesimeyya[10] as the boundary-mark of fields donated to a temple. We may also draw attention to inscriptional reference to a peasant's sons who laid down their lives in defence of their father's land[11] and to the blood feud between peasant families for possession of land with bamboo thickets.[12] The increasing demand for cultivable land is as much evident from a brisk land market as from violent conflict over possession of land.[13] In the neighbouring Cola kingdom the growth of private landholdings during the middle and late periods is said to have created a kind of imbalance which affected the social and economic processes in a large measure. The large accumulation of agricultural land by rich landlords forced many other landholders to lose their *kani* rights in land and slip into the position of evicted tenants or landless cultivators.[14] The growing imbalance in the distribution of landed property, particularly dispossession of resident peasants of their hereditary *kani* rights might explain the changing relations of interdependence between communities and the consequent social turmoil. The situation was aggravated by the emergence of large scale military holdings during the middle and late Cola periods.[15]

Labour Supply

The problem of a slowly changing mode of production can also be viewed in terms of labour as an input in production. The sources of the pre-Christian and early Christian centuries suggest that the productive labour force comprised two distinct parts, one consisting of slaves and the other share croppers and wage earners. During the earlier half of the first millenium, however, slaves do not figure in productive labour; their place was taken by share croppers and wage labourers.

The expansion of private farming brought about changes in the control and deployment of field labour. While the share-cropping system continued in peasant holdings, a new class of servile labour was slowly emerging in the fiefs and freeholdings, mainly from amongst the old class of share-croppers. Conditions favouring the growing servility and immobility of labour appear to have proliferated throughout the early medieval centuries in the wake of the growth of private property in land in the fiefs and Brahmana freeholdings. The extension of arable land, construction and renovation of irrigation works and adoption of new or marginal crops which characterized agricultural expansion in these private domains could not but lead to a relative scarcity of labour. This may have encouraged the relations of bond-service in the fiefs and *agrahāras*. The process of peasant subjection was also helped by the impoverishment of cultivators as a result of the increasing shares of the produce demanded by fief-holders and freeholders which is evident from claims of one-fifth and two-fifth of the surplus in place of the normal one-sixth. One Channapatna taluka record of 1050 shows how a Chola king authorized his feudatories to collect half the produce although he himself was collecting no more than 'one-sixth of the entire produce of the earth'.[16]

Whether the transfers of share-croppers together with fields to their new masters[17] would amount to the growth of serfdom of the west European type can be debated, but not the effects of the growth of servile labour in initiating the process of agricultural expansion and increase in crop production. One may also argue that since serfdom was essentially a form of servile labour brought about by changes in the existing political structure and since the purpose of such servility was to raise production of peasant surpluses it may not perhaps be necessary to look for a stereotype[18] or consider feudalism itself as exclusive to serfdom.[19] If serfdom is understood as an 'obligation laid upon the producer by force and independently of his own volition to fulfil certain economic demands of an overlord in the form of dues and services,[20] such a purpose could be achieved by reducing share-croppers on fiefs and freeholdings to the condition of servile labour.[21] In certain localities and probably to a considerable extent the conditions of servility were reinforced by the right to requisition labour.[22] In the feudal domains the basis of such coercion was the military power of the overlord whereas in the freeholdings such authority was based on custom backed by a juridical procedure and sanctification.

Long periods of oppressive collection of shares and services and subjection in the feudal holdings appear to have brought about a fundamental change in the relations between the landlords and field labourers. Perhaps this alone would justify the characterization of agricultural labourers as bond-servants and bond-workers in the inscriptions of the eighth and ninth centuries. Though such expressions are frequent in later epigraphic records, the beginnings of bonded field labour in the eighth century coincide meaningfully with the expansion of private farms, improved technique of agriculture and increase in crop production. A close look at the epigraphic material would indicate the distinction between plural references to bondservants and references to individual bond-servants mentioned by their caste or profession. The former evidently were agricultural labourers attached to fields while the latter were artisans and service castes attached to the lord's household and providing him the necessary goods and services. We may here refer to the washerman (*asaga*) who was a bond-servant of a *gauḍa* landlord (*nāḍprabhū*) of Avali fief[23] or the blacksmith (*kammāra*) who also served the Avali lord as a bond-servant.[24]

In some localities the lords appear to have used their bond-labourers to cultivate land in captured villages. We may refer to an early ninth century hero-stone from the Sorab taluka to highlight the point.[25] The inscription refers to a refractory chief who, disobeying the orders of his superior, forcibly occupied a certain village while his bonded labourers who belonged to a nearby village, Parige (*pārigeya bandugiyar*)[26] started cultivation in the occupied village. Of greater significance in the present context is the statement that the *bandugiyar* of Parige had destroyed the strength of four bullocks and 'by fraud converted it into six bullocks'. In all likelihood the intruders had extended the cultivable area which was formerly ploughed by four bullocks by encroaching on nearby fields. The area was, however, reduced to its original size by the overlord who had the land ploughed once again by four bullocks, determined its boundaries and transferred it to the family of a hero who had fallen in battle against a rebel chief from the occupied village. His bond-labourers were also driven out from the occupied fields. In another inscription of a later date from the same area the bond-servant (*besa-vagal*) of a village attacked a neighbouring Brahmana freeholding. The *viragal* which was erected to perpetuate the memory of a warrior who fought on the side of the Brahmanas states that many of the *besa-vagal* were killed in the fight.[27] The presence of bonded field labourers on private holdings of rich land owners is also indicated by the inscriptions of the eleventh-twelfth centuries which refer to bequests of agricultural land (*kṣetram*) together with agricultural labour, farm cattle (*dvipadī-catuṣpadī*), grains or crops (*dhānya*), dwelling houses (*gṛham*) and other property (*dhana*).[28] This and many more instances are reported in the early medieval inscriptions, relating to the same region (north-western Karnataka) from where the instance of *bandugiyar* and *besa-vagal* are reported.

In the Brahmana freeholdings, the origins of servile field labour can be traced very early in the transfer of *āddhika* share-croppers along with the plots of land donated to Brahmanas.[29] But the power of coercion increased only later as the demand for such labour rose with the brisk pace of agricultural expansion. This increase in coercive authority is reflected by such characteristic terms as *tottu, bandugiyar* and *besa-vagal*. We may also observe that the *besa-vagal* figure mostly in connection with attacks on Brahmana villages, the *tottu* and *bandugiyar* are enumerated together with different categories of working people inhabiting rural tracts. The *besa-vagal* may also have functioned as a category of rural militia whereas the *bandugiyar* and *tottu* were an exclusive group of bonded field-labourers. The presence of bonded agricultural labourers on Brahmana holdings is also established beyond doubt by the bracketing of farm cattle with farm labour (*emme ettu paśu tottu kaṭine*) in some inscriptions of the twelfth century.[30] That the bonded labourers formed a class apart and an inferior one, can be seen from the use of partisan adjectives to denote different groups of people in the same village who laid down their lives in defence of Brahmanas. Where a folk hero of higher social rank was concerned the terms used were 'dear son' (*priya putra* or *magam*). But where bond-servants were concerned no such compliment is offered.

Labour servility also characterized production on temple estates, though the main thrust was on the enslavement of artisans and service castes in view probably of the crucial collaborative role played by these groups in the consolidation of temple organization. In return the families of masons, metal workers, carpenters and potters received a sanctification of social status and accordingly differentiated themselves from other members of the castes concerned. The two artisan groups whose enslavement by temples was of frequent occurrence during the tenth-eleventh centuries were oil pressers and loom-workers. We do not know whether large-scale bond-service also characterized agricultural production on *devadāna* holdings. The references to the farmers and servants of monastic chiefs[31] might suggest that on the holdings apportioned to priests and pontiffs on a hereditary basis the field labourers were as good as bond-workers.

The shortage of field labour which was already being experienced in the wake of agricultural expansion appears to have been intensified by the beginning of the second millenium. Probably this was partly related to the growth of a market economy which helped to dissociate large groups of artisans from marginal farming activities and convert a part of the field labour into construction labour. The latter was in great demand following unprecedented structural activity during the tenth and eleventh centuries.

The constraint of reduced field labour may have been overcome by captive labour. Judging from the descriptions of village raids, which begin to pour in from the eighth century, it would be noticed that earlier attacks were prompted by demands of farm cattle and foodgrains but the *viragals* of the eleventh and twelfth centuries also mention the rising incidence of captive labour. The people who were captured in the course of these raids could find rehabilitation either in the form of bonded-labour on the estates of feudal lords or in the feudal militia. A Sorab taluka inscription of 1213 refers to a feudal lord who attacked a Brahmana village and captured its cattle, stocks of grain and men (*jana*).[32] In another inscription of the same taluka[33] the two bond-servants (*besa-vagal*) of a *gauḍa* chief who is described as the master (*oḍeya*) of the two men, prevented the cattle and men of a Brahmana freeholding being carried away by a feudal lord.

The growing incidence of bond-service in fiefs, freeholdings and the *devadāna* holdings during the eleventh-twelfth centuries and the simultaneous growth of a partial labour market in the wake of increasing money circulation seem to underline a contradictory situation in certain areas. The effects of the money market may have been first experienced in the artisanal sector. If the construction of tanks and temples involved an expenditure of money, as indeed was happening in some cases, some amount of mobility on the part of construction labour may not have been unlikely. A Bangalore taluka inscription of 1110 mentions the construction of a temple enclosure in a village at the cost of 500 *paṇas*.[34] In another instance the merchant company of the city of Talkad paid an unspecified amount of money for repairing the sluice of an irrigation tank.[35] Whether agricultural labour was also receiving wage payments in money is not clear though the peasant families during the eleventh century were very much in possession of coined money and were even paying money rents. Several inscriptions of this period mention transfers of *paṇam* money rent collected from villages to temples for providing specified services.[36] But garden labourers in certain areas were receiving wage payments in money which the temple earned by loaning out principal sums to traders or whoever else required these. The amount of the loan was part of the temple's liquid capital or charitable funds instituted by rich patrons. A Cola inscription of 1021 from Mysore district mentions the charity of an army officer who deposited 10 *kalañjus* of gold coins with the town council of Mavilangai to provide for a servant to be employed in the garden of the local temple.[37] The record is of added significance in view of the phenomenal growth of garden keeping during the tenth-eleventh centuries and expertise needed in planting and rearing different fruit plants, flower-plants and vine-creepers.

The effects of wage payments in minted money on the mobility of artisanal labour were however much more pronounced than those on constructional labour or field labour. This would perhaps explain the fact that despite increasing enslavement of agricultural and artisanal labour by fief-holders, Brahmana free-holders and temple *devadāna* holders, there were attempts to escape to the emerging towns where wage payments in money had picked up from the close of the eleventh century. Money payments for both labour services and goods produced by the peasants and artisans are too evident in the epigraphic records to need emphasizing. Even such minor professional groups as mat-makers, basket-makers, flower-vendors and vendors of dairy products are seen functioning as large corporate bodies and paying specified amounts of money as tax. Service castes such as washermen were also earning enough cash to make outright money payments to the state.

To a limited extent the emerging money market appears to have liberalised the conditions of bond-service or, at least shattered the immobility of rural artisans. We may refer here to an early twelfth century inscription from the Sorab taluka.[38] The inscription is a *viragal* recording the death of a blacksmith's son who lived in the village Avali but whose death occurred in a fight near a town (*ura*) when the blacksmith's son was going on work (*besa bogalu*). It seems that the *kammāra* was going to the district headquarters Honnapalli to report for chartered duty. The chartered nature of work is suggested by the term *besa-bogalu* or bond-service requisitioned by the *mahāmaṇḍaleśvara* of whose domain the village was a part. Certainly, the record does not suggest any emancipation of bonded artisan labour. What is suggested is the city-bound mobility of village artisans and the rising demand for skilled labour in emerging towns. It will be noticed that although the blacksmith's son represents a kind of migrant labour from the countryside, the blacksmith himself remained bound to his village lord's estate and served him in the capacity of *besa-magam* or bonded son, the suffix *magam* (son) not diluting in any manner the bonded character of the service.

Group migration of artisanal workers to nearby towns also seems to have started during the eleventh-twelfth centuries. Mention may be made of a group of *viragal* carvers who migrated to the new Hoysala capital of Belur where great constructional activity was going on in the earlier part of the twelfth century. There must have been sufficient incentives for the movement of *viragal* engravers who normally remained confined to their villages and lived on meagre payments in grain for their work.[39]

In some cases the temple institutions tried to prevent such migration and force the workers to render service to the temples concerned. One instance of this type is furnished by a Channagiri taluka inscription of 1050. The full significance of this highly damaged record cannot be made out, but what remains of the concluding part is enough to highlight the contradictions of a developing market economy. The record shows that the labourers of a village in the Channagiri locality tried to migrate from the village. In a bid to prevent this movement the local authorities led by a *gauḍa* chief confiscated the tools (*śastravan*) of the concerned workers and deposited these as security in a temple for whose services the artisans seem to have been detained. Following a compromise the names of some of the workers were registered evidently for rendering service whenever required. With the conclusion of this agreement the confiscated tools were returned (lit. allowed to be sharpened). One might also think that all other workers whose names were not registered were now free to migrate to a place of their choice.[40]

NOTES

1. *Annual Report of the Mysore Archaeological Department,* 1935, no. 26, pp. 92-8.
2. *EC,* 9, Coorg 80.
3. *EC,* 9, Channapatna 42 A, AD 1007.
4. Cf. *EC,* 8, Sorab 389 of AD 1172 and Sorab 387 of AD 1241.
5. *EC,* 10, Srinivaspur 29, AD 920; *EC,* 11, Koppa 143, AD 1066.
6. *EC,* 9, Bangalore 100.
7. *EC,* 9, Devanahalli 26.
8. *EI,* 5, no. 3 C, AD 1178.

9. *EI*, 5, no. 3 A, l. 42.
10. *EI*, 5, no. 3 A, l. 42.
11. *EC*, 9, Kankanhalli 71, AD 1259.
12. *Annual Report of the Mysore Archaeological Department*, 1932, no. 21, p. 177, AD 1012, The two *gauḍa* (peasant) families lived in a village of the Chikmaglur taluka.
13. See Ch. 8 below.
14. Noboru Karashima, *South Indian History and Society*, Delhi, 1984, p. 31.
15. Ibid. p. 30.
16. Compare *EC*, 9, Devanahalli 75 and 76.
17. R.S. Sharma, *Indian Feudalism (A.D. 300-1200)*, Calcutta, 1965, p. 57.
18. Harbans Mukhia, 'Was There Feudalism in Indian History?', *Presidential Address* (Section II, Medieval India), 40th Indian History Congress, Waltair, 1979; for a criticism, see R.S. Sharma, 'How Feudal was Indian Feudalism?', *Social Scientist*, vol. 13, no. 2, Feb. 1984, pp. 14-16.
19. Maurice Dobb, *Studies in the Development of Capitalism*, 6th impression, London, 1954 (1st published 1946), pp. 35-6. It may be pertinent to mention that the feudal mode of production never existed in a pure state anywhere in medieval Europe. The feudal formation can be better understood as a composite system in which other modes of production survived and intertwined with feudalism proper. For, the core region of European feudalism was that in which a balanced synthesis of the Roman and Germanic elements occurred. See Perry Anderson, *Passages from Antiquity to Feudalism*, London, 1974, p. 155.
20. Maurice Dobb, op. cit., p. 35.
21. For a good study of new literary material on the subject, see B.N.S. Yadava, 'The Problem of the Emergence of Feudal Relations in Early India', *Presidential Address* (Section 1: Ancient India), 41st Indian History Congress, Bombay, 1980.
22. The growth of forced labour between the fourth and seventh centuries (G.K. Rai, 'Forced Labour in Ancient India', *The Indian Historical Review*, vol. 3, no. 1, p. 26) and increase in the oppressive character of forced labour from the Gupta period in north India (D.N. Jha, *Revenue System in the Post-Maurya and Gupta Times*, Calcutta, 1969, p. 19) would appear significant in this connection.
23. *āvali-nāḍprabhū-kāma-gautana-besa-vaga-asagara-nāgana* or Washerman Nagana who was the bond servant of the *nāḍprabhū* Kama Gauḍa of Avali, *EC*, 8, Sorab 128, AD 1288.
24. *EC*, 8, Sorab 131, AD 1159.
25. *EC*, 8, Sorab 10, AD 800.
26. *Bandugiyar* may be a Kannada term derived from Sanskrit *bandhaka* meaning bound or mortgaged.
27. *EC*, 8, Sorab 251 and 253.
28. *EI*, 5, 3 A, AD 1165.
29. Hirahadgalli grant of Pallava Śivaskandavarmana, D.C. Sircar, *Select Inscriptions*, Calcutta, 1965, vol. 1, p. 461ff.

30. *EC*, 12, Kunigal 1, AD 1157.
31. *Mahantara gelasargga*, *EC*, 10, Srinivaspur 29, AD 920 and *pañchamaṭha-sthāna-gāvuṇḍagalum*, *EC*, 11, Koppa 143, AD 1063.
32. *EC*, 8, Sorab 309, AD 1213.
33. Ibid., Sorab 84, AD 1283.
34. *EC*, 9, Bangalore 85 C, AD 1110.
35. *EC*, 14 (Mysore and Mandya Districts Supplement), *Dynastic List of Inscriptions*, p. 4; the inscription belongs to the reign of Ganga king Nītimārga of the Talkad line.
36. *EC*, 7, Sorab 80, AD 1131 refers to two *gauḍa* brothers paying a fine of 100 *gadyāṇas* to the district administration.
37. *EC*, 14, *Dynastic List of Inscriptions*, pp. 8-9.
38. *EC*, 8, Sorab 132.
39. *Memorial Stones*, S. Settar and Gunther D. Sontheimer, eds., Dharwar, 1982, p. 319ff.
40. *EC*, 7, Channagiri 32, AD 1050.

5

The Technique of Agriculture

The developments which characterized agricultural expansion in the early middle ages fall into three sectors, extension of cultivable land, improvement in drainage technology and increase in crop production. Extension of the cultivable area by forest clearance, waste reclamation, reclamation of coastal land and virgin tracts and establishment of new villages would, however, presuppose some scarcity of agricultural land notwithstanding the oft-repeated claim of land abundance. Scarcity of land cannot, however, be measured only in terms of the availability of surplus land but also in terms of the ability of the peasantry to make use of it. In the *Paṭṭupāṭṭu* poems there are references to vast stretches of grassland intervening between settled tracts and forests.[1] But to reclaim even a part of this virgin land would call for resources which a peasant folk may not be able to mobilize. On the contrary, it would be much easier to develop dry land and waste plots within the village with the help of existing irrigation tanks or by excavating new tanks than to reclaim virgin land and forest tracts lying beyond the boundaries of the village and without any dependable source of irrigation. This is precisely what the cultivators in peasant villages continued to do throughout the period.[2] By contrast, all instances of forest clearance, reclamation of virgin land and development of coastal land during the same period relate in varying degrees to Brahmana freeholders, fiefholders and *devadāna* holders who provided the necessary incentives for the early growth of rural economy.

Extension of the Cultivable Area

The scarcity of cultivable land and food surpluses do not, however, surface in the Sangam works which make pointed references to abundance of crop production despite a low technology with vast stretches of grassland lying unclaimed. The abundance of harvests was evidently related to soil fertility. Some idea of this high fertility is furnished by the poems in the *Paṭṭupāṭṭu* and the *Ethuthokai* which state that the soil was so productive that even one *veli* (acre) of land could yield a thousand *kalams* (roughly a thousand maunds) of paddy and that a patch of land covered by a sitting elephant could feed seven persons through the year.[3] The abundance of produce despite a low technology could not, however, continue for too long in the face of rising demands from a large class of fiefholders and Brahmana freeholders. And since crop production could not be appreciably increased with the existing technological level, improvements in the techniques of agriculture were inevitable. Such improvement can be noticed during the Sangam age itself from references to paddy transplantation, crop rotation, manuring and fallow cultivation. Towards the close of the Sangam period we also hear of sluices and shutters used in tanks for controlled drainage of fields.[4] All this would anticipate the great expansion of agriculture during the three closing centuries of the first millennium.

The first clear reference to reclamation of forest land is furnished by an inscription of the sixth century belonging to a minor Kadamba dynasty of the Goa region.[5] The record entitled a Brahmana to employ four batches of labourers (*preśyakula*) to clear a patch of forest and cultivate it (*araṇyakarsana*). The earliest mention of coastal land brought under rice cultivation is also furnished by this interesting record. The one *hala* of *khajjana* or coastal land which was converted into rice-fields by damming sea water in the shape of a *nullah* was named *vakulakacchakṣetra*, the word *kaccha* being significant in this connection. The next example of forest clearance is implicit in a Goribidnur taluka inscription of 762 which refers to a Kāśyapa Brahmana who received several allotments of different types of land together with a title over forest land which formed the common boundary of all the four villages in which the lands were situated.[6] Compared to these, the later examples of forest clearance and reclamation of virgin land are more explicit and elaborate. For an illustration we may cite a Nanjangud taluka inscription[7] of 904. The inscription praises a Taittirīya Brahmana of the Tanagundur Mahāgrāma which had earlier been settled by a group of Ahicchatra Brahmanas as the promoter of people's welfare (*janodaya*) by executing well devised schemes calculated to deliver benefits. One of these schemes evidently was the construction of a huge tank which put to shame the great ocean. The stated purpose of this tank, which was fed by three small rivers emerging from the nearby Manali forest, was to provide food to the people of the locality. Accordingly, the tract around the new tank was constituted, with the permission of the Ganga king, into a freeholding named *Śiva-Ayyanamangala* and divided into 120 shares of which 60 were given to worthy Brahmanas of Tanagundur and 60 retained by the Brahmana entrepreneur for his sons and grandsons. Another inscription[8] of 935 states that a revenue officer of the Banavasi-12000 administration excavated a tank at Tanagundur and transferred plots below the new tank to a local temple.

A similar instance of agricultural expansion is furnished by the late Pallava Rāyacotta plates of Skandaśiṣya from the Krishnagiri taluka of Salem district.[9] The record which is addressed to the inhabitants of the fort (*koṭṭai*) and the inhabitants of the district (*nāḍu*) mentions the transfer of a village to a Vatsa Brahmana together with the waste land surrounding the village, jungles which had been cleared by burning trees and thickets and dry land under cultivation besides embankments, channels and causeways. It is likely that the village had been established or extended earlier by clearing forest and bringing waste and dry land under cultivation with the help of tanks and channels which too are mentioned in the record. Sometimes such extensions of *agrahāra* land were financed by prosperous merchants settled in these villages. A late eleventh-century Sorab taluka inscription mentions a *seṭṭi* who cleared a patch of forest bordering on the Kuppatura *agrahāra*, excavated a tank and laid rice fields all around.[10]

Reclamation of village waste, even if known earlier, must have been inconsequential in the expansion of agriculture. From the seventh century, however, inscriptions begin to record information on the transfer of waste plots to Brahmanas and folk heroes. The earliest example of this type comes from a late eighth-century inscription from the Goribidnur taluka of Kolar district[11] which registers transfer of different villages to an enterprising Brahmana. The transferred plots in each of the four villages included 12 *kandugas* of rice land (*śāli-ādi-vapana-yogyam*), 30 *kudabas* of waste land (*murpal*), 3 *kudabas* of homestead land (*gṛhakṣetram*) and 30 *khandikas* for sowing millets (*priyangu*) in addition to patches of forest tract. The transfer of *kṛta-akṛta* fields to Brahmanas also appears to be significant in this context.[12] The process of waste reclamation cannot be quantified to ascertain its impact on the overall progress of agriculture, although it seems to have continued throughout the early middle ages. A late ninth century *viragal* from the Sidlaghatta taluka of Kolar district refers to a villager whose brave acts in defence of the village were rewarded by 74 village elders with the transfer of 5 ploughs of rice land and 5 ploughs of waste land (*palu*) to the hero.[13] In another instance the nephew of a village-level chief received one *kanduga* of rice fields and one *kanduga* of waste as a reward for his heroic deeds in defence of the village.[14] The existence of regular plots of village waste is enough indication of a compulsion which induced the peasantry and the ruling aristocracy alike to convert into cultivated plots whatever uncultivated lands were available within the village. A crisis point would be reached when all such scope for extending the arable within the village became exhausted and when any new provision of land would call for the extension of village lands into neighbouring forests and virgin tracts as already noticed.

To the initiative shown by Brahmana freeholders and their feudal patrons, we may add the instances of the lords and their vassals undertaking excavation of tanks for reclaiming forest land and establishing new villages. Such examples do not, however, surface before the close of the ninth century and beginning of the tenth.[15]

In the sphere of irrigation the most significant development was the large-scale introduction of the animal-powered *araghaṭṭa*[16] for deep-well irrigation in northern and western India and of the sluice weir device in tank irrigation in the peninsular region roughly from the seventh-eighth centuries. Other devices which helped agricultural production during the period include substitution of the practice of filling tanks by canal-feeding from nearby rivers, widening the network of irrigation channels drawing water from tanks and rivers and the multiplication of the rain-fed irrigation tanks for bringing fresh land under cultivation in virgin tracts, forests and waste patches and to convert dry land in villages into rice-producing wet fields.

The Drainage System

We have argued elsewhere that the increasing demands on peasant surpluses following the extension of fiefdom and the growth of Brahmana population between the sixth and eighth centuries forced a distinct change in the technique of irrigation[17] and is represented, in the peninsular region by a shift of emphasis from lift-irrigation to drift-irrigation. The *Maduraikañchi* reference to the noise of people who stood in rows to lift water from tanks with the help of baskets tied to well-sweeps and also with the help of bucket-pails softly made but strongly bound[18] does not leave any doubt about the prevalence of an archaic labour intensive device of tank irrigation. These archaic techniques of surface irrigation continued down to Pallava times with slight modification in the form of the *picottah* which was used for lifting water from deep wells and rivers. The use of baskets in surface irrigation is also mentioned in Pallava inscriptions of the later period.[19] It was, however, during the later Pallava period that significant changes appear in the existing drainage technology. It cannot be without some good reason that the earliest references to sluice-weirs in channels drawing water from rivers as well as irrigation tanks are mentioned in the records of the eighth-ninth centuries. The role of the tank management committee (*eri-vāriyā*) which is first mentioned in the inscriptions of the early ninth century would also appear to be significant in this connection.[20]

In Karnataka the first clear mention of tanks with sluice-weir devices is found in a Mulbagal taluka inscription of 750 which refers to the transfer of a plot of land below the sluice of a tank.[21] After the eighth century there is a profusion of references to sluice tanks. Indeed the device became a marker of higher technology and agricultural progress in densely settled localities and settlements dominated by a powerful non-peasant class. The importance of sluice-tanks in raising agricultural output is testified by the description of tanks with four channels and multiple sluices. The first clear mention of a multiple sluice tank is furnished by a Hiriyur taluka inscription of 890 which praises the farmers of a village for constructing a large tank and providing it with four sluices.[22] The reference to the northern sluice-weir of a tank in an inscription of 1080 would also suggest the existence of more than one such device in a single tank.[23]

Another hydraulic improvement relates to the construction of channels for feeding tanks from nearby rivers, a method which is first mentioned in a Pallava inscription of the late seventh century.[24] In Karnataka the earliest mention of a tank fed by river water is found in a Nanjangud taluka inscription of 904 which praises the enterprise of a Brahmana freeholder of the Sthānagundur *agrahāra* in excavating a massive tank which drew water from three rivulets emerging from a nearby forest.[25] It needs no emphasis to state that the device reduced the dependence of cultivators on annual rainfall for filling their tanks. The perennial supply of water ensured crop production in the area.

The expansion of tank irrigation was also accompanied by the problem of maintenance. This is reflected by inscriptional references to constant operations and repairs to breaches and broken sluices. Although the reasons are not clear the structural damages appear to have been caused by excessive rainfall. At some places the problem was overcome by replacing earth-work by brick work and stone masonry. This was undertaken by the farmers both individually and collectively in peasant villages and by fiefholders and freeholders in their respective domains. Sometimes repair was undertaken jointly by the lords and peasants and by peasants and Brahmana freeholders. Such collaboration is also noticed between the overlord and his vassal. A late ninth-century inscription of a Ganga king mentions the good work of village chief and two palace officials in constructing a new tank and its stone sluices.[26] In another example a Sāmanta rebuilt a village tank by employing stone workers.[27] A late ninth-century Hiriyur taluka inscription refers to the initiative of villagers in excavating a large tank and its four channels in their village.[28] The work was rewarded by a locality chief who granted permanent sowing rights on certain plots irrigated by the new tank. While transfer of plots irrigated by tanks or of the one-tenth part of the produce of the lands or the grants of permanent sowing rights in these plots appear to have financed repairs to tanks and silt clearance during the eighth-tenth centuries, the institution of commercial credit funds for the same purpose can be noticed in the inscriptions of the eleventh century. The enterprise of individual merchants and merchant companies in the management of irrigation which can be noticed from the eleventh century would also appear to be significant in this connection.[29]

Probably a much greater problem was to retain and increase the storage capacity of tanks by regular dredging and by raising the height of embankments. Several Pallava inscriptions of the ninth century mention the institution of agricultural credit and the apportionment of the products of certain lands to facilitate dredging operations.[30] In very large tanks boats were used to carry silt ashore.[31] The dredging of a tank was necessary as much to retain and increase storage capacity as to prevent oversilting and consequent tank-bursts. In Karnataka villages the maintenance work was facilitated by grants of permanent sowing rights (*bittuvatta*) on plots irrigated by tanks or the transfer of one-tenth part (*dasabandha*) of the produce from concerned irrigated lands. We do not, however, hear of the constitution of tank committees as in the neighbouring Tamil Nadu. This lack of organizational effort may partly account for the frequent instances of breached tanks and broken sluices. The weakness on the organizational side of tank management was sought to be compensated in some areas by constructing stone embankments and stone sluices wherever resources could be mobilised.

NOTES

1. *Perumpanattrupadai*, 200-10, in J.V. Chelliah, *Paṭṭupāṭṭu*, Madras, 1962.
2. *EC*, 11, Hiriyur 33, AD 870 refers to a group of peasant families who constructed a large tank in their village and provided it with four channels; also *EC*, 5, Channerayapatna 251, AD 925.
3. *Perumpanattrupadai*, 290-9, in Chelliah, op. cit.
4. The sluices and shutters are first mentioned in the *Padirupāṭṭu* which on the basis of the *padigam* of the prologue can be assigned to the seventh century, see K.K. Pillay, *A Social History of the Tamils*, vol. 1, Madras, 1975, p. 196.
5. *EI*, 33, 3no. 53.
6. *EC*, 10, Goribidnur 47.
7. *EC*, 12, Nanjangud 269.
8. *EC*, 8, Shikarpur 194.
9. *EI*, 5, no. 8, p. 52. Compare these instances with L.B. Alayev's view that the construction of an irrigation system usually was beyond the labour resources of a single household and hence undertaken by a village or group of villages, L.B. Alayev, 'The Systems of Agricultural Production, South India', in Tapan Raychoudhuri and Irfan Habib, eds., *The Cambridge Economic History of India*, vol. 1, Delhi, 1984 (rpt.), p. 227. The view that irrigation was work of religious merit seems to overstate the importance of religion in traditional India and suggests that the desire for religious merit outweighed the importance of fulfilment of material needs.
10. *EC*, 8, Sorab 317, AD 1070.
11. *EC*, 10, Goribidnur 47, AD 762.
12. *EC*, 12, Davangere 66, AD 694.
13. *EC*, 10, Sidlaghatta 32, AD 870.
14. *EC*, 10, Mulbagal 108, AD 950.
15. See Ch. 3 above.
16. The *araghaṭṭa* seems to have been introduced to agricultural technology about the fifth century, though its use became widespread only during the early middle ages. For a useful discussion see Lallanji Gopal, *Aspects of the History of Agriculture in Ancient India*, Ch. 5, Varanasi, 1980. Chottapadhyaya's good study shows that in Rajasthan the adoption of the *araghaṭṭa* device began in the seventh century and by the close of the twelfth century it became widespread in the area, B.D. Chattopadhyaya, 'Irrigation in Early Medieval Rajasthan', *Journal of the Economic and Social History of the Orient*, vol. 14, pts. 2-3, pp. 293-316. Consequently Irfan Habib gives up his insistence on the equation of the *araghaṭṭa* with the noria and the introduction of the wheelpot device in India in the thirteenth century, Irfan Habib, *Presidential Address* (section II: Medieval India), 32nd Indian History Congress, Varanasi, 1969, pp. 12-19 and 'The Peasant in Indian History', *Presidential Address*, 43rd Indian History Congress, Kurukshetra, 1982, p. 30, fn. 2.

17. The idea of the constant factor in technology (Burton Stein, *Peasant, State and Society c. 800-1300*, Delhi, 1980, p. 24) has rightly been questioned by Irfan Habib, 'The Peasant in Indian History', *Presidential Address*, Indian History Congress, 43rd Session, Kurukshetra, 1982, p. 19.
18. Maduraikāñchi, 80-90.
19. C. Minakshi, *Administration and Social Life under the Pallavas*, Madras, 1938, p. 104.
20. The first Uttiramerur inscription which refers to *erivariya* belongs to the reign of Dantivarmana (795-845), C. Minakshi, op. cit., p. 106.
21. *EC*, 10, Mulbagal 255.
22. *EC*, 10, Hiriyur 33.
23. *Annual Report of the Mysore Archaeological Department*, 1934, no. 76, p. 236.
24. C. Minakshi, *Administration and Social Life under the Pallavas*, Madras, 1938, p. 102. The data might be of the second quarter of the eighth century, depending on the identification of king Parmeśvara Varmana. One ruler of this name ruled from 670 to 680, another from 720 to 731.
25. *EC*, 12, Nanjangud 269.
26. *Annual Report of the Mysore Archaeological Department*, 1932, no. 11, p. 167.
27. *EC*, 12, Tiptur 106.
28. *EC*, 11, Hiriyur 33.
29. *EC*, 14 (Mysore and Mandya district Supplement), *Dynastic List of Inscriptions*, p. 4; *EC*, 10, Mulbagal 208, AD 1000; *EC*, 10, Chik Ballapur 13, AD 1027; *ARMAD*, 1934, no. 4, p. 167.
30. Minakshi, op. cit., p. 107.
31. Ibid., p. 106.

6

Increase in Crop Production

The main factors in increasing crop production during the early middle ages may be identified as expansion of wet cultivation, a greater socialization of wild and marginally grown cereals and the introduction of new food crops, vine-crops and garden products. The great expansion of wet cultivation has already been noticed in the previous chapter. The effects of this development can be inferred from the additional surplus offering to non-producing consumers in the fiefs, freeholdings and temple *devadāna* holdings from the ninth century. The multiplicity of rice-oblations (three in a day) and apportionment of rice lands or their produce to a large number of functionaries in the prolific temple institutions appear to dominate the inscriptional material of the tenth and eleventh centuries. In some localities increased production of irrigated rice stimulated the process of long distance commodity exchange, as we see in the descriptions of certain Arab travellers. Ibn Khurdadbeh for instance, refers to the export of rice from certain parts of Andhra to Sarandib or Ceylon in the ninth century.[1] In most areas, however, the process of commodity exchange picked up at a later date to judge from the large dumps of food-grains, spices, garden-products and vine crops in market places and also from the collection of heavy tolls on these goods; both of these are fairly evident in the inscriptional records of the eleventh century.

New Cereal Crops

Since a major portion of the increased rice crop was claimed by the multiplying feudal houses, Brahmana freeholdings and temple institutions, some effort had to be made to supplement the staple food reserve of the remaining population, which too was increasing to judge from the growing density of rural settlements and foundation of new villages. The mandatory cultivation of major millets like *ragi* and greater attention to inferior cereals which were earlier wild or grown in marginal plots would thus appear to be self-explanatory. The inferior cereals included different wild and uncultivated varieties of rice such as *śyāmāka, nīvāra, kangu, kodrava* and *karaduṣa*. The millets included *priyangu (panicum italicum), ragi (eleusine coracana)* or the finger millet, *jowār (sorghum vulgare)* or the great millet and *bajra* or bulrush millet.

The earliest mention of *priyangu* (panicum italicum) is found in the later Vedic literature[2] where it is considered an inferior cereal. The low reckoning of the grain is also noticed in the medical works of Caraka and Suśruta.[3] A change is discernible in the *Vāyu Purāṇa* which distinguishes *priyangu* from *śyāmāka, nīvāra* and *karaduṣa* by stating that the former was a cultivated cereal whereas the latter grew wild.[4] Although the *Vāyu Purāṇa* is earlier than the *Suśruta Saṁhitā*, this particular chapter seems to be a later addition and may therefore be pointing towards a socialization of wild cereals. This is also confirmed by epigraphic data which refers to the cultivation of *priyangu* in certain localities. A late eighth century inscription from the Kolar taluka refers to *priyangu* fields donated to a Brahmana along with rice fields, gardens and waste plots in four adjacent villages.[5] Another cereal crop consumed during the early middle ages was the foxtail millet (*kangu*) of which there is neither any palaeobotanical evidence nor any references in the literature of the pre-Christian centuries. In the beginning of the Christian era the grain is mentioned by Strabo and Diodorus.[6] In the *Aṣṭānga Saṁgraha*, a text of the seventh century, *kangu* is described as an inferior grain alongwith *kodrava* and *śyāmāka*.[7] In a work of the ninth century, *kangu* is listed with *śyāmāka, nīvāra* and *kodrava,* the consumption of which is said to cause coughs, colds and gastric ailments.[8] Despite such disapproval *kangu* appears to have been one of the regularly cultivated food crops of the early middle ages and consumed by the poorer strata of the rural population. A Kadur district inscription mentions four *kandugas* of rice land (*vrīhikṣetram*) and two *kandugas* of *kangukṣetram* as the share of a blacksmith who engraved a charter of land transfer to a Jaina *basadi*.[9] The *Mānasollāsa* would, however, suggest that by the close of the eleventh century *kangu* had entered the royal and aristocratic households where a milk and sugar preparation of *kangu* was greatly relished. This early twelfth-century work authored by a western Cālukya king of Karnataka also praises similar milk and sugar preparations of *śyāmāka*, *nīvāra* and *gandhaśāli*. The characterization of *kangu*, *śyāmāka* and *nīvāra* as superior grains (*sutaṇḍula*)[10] is in sharp contrast with the earlier descriptions of the same varieties as inferior grains *kudhānya*.

The early popularity of *bājrā* or bulrush millet in the peninsular region is evident from carbonised specimens of the grain from different neolithic and early historical sites in the area.[11] But during the historical period the crop remained confined mainly to the lower strata of the population. The Sangam works whose dates range between the third and the seventh centuries seem to associate the crop with people of the forest region and the pastoral groups. In the advanced agricultural tracts (*marudam*) it was no more than a marginal crop.[12] This impression is confirmed by absence of any reference to *jowār* until the beginning of the Christian era when Caraka refers to the *sorghum vulgare*. In the peninsular region, however, there is no reference to this millet in either Sanskrit or Prakrit literature until the sixth-seventh centuries. Thereafter one can observe spate of references in literature and inscriptions.[13] By the eleventh century *jowār* had earned considerable access to the higher strata of the population and was being produced on a large scale to infer from references to *jowār* shops and *jowār* merchants in the inscriptions of the eleventh-twelfth centuries.[14]

Ragi (*eleusine coracana*), also known as the finger millet, seems to be a native of Karnataka despite suggestions about its migration from Africa.[15] Not only the name *ragi* is a Kannada term which is retained in modified form in neighbouring languages (Tamil *ragi*, Telugu *ragulu*, Marathi and Gujarati *nagli*),[16] but the largest area under *ragi* cultivation is also in Karnataka.[17] The discovery of carbonized seeds of *ragi* along with its wild progenitor from neolithic Hallur (*c.* 1800 BC)[18] might also support the independent origin of the crop in the Karnataka region, from where it appears to have spread to Andhra Pradesh, Maharashtra and Tamil Nadu. As the hardiest crop most suited to dry farming and of great nutritive value and with a storage life of up to fifty years the *ragi* millet appears to have been of considerable help in neutralizing the effects of growing scarcity of staple food crops for poorer villagers. It still continues to be eaten as a staple.

The mandatory cultivation of *ragi* may thus have been forced on the peasant in order to free the rice crop for consumption in temples and feudal houses. A late tenth century inscription from the Sorab taluka registers the order of a *mahāsāmanta* which states that if any land under *ragi* cultivation in the Gede-12 locality remained waste, all the chief farmers in the district were to pay fines and undergo punishment.[19] Gede-12, it may be mentioned, was one of the eight estates of the *mahāsāmanta* whose order is recorded here. A thirteenth-century Pāṇḍya inscription also shows that *ragi* was under extensive cultivation.[20]

Sugarcane

The cultivation of sugarcane was introduced into the peninsular region by the ancestors of Adigaman Neduman Anji.[21] According to the *Puranānuru*, a Tamil poem of the third century AD, Adigaman was one of the last seven Maravar chiefs known for their philanthropy. Going by the date of the *Puranānuru*, the ancestors of Adigaman can be safely placed in the first-second centuries AD. Sugarcane was quickly assimilated into the plant economy, for the same poem mentions its popularity in a later passage. This is also evident from the *Pattinapalai* (1-10) which refers to lush green and never failing fields of sugarcane by the side of spacious tanks. The *Pattinapalai*[22] which is assigned to the third century would, however, suggest that in the earliest stage of its adoption sugarworking was one of the many activities of the agriculturists who extracted juice from the sugarcane by some improvised device and boiled it in vats set in the harvested fields. The description of waste water flowing from these vats into adjoining fields and making the standing crops pale and fade away only highlights the crude nature of sugar preparation in early Tamil Nadu villages. At a later stage the manufacture of jaggery appears to have been dissociated from the peasants' domain of activities and concentrated in the hands of a professional class who worked sugar-presses in village huts and sold both sugarcane juice and crystal sugar to customers who approached these huts.[23] The *Gāthāsaptaśatī* reference[24] to the owner-operators of sugarcane presses who took a portion of the manufacture as the cost of their labour also points in the same direction. This may have facilitated the commodity-production of jaggery and crystal sugar of which the inscriptions provide unmistakable evidence from the tenth century.

Betel Leaves and Areca Nuts

Among the crops which were of a comparatively recent origin and marginal utility until the beginning of the feudal era, but whose cultivation rapidly expanded on account of new social manners and ritual requirements, we may include betel-leaves and areca-nuts. The absence of *tāmbula* (betel-leaf) and *guvāka/ puga* (areca-nut) in the literature of the pre-Christian era would show that the two articles were not used on any scale until at least the beginning of the Christian era when these may have entered the Indian market as imports from the countries of their origin.[25] It may have taken the two imported items another two to three centuries to enter the agricultural sector.

The *Paṭṭupāṭṭu* evidence would suggest that marginal cultivation of areca-nut had begun in the peninsular region about the fifth or sixth centuries[26] to judge from references to fields of areca palms together with those of coconuts, plantains, sugarcane and ginger. More positive evidence is furnished by the inscriptional records of the early middle ages. A Gubbi taluka inscription of 812[27] mentions tall betel plants as the boundary of a village transferred to a Jain temple.

However, this slow pace of adoption is unimpressive when compared with the numerous instances of the creation and donation of betel-vines and areca-gardens to temples in the inscriptions of the eleventh and twelfth centuries. A comparative view of temple offerings towards the closing centuries of the first millennium and those noticed in the eleventh century and later would at once suggest the great demand of betel-leaves and areca-nuts in mandatory temple rituals. The earlier oblations comprised boiled rice, incense (camphor) and perfumes (sandal paste). But the later documents invariably mention both betel-leaves and areca-nuts. Even a peripheral view of the inscriptional literature would convince a reader how the scale of temple demands had transformed articles of marginal utility into essentials produced in marketable quantities.

Besides the religious compulsion behind commodity production of the two articles, the social factor also deserves consideration. Abu Zaid, an Arab chronicler of the early tenth century, refers to betel offerings as a token of honour and friendship.[28] An inscription of Rājarāja Cola mentions the old custom of exchanging *tāmbula*.[29] Chou-Jukua, an early twelfth-century Chinese traveller, refers to the popularity of betel chewing among kings[30] and nobles. The betel-leaf and areca-nut also owed their new-found status to their medicinal properties. Alberuni notices that Indians ate betel-leaves with lime after dinner to strengthen their power of digestion while the chewing of betel-nut acted as an astringent on the teeth, gums and stomach.[31]

The growth of cottage industries centred on large-scale production of areca-nut is evident from the inscriptional records of the tenth-eleventh centuries. An Arsikere taluka inscription of the eleventh century mentions details regarding harvesting and processing of areca-nuts by two different classes of workers. The *koylasis* were the people who harvested the crop while wholesale dealers or *moṭṭakāras* were associated with the processing of areca-nuts for the market.[32]

Coconut and Orange

Of the fruit crops subjected to commodity-production coconuts and oranges deserve special mention. Of the two fruits, coconut entered the temple ritual and social customs earlier and in a much bigger way, but oranges do not appear in the orchards of the peninsular south until the eleventh century. Indeed the orange never attained even a semblance of the ritual or social status which the coconuts, betel-leaves and areca-nuts had acquired with the growth of social customs and expansion of temple institutions. The coconut, like the betel-leaves and betel-nuts was introduced into the peninsular region[33] about the beginning of the Christian era or a little earlier. The nutritive value of the fruit helped its quicker adoption.

The orange is mentioned for the first time in Indian literature about the first century of the Christian era. The medical work of Caraka enumerates a long list of fruits, many of which were introduced for the first time. The orange or *nāgaraṅga* (Hindi *narangi*) is one of these new arrivals. The fruit does not, however, find a place in Suśruta's list of best fruits — grapes, dates, pomegranates and myrobalanas. These references do not, however, suggest that orange was cultivated on any scale in the subcontinent. It appears that the fruit was a native of Kashmir and remained confined to the valley until its extensive patronage by aristocratic families towards the close of the first millennium.

The diffusion of orange cultivation in the peninsular region, vividly described in inscriptions of the tenth-eleventh centuries, can be attributed to the requirements of delicacies in feudal cuisine. Probably this is evident from the raising of oranges in the exclusive domains of feudal lords. A Sorab taluka inscription of 1172 refers to Elamballi which was a *vṛtti* (fief) and a jewel of the Nagarkhaṇḍa-*nāḍ*, well-known for its betel vines and the fruits of areca palms and orange trees (*nāraṅga*).[34] That Elamballi was a prosperous feudal estate is evident from contemporary inscriptions. Probably orange cultivation in the locality began at the initiative of a merchant who earlier purchased the *vṛtti* ostensibly by paying the required price to its peasant owner, but actually occupying the fief by fraudulent methods. Another prosperous locality where oranges were grown about the same time was also the domain of a *daṇḍanāyaka* lord. An inscription of 1217 refers to this district as Jiduling *kampana* with orange and plantain groves and areca palms which meet overhead and create shade.[35]

Towards the close of the millennium, orange cultivation was introduced into the Arab-Islamic heartland. Al-Masudi writes that after AH 300 (AD 915) the orange tree was imported from India and planted in Oman. Since Oman was the chief port which dealt with Indian products, the diffusion of orange might have been from southern India, particularly Karnataka, whose orange cultivation began well before the tenth century and which formed the heart of Rāṣṭrakūṭa (Balhara of the Arab traders) kingdom. Here merchant entrepreneurs from the Islamic lands received great encouragement. It is, however, possible that early south Indian oranges were grown in limited family gardens of chiefs and commodity production of the fruit reported in the inscriptions of the eleventh century may have picked up when Arabs showed an interest in this fruit. From Oman the plant was taken to Basra and Iraq and it became plentiful in the houses of Tarsus, Antioch and the Syrian and Palestinian coasts, and in Egypt where it was unknown before. The fine fragrance and the beautiful colour which it had in India, however, disappeared.[36]

Commodity-production of food crops was mainly the consequence of internal compulsions of the early feudal order, but the commercial production of luxury goods was as much the result of internal demands of temples and feudal households as it was of the rising demand for Indian goods in international markets. The redevelopment of India's international trade in luxuries and prestige goods was set in motion by Arab traders who used India both as an entrepot in world-wide exchange of commodities and as a producer of goods. The market in luxuries, particularly spices, had also expanded considerably since the days of the Roman empire.

Spices

The demand for spices was no longer confined to the upper strata of the society, but had become a normal feature of the people's diet in Europe, Western Asia and China. The market for black pepper, a monopoly of the west coast of India, was fast developing, with China as the major consumer. In the city of Kinsay alone the inhabitants consumed pepper at the rate of 10,000 pounds a day, all of which came from India.[37] The ship-loads of coarse spices which went in the direction of the Persian Gulf and Alexandria did not account even for one-tenth of those sent to China.[38] Indian ginger, which in earlier times did not figure in the foreign markets, sold at a very high price in the markets of medieval Europe.[39] Export of ginger is mentioned by Marco Polo, Nicolo Conti and Vasco de Gama.[40]

Perhaps the clinching evidence for commodity production of cereals, garden crops, spices and prestige items is furnished by a Shikarpur taluka inscription of 1150[41] which refers to large dumps of these articles in separate market streets and the collection of specified amounts of coined money in the denominations of *hāga, visa* and *paṇa* on each of these commodities. Some of the more important items, besides the different varieties of grain brought in as head loads, cartloads and bullock loads, were mustard seed, cummin, coriander, dry ginger, green ginger, long pepper, black pepper, sugar and sugar-candy, cardamom, turmeric, camphor, musk, sandal and saffron, pearls and drugs and roots of medicinal value. The inscription refers to foreign merchants, local merchants, cloth merchants, gold merchants, betel merchants and flower-merchants. A Bagewadi taluka (Dharwar district) inscription of the twelfth century makes copious references to tolls collected in cash and kind from various groups of merchants and artisans in the Maningavalli (Managoli) *agrahāra.*[42] The inscription refers to taxes collected on gold merchants, guilds of weavers, guilds of oilmen, toddy sellers, dairy merchants and others.

NOTES

1. K.A.N. Sastri, *Foreign Notices of South India*, Madras, 1939, p. 119.
2. Om Prakash, *Food and Drinks in Ancient India*, Delhi, 1961, p. 11, fn. 5.
3. *Caraka Saṁhitā* 27. 25-17, *Suśruta Saṁhitā* 46. 21.
4. *Vāyu Purāṇa*, 8. 153-545.
5. *EC*, 10, Goribidnur 47, AD 762.
6. N.N. Kher, *Agrarian and Fiscal Economy in the Mauryan and Post Mauryan Age*, Delhi, 1973, p. 382.
7. *Aṣṭāṅga Saṁgraha*, VI. 14-16 cited in Om Prakash, op. cit., p. 170 fn.
8. *Aṣṭaṅga Hṛdaya*, VI. 11-12 cited in ibid.
9. *EC*, 6, Mudgere 36, AD 744.
10. *Mānasollāsa*, III. 1373-4.
11. *Indian Archaeology: A Review*, 1976-7, p. 90ff.

12. *Perumpanattrupadai*, 190-200, in J.V. Chelliah, op. cit.
13. P.K. Gode, *Studies in Indian Culture*, vol. 1, Hoshiarpur, 1961, pp. 281-2. The table of references shows that of 15 literary notices to *jowār* between AD 100 and AD 1200, 14 belong to the period 500 to 1200.
14. *KI*, 2, no. 10, p. 33.
15. Bridget Allchin and Raymond Allchin, *The Rise of Civilization in India and Pakistan*, New Delhi, 1983, p. 292.
16. B.G.L. Swamy, 'Sources for a History of Plant Sciences in India', *Journal of the History of Science in India*, vol. 8, nos. 1 and 2, 1973, p. 69.
17. M.S. Randhawa, *A History of Agriculture in India*, New Delhi, 1980, p. 235.
18. Note the insistence of Allchins on the absence in India of the wild relative of *ragi*, Bridget Allchin and Raymond Allchin, op. cit., p. 279.
19. *EC*, 8, Sorab 477, AD 991.
20. *EI*, 24, no. 22.
21. K.K. Pillay, *A Social History of the Tamils*, vol. 1, 2nd edn., Madras, 1975.
22. *Pattinapalai*, p. 10.
23. *Perumpanattrupadai*, 290-300.
24. *Gāthāsaptaśatī*, 6. 54 (*Jantia Gulam*).
25. *Dictionary of the Economic Products of India*, vol. 6, pp. 247-56; betel leaf is said to be a native of Java.
26. *Pattinapalai*, 1-10.
27. *EC*, 11, Gubbi 61.
28. K.A.N. Sastri, *Foreign Notices of South India*, op. cit., p. 129.
29. *EI*, 6, no. 35.
30. Sastri, op. cit., p. 136.
31. *India Alberuni*, ed. Q. Ahmad, Delhi, NBT, 1983, p. 237.
32. *EC*, 5, Arsikere 77, 78 etc.
33. It has been argued that since all the south Indian and Ceylonese languages preserve the root *ten* (south) in their respective terms for coconut, the fruit must have migrated from the South Pacific islands, B.G.L. Swamy, 'Sources for a History of Plant Sciences in India', op. cit., p. 69.
34. *EC*, 8, Sorab 389.
35. *EC*, 8, Sorab 135.
36. Al-Masudi, *Muruz-al-dhabab*, ed. de Meynard, Paris, 1861, vol. 2, pp. 438-9, cited in S.M. Ziauddin Alavi, *Arab Geography in the Ninth and Tenth Centuries*, Aligarh, 1965, p. 94.
37. C.H. Yule, ed., *The Book of Ser Marco Polo*, ii (London, 1875), p. 186.
38. Ibid., p. 379.
39. Ibid., p. 363 and note B on p. 370.
40. Ibid., p. 363; Nicolo Conti, *India*, pp. 1-39; and Vasco de Gama, *The Three Voyages*, p. 184, cited in A. Appadorai, *Economic Conditions of Southern India*, vol. 2 (Madras, 1936), pp. 527-8.
41. *EC*, 7, Shikarpur 118.
42. *EI*, 5, no. 3a, 3b, 3c, twelfth century AD.

7

The Growth of a Market Economy

Money Circulation and Mints

The revival of the urban market economy from the beginning of the eleventh century appears to have coincided with a recognizable increase in the circulation of metallic money. Attention has been drawn to the almost total absence of indigenous currency in large parts of southern India between the seventh century and the tenth century.[1] In some of these areas, particularly the central and western parts of the Deccan, the complete discontinuation in the manufacture of indigenous lead and copper coins[2] of which there was a great profusion during the Sātavāhana era constituted a glaring reality of the currency history in the region. In line with this is the evidence of Brahmapuri excavations which shows the presence of coined money in Sātavāhana layers and in the eleventh century Śilāhāra layers but none in the intervening Cālukya-Rāṣṭrakūṭa strata.[3] This absence of low value indigenous coins is also reflected in the descriptions of Hiuen-tsang in the second quarter of the seventh century[4] and Sulaiman in the early tenth century.[5] While Hiuen-tsang notices the use of gold, silver, cowries and small pearls in the commerce of the country, Sulaiman mentions that in the Balhara country all buying was done in bullion and that the Balhara king had plenty of *dirham* gold coins. It appears that a gold currency of some sort, represented by the *gadyāṇaka*, *dirham* and *dramma*, continued in high value transactions like the purchase of horses, elephants and prestige goods requisitioned by palaces, forts and garrisons. A limited circulation of the *dirham* is also mentioned by Ibn

Khurdadbeh who travelled in India between 844 and 848.[6] Ibn Khurdadbeh's references to a king who collected 200 pieces of gold every day from his people, melted these into ingots and deposited the ingots in his treasury under the sea is interesting since it suggests a low commercial profile and exterjection of metallic money from the channels of circulation. Destablization of currency can be seen also from Sulaiman's observation that although the Balhara king had plenty of *dirhams* he gave neither food nor pay to his vast armies, whereas in China the troops received the same pay as the troops of the Arabs. This may again indicate the absence of low value coinage which in Karnataka reappears only towards the close of the eleventh century in the shape of the *hāga/pāga* and *visa* small value coins. What is particularly significant in this passage is the predominantly feudal character of military mobilization. The traveller writes that the king only calls up the troops in case of war and that they take the field and realize for themselves the cost of their maintenance.[7] This seems to resemble the many instances of kings and lords sending out summons to vassals and warriors to rush against named enemies and rewards of agricultural land which followed victories and deaths.[8]

It is in this context that the increase in money circulation, growth minting activity and the attendant development of a market system during the eleventh century have to be considered. It has rightly been stressed that the coinage of this late period presents a sharp contrast with the currency situation of the sixth-ninth centuries. Of the several new trends the most striking is the consistent and regular use of coined money in all major areas of economic life.[9] The increasing incidence of revenue payments in minted money, money payments for construction labour and a flourishing credit market are all indications of the growing relevance of money.

The Credit Market

The beginnings of large-scale commercial credit can be traced on the basis of inscriptional references to *sabhās* of Brahmana villages and the temple institutions which accepted gifts and gratuitous loans of principal amounts and earned handsome interest on these sums. Institution of credit funds by merchants and merchant companies are already noticeable in the tenth century.[10] Significantly, the interest earned on principal was meant not merely to run charities of varying nature but also to pay wages to constructional and garden labourers.[11] This certainly is an indication of new uses to which money was being put and of the possession of some liquid capital by merchants. The records also suggest the role of Brahmana assemblies and temples as early credit establishments. The interest earned by the *sabhās* together with the proceeds of the sale of *agrahāra* land, helped Brahmana landlords to accumulate substantial hard cash, the benefits of which began to surface in the eleventh century in the wake of market development. The most striking feature of temple participation in the credit market was the uninhibited manner in which loans were accepted or interests collected. This is in contrast with the practice of contemporary Church in Europe. Probably the rejection of usury by the Church as a sinful act did not create problems so long as money was not indispensable to the relations of exchange. But with the development of commercial credit during the eleventh century the Church found it difficult to adhere to its own ethical formulation and consequently there were occasional violations of the rule.[12] In India, however, the temple priests set aside the orthodox brahmanical abhorrence of usury and freely accepted gifts and gratuitous loans for earning interest. In fact, the brahmanical temple did no more than to emulate the example of earlier Buddhist and Jain monasteries which never failed to appreciate the value of usury as a source of wealth.

Although no uniformity in credit relations during the early middle ages can be expected, certain trends in the credit market are perceptible. One of these was the rising rate of interest from the ninth century. A Kanheri inscription[13] of the ninth century shows that 29 *drammas*, were collected annually on a deposit of 160 *drammas,* the rate of interest thus working out to 17 per cent. An early tenth century Bāṇa epigraphic record[14] from south Karnataka shows that on a deposit of 20 *kalañjus* of gold coins, 5 were to be collected annually, the rate of interest in this case being 25 per cent. Further south-west, the rate of interest was still higher. An early-tenth century inscription of Parantaka I from the Annamalai region states that a local temple was earning interest at the rate of 40 per cent annually for paying to the village assembly 6 of the stipulated 18 *ilakkāsus*[15] of tax for enjoying the usufruct of lands belonging to the *sabhā*. The rate of interest in this case works out to be as high as 40 per cent. These instances show that the money-market had infiltrated the countryside in the wake of commercialization of peasant production. The rate of interest on loans advanced by temples continued to rise despite increase in money supply. A Channapatna taluka record of 1164[16] shows that for burning a twilight lamp in a temple of the village Malavur an interest of one *pāgam* was to be collected on a deposit of 4 *paṇams*. The record specifies that the interest was payable on a monthly basis. The system of monthly collections of interest was fairly widespread about this time,[17] no matter whether the interest was paid in cash or in kind. Considering that the *pāga* or *bāga* was one-fourth of a *paṇa*[18] and that this interest was chargeable every month, a total of 3 *paṇams* would have to be paid on a principal of 4 *paṇams*, the rate of interest thus being as high as 75 per cent. It is evident that the interest rates were rising just about a time when the money market was in a developing state and the supply of money had also considerably improved.[19] The credit market in foodgrains also indicates similar trends with rates of interest in the vicinity of 30 per cent and above. The purpose of consumption loans generally advanced by temples appears to have been to raise stocks of grain by fleecing peasants during the lean season. A late ninth-century inscription of the Pallava dynasty mentions an annual interest of 100 *kadis* on a deposit of 400 *kadis* of rice.[20] A higher rate is indicated by a Channapatna taluka inscription which refers to 320 *kalams* of paddy advanced by a temple to the *sabhā* of a neighbouring Brahmana village.[21] The Brahmanas were asked to pay an annual interest of 100 *kalams* on the deposit after three years from the date of the deposit. The rate of interest in this case is over 30 per cent. Probably the Brahmanas charged a higher rate from the villagers among whom the loan may have circulated.

The reasons for increasing rates of interest lay not in the

decline of trade or diminished supply of metallic money as suggested by some scholars[22] but in the desire to earn higher profits and in the compulsions of a growing market. We may also draw attention to the scarcity of cultivable land in the settled areas and the hard cash required for its purchase. In many examples the purchaser was the temple itself. We have already drawn attention to temples paying money rent to *sabhās* for occupying *sabhā* lands. We may also mention that in the twelfth century many of the temple services which were earlier managed from the products of the land were now being managed from interest on principal amounts loaned out to traders or whoever else needed them. In the present state of our knowledge it cannot, however, be determined whether such high rates of interest were a normal feature of the credit market or were restricted to the earnings made by sanctimonious temple institutions.

The Minting of Coins

The expansion of commercial credit and the importance of low value coins in the relations of exchange might also explain the growth of mints in the latter half of the eleventh century. The shops of goldsmiths which appear to have manufactured a limited gold currency during the earlier period, however, continued to dominate mintage activities with the state exercizing a supervisory control. The absence of a central mint and the multiplicity of privately worked minting shops of which sometimes there was more than one in a district, may have created problems in the exchange market. The role of the private money changer, the earliest examples of which go back to the second half of the eleventh century, would become meaningful in this context. Probably the profession of money-changing was as lucrative in India as it was in contemporary Europe.[23] In either case the right of money-changing was granted by the state which claimed a part of the earnings as tax. We may refer to a Shikarpur taluka inscription of 1098 which mentions the remission of one *visa* on every sum of money changed in the locality.[24] The remission which figures along with several other tax remissions in the institution of a temple fund, was evidently only a part of the state's share in the profits of private money-changers.

A relationship between minted coins and the money in actual circulation is also fairly evident from a comparison of inscriptions from the same region and the same period. For illustration, a Managoli inscription of 1170 from the Bagewadi taluka of Dharwar district mentions specified amounts of *haṇa* (*paṇa*), *visa* and *hāga* as part of the state's collection of commercial taxes on the sale of different consumer goods and luxury articles.[25] A Shikarpur taluka inscription of 1150 similarly mentions the *pāga, visa, paṇam* and *kani,* of which specified amounts were collected on the sale of different commodities.[26] The *gadyāṇa* which was a high-value gold coin during the twelfth-thirteenth centuries, seems to have been gradually replaced by the gold *paṇa.* Many of these coins were being manufactured by newly established mints in the region and in some cases the coins were named after the mints which issued them. For example, the Lokkundi mint which is frequently mentioned in the inscriptions of the eleventh-twelfth centuries issued coins which were known as the *lokkigadyāṇa,*[27] *lokkipaṇa*[28] and *lokkiya-visa.*[29] It may be mentioned that Lokkundi had developed as an important mint town of Dharwar district in the twelfth century and was evidently catering to the currency requirements of the region. Despite the large number of mints appearing in the inscriptions of the twelfth century and the considerable increase in the circulation of coined money, the regional character of the money market cannot be denied. Judging from the distribution of mints and market towns one can notice the commercial viability of certain regions such as north-western Karnataka, which claimed six of the nine mints founded in different parts of the state during the eleventh-twelfth centuries[30] and which had the largest number of market towns which emerged about the same period.[31]

The Rise of Commercial Tolls

In European feudalism, increasing references to tolls during the eleventh century are said to underline the growing marketization of rural production.[32] A parallel situation seems to have developed in India also where we come across references to collection of tolls from the beginning of the eleventh century. Tolls were collected, in both cash and kind, on peasant goods as well as artisanal products. The two generic terms for commercial tolls used in Karnataka inscriptions are *perjjuñka* and *vaḍḍarāvula-sunka*, the suffix *sunka* being a vernacular form of Sanskrit *śulka* (toll). Both the terms mean heavy custom dues which were levied in the beginning on paddy, areca-nuts and betel leaves. From the close of the eleventh century, however, a large number of goods were subjected to tolls at the feudal headquarters and large villages which show a marked tendency to develop into major trading marts. The goods subjected to customs dues during the eleventh and the twelfth century included drugs, clothes, spices, perfumes, oil-seeds, jaggery, white sugar, gems of every description and also grain, areca-nuts and betel leaves. The point is brought into sharp focus by a comparative study of inscriptions found at Belgami. Belgami or Balligave was an obscure Brahmana village which was raised to the status of a feudal headquarters by a *mahāmaṇḍaleśvara* lord towards the beginning of the eleventh century. Of the numerous temple endowments registered during the eleventh century not a single one mentions the collection of heavy customs dues until the last quarter of the century. During the first two quarters Belgami witnessed transfers of land to different temples.[33] By 1054, however, we hear of a senior merchant of the place and also the transfer of local shops and gardens. By the eighties the commercial tolls began to dominate the revenues of the state and consequently more transfers of toll incomes to temples are recorded.[34]

Commodity Production of Artisan Goods

Commodity production of artisan goods which is indicated by increasing collections of commercial tolls and the corporate basis of artisan activity, constituted an important aspect of the growth of the market economy during the eleventh century. Large groups of weavers, oil-pressers, tailors and smaller bodies of smiths and potters who dominate the emerging towns during the eleventh century invite comparison with single families of village artisans who figure as folk heroes in the *viragal* records of the eighth-tenth centuries. From grants of land to these people it would be clear that before the eleventh century the artisans combined domestic crafts with family farming besides military duties as and when demanded. But the market economy of the eleventh century helped a progressive dissociation of the two and confined the artisans to commodity production of their goods.

The liberalizing effect of the market was not, however, without constraints, to judge from increasing subjection of artisans and service castes by the dominant temple institutions. Though enslavement by temples made the concerned families immune from the payment of tolls to the state it also took away their freedom to market their goods after payment of dues. One would notice that the incidence of artisan subjection increased just about the time when the artisans had started banding together for organized commodity production. We have discussed elsewhere in this study the effects of these contradictions on the interdependence of classes in giving rise to a potential conflict situation.

The pertinent question which arises in this connection is whether increasing circulation of minted money helped reduce the chances of enslavement by temple institutions. Taking an overview of the inscriptional evidence a few trends would come to the surface. During the tenth and the early eleventh century inscriptions generally mention the transfer of artisan families to temples. From the close of the eleventh century oil-mills and looms were asked to remit a part of the goods produced by them, or the income thereof, to temples. During the twelfth century payment of money dues becomes the normal practice though the subjections did not stop. Where there was a large number of artisans belonging to a single craft, one family was permanently enslaved and the rest were asked to pay fixed shares of the commodity or fixed amounts of cash to the temple. Evidently the temple authorities wanted to make the best of the existing conditions, utilizing money payments for defraying expenses and meeting the requirements of lamp oil from the one mill that was attached. In any event, the larger body of artisanal workers in a particular locality was spared subjection in return for cash and to this extent at least the conditions in the artisan sector of commodity production were liberalized.[35]

Although we are on less sure ground about progress in the techniques of craft production in encouraging marketable turn out of artisan goods, some evidence is forthcoming to show that in certain fields there had been a welcome change in the method of production, for instance in oil-pressing industry. The earlier technique seems to have been to use manually operated mills which the inscriptions call hand oil-mills for extracting oil from oil-seeds. But the records of the eleventh-twelfth centuries make pointed references to the use of bullock oil mills for pressing. This certainly is the signal for the large-scale use of rotary motion in selected sectors of agro-industrial activity. While the hand oil mill did not pass out of fashion, as can be seen from joint references to bullock oil-mills and hand oil-mills, the frequency of oil-mills worked by single bullocks and a pair of bullocks cannot but highlight the widespread application of animal power to rotary motion. The appearance of two-bullock mills[36] would suggest the appearance of heavier presses as indeed can be seen from the mention of stone oil-mills in the inscriptions of the eleventh-twelfth centuries. The heavy stone press which replaced hand-operated wooden presses must have been developed for increasing the output of oil from single mills. The rise of oil miller subcastes specializing in the operation of single-bullock mills, double-bullock mills and stone mills is further indication of the expansion of the craft and the professional expertise which characterized such expansion.

Another craft which underwent considerable expansion and specialization about this time was weaving. The earliest instance of the promotion of looms is furnished by a Challakere taluka inscription of the eleventh century[37] which refers to the grant of a site for establishing a loom. In later times we come across a large variety of textiles and the weaver subcastes which specialized in their production. In some cases the weavers themselves undertook to market their goods and consequently acquired a distinct merchant status.[38]

Social Participation in Market Development

The great initiative of peasant families in the development of the market system, which seems to approximate similar developments in contemporary Europe,[39] could not but influence the formation of a class of merchants from among the ranks of the peasantry. It is significant enough that of the ten classes of merchants enumerated in a Shikarpur taluka inscription of 1150 as many as three belonged to the peasantry namely *gāvuṇḍas*, *gāvuṇḍa-svāmīs* and *seṭṭiguṭṭas*.[40] The other groups are perfume-sellers (*gandigas*), betel leaf sellers (*gatrigas*), general merchants (*seṭṭis*), merchant militias (*bīras* and *ankakāras*) and Bīra-Baṇajigas. The point is substantiated further by another record of about the same date,[41] which describes the seventy *okkals* (cultivators) of a village as belonging to the honoured lineage of *seṭṭiguṭṭas*. The *seṭṭiguṭṭa* too was a class of professional merchants who figure in numerous joint references to merchant associations. Clearly a sizeable section of the peasant commodity producers was taking upon itself the responsibility of marketing its own products. The robbing of peasants returning from a village fair in the evening[42] probably after disposing of their stocks may appear to be significant in this context. Interestingly enough the early references to *santhe* or village markets also appear in the inscriptions of the eleventh-twelfth centuries. In some cases the constraint of an undeveloped market-system was overcome by inducing professional groups of merchants to settle in villages. A T Narsipur taluka inscription of Hoysala Vīraballāla refers to the Brahmana assembly of a *chaturvedīmaṅgalam* which donated some plots of land exempt from taxes to Salattigandar who appear to have been a class of itinerant merchants like the *nānādeśīs*.[43]

It is unlikely that an itinerant merchant would permanently settle down in a village unless the locality was producing marketable quantities of goods. The incentives to merchants also become significant in view of the fact that the same Brahmana assembly also offered several tax concessions to stone masons and the artisans of the five classes. While the inducement to stone masons may have been prompted by the need for skilled labour for the construction of tanks and temples, the encouragement to the artisans of five classes may have been prompted by demand for artisan goods in the locality. The necessity to develop a market system must have been a compelling one to judge from the instances of cooperation among peasants, merchants and chiefs in the establishment of markets and urban centres. In one of the several instances the grateful peasants of a village made certain grants of land to a bangle-merchant who had converted their village into a market town or *paṭṭana*.[44] The peasants also undertook to pay to the *seṭṭi*, with the consent of the king, the taxes which they earlier paid to the treasury. In another instance, the peasants (*gauḍas*) of the village Mugur are said to have converted their village into a town and established a market (*saṇthe*) there.[45] An earlier example of this type is furnished by a Tamil inscription of 1036 which mentions the establishment of a *nagaram* in the eastern part of the great *brahmadeya* of Chidambaram.[46]

The instances of feudal lords promoting the growth of market towns are, however, far greater than those relating to peasants. This is evident from tax concessions and the delegation of administrative authority by kings and chiefs to both individual merchants and merchant associations. The concessions came almost invariably in recognition of the merchants helping in the development of market places. The characterization of chief merchants as town lords or *paṭṭanasvāmī* in all the records would also emphasize the new collaborative links between merchants and chieftains.[47] The merchants, on their part, tried to enrich the treasury by paying tolls in both cash and kind. In one inscription a large merchant association is said to have filled the emperor's treasury with gold and jewels and his armoury with weapons and by preventing loss to the customs houses.[48] In certain cases the merchants were called upon to share the responsibilities of feudal underlords in administering territories after a ceremonial act of vassalization.[49]

The Emerging Towns

The initiative shown by peasants, merchants and chiefs in the establishment of market places would suggest that the urban development of the eleventh-twelfth centuries owed mainly to the compulsions of an incipient market system felt increasingly in the wake of large-scale commodity production. A line of distinction, however, needs to be drawn between urban settlements of the earlier period and those of the eleventh and twelfth centuries. During the latter half of the first millennium towns were represented by forts of the *koṭṭai/dūrga* type and garrison headquarters of the *skandhāvāra/neleviḍu* type. The forts were masonry constructions of stone usually on the top of a hill and therefore great seminal points of feudal authority. The *skandhāvāra* garrisons on the other hand were of a fleeting character the chief purpose of which was mobilization of local militias for conducting warfare in areas away from the stone-built forts.

In terms of surplus mobilization, however, neither could look beyond the immediate neighbourhood which provided the necessary subsistence to the families of chiefs, military and other palace officials, a marginal priestly class and a subjected workforce in households, fields and family craft-shops. Compared to this the *nagara/paṭṭana* settlements of the eleventh-twelfth centuries were considerable centres for accumulation of surplus from across the immediate neighbourhood and also of the distribution of surplus over long distances.[50] This might explain the fact that although the *koṭṭai/neleviḍu* continued in later times depending on the uneven growth of the market system there is not much evidence of the *nagara* and *paṭṭana* during the eighth-tenth centuries. It would also appear that many of the feudal garrisons and *agrahāras* developed into market places and accordingly were described as *pura, nagara* and *paṭṭana* and not *koṭṭai* or *neleviḍu*. We have referred to Belgami in the Shikarpur taluka, which began as the headquarters of a *mahāmaṇḍaleśvara* in the beginning of the eleventh century and by the close of the century was transformed into a great centre of trade. In keeping with this development the settlement changed its designation from Balligave, Balligrāma, and Ballipura in early inscriptions to Ballinagara in the records of the late eleventh and twelfth centuries.[51]

For more positive evidence we may turn to a Cālukya inscription of 686 which describes Puligere as *skandhāvār* or army camp, but the same place is characterized as a *nagara* in an inscription of 968 and as *rājadhānīpaṭṭana* in a record of 1138.[52] We may also refer to the *agrahāra* acquiring the character of an urban place (*pura*) with the development of markets.[53] That the trading mart was the basic factor in the expansion of urban networks during the opening centuries of the second millennium can be seen from a permutation of the two terms in the description of emerging towns during this period. Some of the more important terms are *rājadhānīpaṭṭana, banañju-vaṭṭana* and *erivīrapaṭṭana* besides *mahānagara.* A dynastic headquarters superimposed on a *paṭṭana* was called *rājadhānīpaṭṭana*, a settlement dominated by merchant colonies was known as *banañju-vaṭṭana* and a town dominated by military settlements was called *erivīrapaṭṭana*. Although in terms of commercial value these different *paṭṭanas* were of uneven merit the association of the political and mercantile elites with the emerging market towns cannot be without significance. The *paṭṭana* and *nagara* settlements are distinguished by the presence of a large urban population, an indication of which is given by expressions such as *aśeṣa nagara-jana* in Calukya-Hoysala inscriptions[54] and *janākīrṇa* in the Kalacuri-Cedi inscriptions.[55] A dominant section of this large population consisted of new classes of merchants and artisans.

Since the *nagara* and *paṭṭana* were basically market centres and for that reason could not remain closed to the outer world of exchange relationships, these were largely free from the insularity of the earlier and contemporary *pura/dūrga/neleviḍu* settlements. Correspondingly the defence requirements of *nagara/paṭṭana* settlements appear to have been much fewer comparatively. One might argue that the people who indulged in village raids and feudal warfare were slowly appreciating the role of emerging towns in the redevelopment of a market economy. We may once again draw attention to the great collaborative efforts made by peasants, merchants and chiefs in the establishment of towns and markets. This new awareness reduced, if it did not completely eliminate, the possibility of violent attack against market-places. In this respect it would emerge that the need for defending merchants and merchandise was as great in Europe as it was in

India. But whereas in Europe the emphasis was on city walls[56], in India the purpose was adequately served by merchant militias and armed bands of caravaneers whose graphic descriptions constitute an important theme in many inscriptions.[57] The absence in India of conflict between merchants and temples and the absence of municipal insurrections against feudal oppression which characterized urban revival in medieval Europe[58] may also be noted.

NOTES

1. B.D. Chattopadhyaya, *Coins and Currency Systems in South India*, New Delhi, 1976, p. 118.
2. Ibid., p. 124.
3. H.D. Sankalia, *Excavations at Brahmapuri* (Kolhapur), Poona, 1952.
4. Thomas Watters, *On Yuan Chwang's Travels in India* (2nd Indian edn.), New Delhi, 1973, vol. 1, p. 178.
5. K.A.N. Sastri, *Foreign Notices of South India*, Madras, 1939, pp. 123-7.
6. Ibid., p. 121.
7. Ibid., p. 127.
8. R.N. Nandi, 'Feudalization of the State in Medieval South India', *Social Science Probings*, pp. 33-59.
9. B.D. Chattopadhyaya, op. cit., p. 110.
10. *EC*, 10, Mulbagal 122, AD 969; *EC*, 14, *Dynastic List*, p. 56, AD 933, etc.
11. See Ch. 4 above.
12. Henri Pirenne, *Economic and Social History of Medieval Europe*, London, 1937, p. 122.
13. A.S. Altekar, *Rāṣṭrakūtas and Their Times*, Poona, 1935, p. 315.
14. Ibid.
15. *SII*, 3, p. 242.
16. *EC*, 9, Channapatna 88 B.
17. *EC*, 9, Channapatna, 97 A, AD 1050.
18. A. Appadorai, *Economic Conditions of Southern India*, vol. 2, Madras, 1936, p. 716.
19. B.D. Chattopadhyaya, op. cit., p. 118.
20. *SII*, 3, p. 13.
21. *EC*, 9, Channapatna 129.
22. R.S. Sharma, *Perspectives in the Social and Economic History of Early India*, Delhi, 1983, p. 217.
23. Henry Pirenne, *Economic and Social History of Medieval Europe*, p. 130.
24. *EC*, 7, Shikarpur 13.
25. *EC*, 5, no. 3.

26. *EC*, 7, Shikarpur 118.
27. *South Indian Inscriptions*, vol. 20, no. 320.
28. Ibid., vol. 15, no. 160.
29. Ibid.
30. M. Liceria, 'Social and Economic History of Karnataka', unpublished Ph.D. thesis, Patna University, 1970.
31. Om Prakash Prasad, 'Towns in Early Medieval Karnataka', Ph.D. thesis, Patna University, 1980.
32. Georges Duby, *The Early Growth of European Economy*, London, 1974, p. 179.
33. Cf. *EC*, 7, Shikarpur 125, AD 1010; Shikarpur 126, AD 1036, etc.
34. *EC*, 7, Shikarpur 111.
35. See Ch. 5 above.
36. *EC*, 5, Hassan 54 for hand oil-mill or *kaigāṇa*; *EC*, 5, Belur 114 for tread oil-mill; *EC*, 3, Mysore 9 (Old Series) for bullock oil-mill or *ettugāṇa*.
37. *EC*, 11, Ch. 21.
38. Vijaya Ramaswami, 'Some Enquiries into the Conditions of Weavers in Medieval South India', *The Indian Historical Review*, vol. 6, nos. 1 and 2, p. 126.
39. Georges Duby, *The Early Growth of European Economy*, London, 1974, p. 130.
40. *EC*, 7, Shikarpur 118.
41. *EI*, 5, no. 28 C.
42. *EC*, 9, Kankanhalli 54, AD 1291.
43. *ARMAD*, 1939, no. 53, p. 203.
44. *EC*, 14, *Dynastic List of Inscriptions*, p. 19. The record is dated 1251.
45. Ibid., p. 21. The inscription is dated 1277.
46. Burton Stein, *Peasant State and Society in Medieval South India, c. 800-1300*, Delhi, 1980, p. 250.
47. *EC*, 6, Kr. 3, 12th *c*. and *EC*, 6, Kr. 27, 12th *c*. (New Series); *EC*, 3, Mg. 15, AD 1164 (New Series); *EC*, 6, Kd. 102, AD 1142 (New Series), etc.
48. *EC*, 7, Shikarpur 118.
49. *EC*, 8, Shimoga 36 and Shimoga 40, 12th *c*.; *EC*, 3, Nanjangud 156, AD 1114.
50. The fact that the *nagara* urban places and the *nagaram* merchant companies which operated from these centres were a typical product of a developing market system is sometimes glossed over in a attempt to trace *nagaram* activities in the late Pallava period. See K.R. Hall, *Trade and Statecraft in the Cola Kingdom*, Delhi, 1980, p. 76.
51. *EC*, 7, Shikarpur 90-167.
52. Compare *Indian Antiquary*, vol. 2, 1878, p. 112 and *Bombay Karnataka Inscriptions*, no. 15 of 1935-6 cited by G.H. Yazdani (ed.), *Early History of the Deccan*, London, 1960, p. 401.
53. *EI*, 5, nos. 3 A, 3 B, 3 C and 3 D show that Maningvalli (present Managoli) is mentioned as Maningavalli *agrahāra* in the beginning but in later records

the place is described as Maningavalli *koṭṭai* and Maningavalli *pura* to highlight its fortified urban character which is also evident from changes in its social composition. Similarly the *agrahāra* of Malavura which witnessed great structural and commercial activity during the eleventh and twelfth centuries developed into an urban place to justify its present characterization as Malurpatna. *Annual Report of the Mysore Archaeological Department,* 1932, pp. 11-14. For the conversion of *brahmadeyas* into *nagara* market centres see Burton Stein, op. cit., p. 250.

54. *EC,* 7, Shikarpur 113, 118, 119.
55. I owe this information to Professor R.S. Sharma.
56. Henri Pirenne, *Economic and Social History of Medieval Europe,* London, 1937, p. 54ff.
57. *EC,* 7, Shikarpur 118, etc.
58. Pirenne, op. cit., p. 54f.

PART III

Social Conflicts and Subcaste Formation

8

From Collaboration to Conflict

In the early growth of rural economy some measure of collaboration between the new classes of surplus-appropriators, the fiefholders, freeholders and the *devadāna* holders was as essential as it was unavoidable. During the earlier phase the chief purpose of such interdependence was to increase crop production, the efforts being mainly concerned with the extension of the cultivable area and development of the drainage network. However, these acts of collaboration and interdependence also contained the seeds of conflict. Tensions began to surface as the production of peasant goods fell short of the rising and overlapping claims of non-peasant surplus appropriators.[1] In some localities the crisis appears to have been aggravated by famines and epidemics but in most areas it was the effect of feudal depredations which disrupted production for some time. Burning down of entire villages and standing crops, and armed attacks against Brahmana freeholdings and peasant villages for collection of dues and rents are very much in evidence during the opening centuries of the second millennium.

The epigraphic records would suggest that there were conflicts between Brahmanas and feudal lords, amongst Brahmana freeholders of neighbouring villages, and between peasants and their feudal lords.

Brahmana-Peasant Conflicts

The conflicts which involved Brahmanas against peasants seem to highlight the resentment of old resident peasantry against encroachment on their traditional rights by non-cultivating

Brahmana families imposed over them. A Karnataka inscription of 1251 refers to the *gauḍa* peasants of a village who protested against the conversion of their village into a Brahmana freeholding and refused to accept the new landlords. Hearing this the enraged king sent an army which pillaged the village, defiled women and attacked even children.[2] Protests over the destruction of common property and infringement of communal rights are also reported. A Hassan taluka inscription of 1230 mentions the death of two *gauḍa* peasants of a village who tried to prevent the agents of Brahmanas from cutting palmyra trees in their village.[3] In a Telugu-Coda inscription from the Anantpur district of Andhra Pradesh we hear about the forcible occupation of *umbali* lands by the Brahmanas of a village. The three *gauḍa* families who were the rightful owners of these lands resolved to assault the Brahmana usurpers and to provide compensation in the event of the death of any *gauḍa* hero in the fight with the Brahmanas. The inscription reports the killing of two *gauḍa* peasants in self defence by Brahmana landlords.[4] Violence and bloodshed also resulted from disputes over the control of irrigation tanks. A Hassan taluka inscription of 1212[5] records a fight between the peasants of a village and a fiefholder of the locality for possession of an irrigation tank. The fight resulted in the killing of the chief whereupon the Hoysala king ordered the construction of a new tank and a *viragal* set up to commemorate the death. Evidently the fiefholder failed to take possession of the disputed tank and instead a new tank was built by the Hoysala overlord as an act of favour to the family of the departed chief. Another Hassan taluka inscription of 1080 relates to the dispute between a Brahmana and a peasant family over the drawing of water from a village tank. In the fight which followed, a member of the peasant's family was killed[6] and buried at the spot; the dispute was resolved by dividing the water of the tank into two equal shares. It is significant that although peasant action was generally in defence of traditional land rights sometimes it was aimed at capturing Brahmana land in the same village or in a neighbouring one. A Telugu-Cola inscription from Andhra Pradesh[7] refers to the *gauḍa* cultivators who deserted their village Inombrolu on the outbreak of plague and settled down in a neighbouring Brahmana village on the condition that they would pay an agreed compensation to the Brahmana landlords. Subsequently the Brahmanas themselves fled their village on the outbreak of famine. Later, when conditions improved in the countryside the 52 Brahmanas returned and asked the immigrant cultivators for payment of the compensation; this was promptly refused. The Brahmanas then appealed to the king who asked the peasants to pay the amount.

Resorting to violence for redress of grievances could not, however, be a matter of choice for the Indian peasant who lived under the gripping influence of a Brahmana dominated ideology and in habitual subservience to brahmanical norms of social discrimination. The peasant in traditional India was thus incapable of mobilizing common action across distant localities; he was still less capable of any thought of changing the established order. Necessarily, the sporadic incidents of peasant protest remained isolated attempts to counter abuses of landlords. The instances are nevertheless significant inasmuch as these underline the rising impatience of the resident peasantry with an intruder intermediary class which had long been encroaching on the peasant's traditional land rights and communal property. In an age when a part of peasant goods was being earmarked for the market and also when the peasant was collaborating with an enterprising trading class in the foundation of new markets and towns, the presence of a large and oppressive surplus appropriating class in advanced peasant localities must have been particularly odious to the enterprising peasant.

Sāmanta-Brahmana Conflicts

The rising demand for and rigorous collections of rents, dues and tributes which constituted the chief support of the state would also point towards a situation in which the existence of a large number of rent-free holdings was a serious detriment to fiscal resources of the state. Not surprisingly, the sanctimonious pockets of brahmanical authority which had long been nourished by kings and feudal lords were becoming targets of armed attack from the same class of patrons. That the freeholdings were increasingly being subjected to state demands for rent is amply clear from the flight of Brahmana landholders from *chaturvedīmaṅgalam* on failure to pay rents, their plots being subsequently redistributed among new holders or sold out to temples.[8] The quest for fixed annual rent from the freeholdings may have been prompted by the fact that through constant sale of *agrahāra* land and collections of fines and other dues in cash from peasant communities, the freeholders were in possession of liquid capital of which the state wanted a share. Brahmanas' refusals to pay rents and dues invited attack from kings and feudatories. A Sorab taluka inscription of 1177 refers to a feudatory Gāvuṇḍasvāmī Daṇḍanātha who attacked the immemorial *agrahāra* of Kuppatur and like an *asura* was destroying the sacrifices of Brahmanas and defiling women. In retaliation the Brahmanas of Kuppatur captured a few of the attackers; the infuriated Daṇḍanātha sought reinforcements from a friendly chief, Hadu Deva of Ucchaṅgi fort. Helped by the reinforcements, the Daṇḍanātha surrounded the village in three circles, pillaging it and distraining its cattle, liberating the captured followers and forcing the Brahmanas to pay the rent. It is pertinent to remember here that while the freeholdings did not pay anything to the state, Brahmanas freely extended their fields into the outlying forests and virgin lands, enhancing the possibility of higher annual rent if it was collected. The village Kuppatur which was attacked in 1177 by a feudatory must have been doing this for a long time. In 1071 the Brahmanas authorized a *seṭṭi* to clear a part of the nearby forest, excavate a large tank and constitute rice-fields around it.[9] Such enrichment of freeholdings was unlikely to be relished by neighbouring chiefs, and four years later the *agrahāra* was attacked by an army led by twelve *nāyakas*. The *seṭṭi* benefactor of the Kuppatur Brahmanas who fought on this occasion lost his life.[10] Similarly extensions of cultivation into neighbouring villages gave rise to violent conflicts between Brahmanas and peasants. Kuppatur itself was involved in two such conflicts between 1141 and 1143.[11] Encroachment on neighbouring pastures also led to frequent violent incidents. One Shimoga district inscription refers to the cattle of a Brahmana village straying into a neighbouring village and grazing there.

The angry chief of whose domain the village appears to have formed a part immediately attacked the Kumbise freehold and killed two supporters of Brahamanas.[12] Instances of violence against Brahmana freeholdings are also widely reported from neighbouring Tamil Nadu. In one case the Brahmanas of a *brahmadeya* were tortured by a feudal lord who drowned them in water, scorched them in the sun and finally imprisoned them. They managed to escape with the help of escorts and report the matter to the king at Thanjavur.[13] However, unlike the meek holders of *brahmadeya* land, the *agrahāra* freeholders in Karnataka had grown to a position of considerable armed resistance. With fortified settle-ments and small rural militias, many of these villages gave resistance to the attacking armies of kings and feudal lords. This would also explain a decline in the patronage of these rural bastions of Brahmana power.

Forcible Collection of Rent

In the context of an emergent urban market economy, which called for the envigoration of the role of the state,[14] the revenues of the state appear to have been in a precarious condition forcing the necessity of an armed collection drive. In different cases, these expeditions were prompted by the appropriations of rent by ambitious rival chiefs, misappropriation by local officers and unwillingness or inability of peasants to pay the apportioned rent. A Sorab taluka inscription of 1112 refers to a *mahāmaṇḍaleśvara* chief ordering his army to collect tribute from the Hayve locality.[15] A junior commander is stated to have been killed in the engagement that followed. A late twelfth-century inscription from the same area mentions a Kalacuri king who ordered his two generals to launch a rent-collection (*siddhāya*) drive in the district (*nāḍ*) of Banavāsī.[16] Although widespread peasant revolts were yet far off, some of the violent incidents seem to anticipate the common militant action of peasants and landlords which underlined all major conflagrations of the later middle ages. The refusal of the district headmen (*nāḷgāvuṇḍas*) to deposit collected rent, and the dispatch of an army to punish them and recover the amount[17] approximate an early fourteenth-century peasant uprising described by Barani in which the *muqaddams* (headmen) of the Doab region collected the *khots* (peasants) around them and resisted oppressive collections of enhanced land tax in 1330.[18] The oppressive collections of rents, taxes and dues sometimes forced peasants and artisans to combine in common action against the state.

A Vijayanagara inscription of 1351 from Vridhachalam in the South Arcot district registers an agreement between the *Valangai* peasants and small trading castes and the *Idangai* artisan castes to jointly resist the forcible collection of tax by government officers. The members of the two factions resolved to inflict corporal punishment on those who helped the tax collectors. The same punishment was also laid down for all those who consented to write the accounts of revenue.[19] A Mayavaram taluka (Thanjavur district) inscription of the time of Devaraya I records a similar agreement between the *Valangai* 98 castes and the *Idangai* 98 castes to resist oppressive and illegal collections of *Idangavāri* and *Inavāri* from the members of the two factions.[20] Coming together of the *Valangai* and *Idangai*, whose violent and bloody conflicts are too well known to be described here, cannot but highlight the growing incompatibility of interests between the landowning and surplus-appropriating classes on the one hand and the producer-distributor classes on the other.

Much more significant than the sporadic risings and acts of resistance were the formation of new social alliances and the rise of protestant sects. Significantly, it was in the eleventh century that the supra-caste unions of *Valangai* peasants and *Idangai* artisans make the first appearance. It is also apparent that most of the activities of the *Valangai* and *Idangai* during the eleventh-twelfth centuries are reported from the lower Kaveri basin which is said to have witnessed social turmoil in the wake of the expansion of private farms of rich landlords and the dispossession of the old resident peasantry of their *kani* rights.[21] That these mobilizations across peasant localities were aimed against the oppression of a powerful landlord class emerging from the fiefs, freeholdings and temple *devadāna* holdings is not concealed by the overstated incidents of violence between the *Valangai* and *Idangai* themselves.

The growing impatience of the peasants with the exploiter landlord class is also evident from the formation of the Tamil Śaiva Siddhānta sect during the twelfth century. It was characterized by the domination of Vellāla peasants in prebendary organization and the adoption of Tamil language in preference to Sanskrit in worship. The attempts of the Brahmanas to capture monastic establishments of the Śaiva Siddhānta and prevent its further growth[22] appear significant in this connection.

In Karnataka, the artisans' quest for occupational security and status-relief assumed the form of a powerful religious upsurge known as the Vīraśaiva movement, the chief supporters of which were traders, artisans and peasants led by a few disaffected *smārta* Brahmanas of Karnataka.[23] The sect which originated in the north-western region of Karnataka about the twelfth century was the product of a social situation in which the revival of commodity production had considerably added to the importance of trading and artisan castes but whose profits and interests were constantly subjected to infringement by Brahmanas and temples. Understandably therefore there is no place in the Vīraśaiva sect for traditional Brahmana priesthood or temple-centric cults of brahmanical deities. The anti-brahmanical character of the sect is also evident from its opposition to the conventional ordering of the social structure on the basis of caste endogamy. The early Vīraśaivas were in fact an undifferentiated fraternal community although later on it became vulnerable to brahmanical norms of social differentiation.[24]

NOTES

1. Attention has rightly been drawn to the plurality of peasant exploitation which in a social world dominated by overlapping claims and powers created latent interstices and discrepancies, see Perry Anderson, *Passages from Antiquity to Feudalism*, Verso, London, 1974, p. 149.
2. *MAR* (1936), no. 19, p. 84.
3. *EC*, 5, Hassan 122.
4. *Catalogue of Inscriptions*, Government of Andhra Pradesh Archaeological Series no. 22 cited in K.Satyanarayana, *A Study of the History and Culture of the Andhra People*, New Delhi, 1975, pp. 322-3.

5. *EC*, 5, Hassan 42.
6. *EC*, 5, Hassan 34.
7. *Annual Report on Epigraphy*, 1908, pp. 70-1.
8. K.A.N. Shastri, *Cholavaṁśa* (Hindi), Delhi, 1979, pp. 417-18.
9. *EC*, 8, Sorab 317.
10. *EC*, 8, Sorab 314.
11. *EC*, 8, Sorab 252 and 253.
12. *EC*, 8, Sorab 178.
13. K.A.N. Sastri, op. cit., p. 415.
14. In Tamil Nadu this seems to be characterized by the introduction of *maṇḍalam* and *valanāḍu* administrative units about the beginning of the eleventh century and reorganization of provinces on that basis. Y. Subbarayalu, 'Mandalam as a Politico-Geographical unit in South India', *Proceedings of the 39th Indian History Congress*, Hyderabad, 1978, pp. 84-6.
15. *EC*, 8, Sorab 468.
16. *EC*, 8, Sorab 139.
17. *EC*, 8, Sorab 425, AD 1202.
18. Irfan Habib, 'The Peasant in Indian History', *Presidential Address*, 43rd Session, Indian History Congress, Kurukshetra, 1982, p. 45.
19. Annual report on Epigraphy no. 92 of 1916 cited in the *Journal of the Andhra Historical Research Society*, vol. 4, p. 82.
20. Annual Report on Epigraphy no. 28 of 1926, cited in ibid., pp. 82-3.
21. N. Karashima, *South Indian History and Society*, Delhi, 1984, p. 530.
22. The arguments are based on the evidence collected by Burton Stein, *Peasant, State and Society in Medieval South India, c. 800-1300*, Delhi, 1980, pp. 235-9, though Stein himself would not view all this as anything new, whether it be *Valangai-Idangai* unions or the peasant dominated Śaiva Siddhānta movement, he is inclined to explain these in terms of changing social alliances and a harmonious and assimilative social evolution (p. 239).
23. See R.N. Nandi, 'Origin of the Vīraśaiva Movement', *The Indian Historical Review*, vol. 2, no. 1.
24. The present community is divided into three distinct groups, the *jaṅgam* priestly order, the *pañcaṃśāli* trading communities and the non-*pañcaṃśāli* artisans and peasants, none of which interdines or intermarries with the others. There is a fourth group, comprising shoemakers, fishermen and a few untouchables, who can neither invest themselves with the sacred *liṅgam* nor perform the eight sacraments (*aṣṭāvaraṇa*) of a full Lingayat. See Edgar Thurston and K.V. Rangachari, *Castes and Tribes of Southern India*, Madras, 1907, see under Lingayat.

9

The Formation of Brahmana Subcastes

The process of subcaste formation among Brahmanas seems to have been accelerated in the wake of their extensive migrations from about AD 400. The fourth and fifth centuries marked a period of crisis for the client-serving Brahmanas whose *yajmāni* interests were seriously undermined by the decay of urban centres and the consequent loss of a prosperous urban clientele. The decline of urban markets also snapped ties with the hinterland leaving the countryside to fend for itself. This might explain why, between the fifth and seventh centuries, most of the migrations took place from important urban centres that had passed into a state of decline.[1] The client-seeking Brahmanas who migrated to distant places either secured plots of land and settled down as inseparable parts of the village community or participated in temple service in district headquarters and capitals where feudal patronage helped them gain agricultural surpluses. In either case the basis of subsistence was habitual association with agricultural holdings. In a stagnant rural society, which was almost shut out from the outer world, it was only likely that great importance would be attached to the territorial basis of social identity. Indeed the regional basis of social exclusiveness can be seen as the most dominant feature of the whole process of social differentiation during the early medieval period.

The majority of subcastes which are affiliated to either the Pañca Gauḍa or the Pañca Draviḍa divisions of Brahmanas appear to have been formed or in the process of formation during the early medieval centuries. The concept of Pañca Gauḍa and Pañca Draviḍa divisions itself does not seem to go beyond the early medieval period. The earliest references to Kānyakubja or Sarayupārī sections of the Pañca Gauḍas are found in the inscriptions of the post-Gupta period. Similarly the different divisions and subdivisions of the Pañca Draviḍas become more and more identifiable from the sixth-seventh centuries. The term Pañca Draviḍa covers all the regional divisions and subdivisions of South Indian Brahmanas except those who speak Oriya or Konkani.[2] Konkanis are classed as a branch of the Pañca Gauḍas who migrated to the Konkan region from Trihotrapura or modern Tirhut division in Bihar.

The five major divisions of Pañca Draviḍas are (i) Dravida or Tamil Brahmanas, (ii) Andhra Brahmanas, (iii) Karnataka Brahmanas, (iv) Marathi Brahmanas and (v) Gujarati Brahmanas.[3] The inclusion of Gujarati Brahmanas is interesting. Of the five Draviḍa divisions, those of Karnataka, the Śiva Brahmana subdivision of the Tamils, the Karādi and Virkar subcastes of Marathi Brahmanas and the Nagar Modha Gujarati Brahmans are mentioned in the epigraphic records in varying measures. Except the Śiva Brahmanas, all are regional divisions and subdivisions which formed as a result of migrations or prolonged settlement. The Konkani and Sārasvata sections of the Pañca Gauḍas also become identifiable about the tenth-eleventh centuries.

Karādi Brahmanas

The Karādi Brahmanas, who constitute today a prominent Marathi Brahmana subcaste, are listed as a migratory group along with the Deśastha sub-section.[4] They are more numerous in the south Kanara district and are stated to have come southward from Karhād.[5] Their identity can be traced as far back as 871 when the Rāṣṭrakūṭa king Amoghavarṣa granted a village to the heads of three Brahmana families who are described as having emigrated from Karhād.[6] Two of the beneficiaries, Narsiṁha Dīkṣita and Rakṣāditya Kramavid, belonged to the Bhāradvāja *gotra* with the Bhāradvāja, Bārhaspatya, Āngirasa and Agniveśya *pravaras.* Āngirasa, which is given here as a *pravara,* is used as a *gotra* by the Dhamanakara subcaste of the Karādi Brahmanas.[7] The *gotras* and *pravaras* of the Brahmanas of Karahātaka mentioned in the above inscription appear to have been authentic. For, Āśvālāyana says that Bhāradvāja has four *pravaras*, Bhāradvāja, Bārhaspatya, Āngirasa and Agniveśya.[8] Nearly a century before the issue of this charter, the Brahmana residents of Karhād were going about in search of land grants and new settlements. In 781 the Rāṣṭrakūta king Dhruva donated a village named Vinga to Brahmana members of the *Cāturvidya samudāya* in the town of Karahātaka.[9] The village, which lay only 70 miles from Karhād, was regranted in 1079 to the resident Brahmanas. The original donees of the village Vinga belonged to Gārgya *gotra* and Bahvṛca section of the Brahmanas of Karhād. In yet another Rāṣṭrakūta grant, dated 929, the Karādi or Karhād Brahmanas are referred to as *karahāṭaka-pramukhabrāhmaṇa*,[10] meaning the foremost among the Karahātaka Brahmanas.

The evolution of Karādi Brahmana identity in this early period is also borne out by a reference to the name-ending *ghaisās*. In inscriptions, *ghaisās* is used as a surname of Karhātaka Brahmanas. Vāsudeva Ghaisās, the son of a certain Bhaṭṭopādhyāya, received a grant of land in 1093.[11] Prabhākara Ghaisās of Karahātaka and Vasiyana Ghaisās figure in a record of Śilāhāra king Bhoja II.[12] The surname *ghaisās* is still traceable among the Deśastha, Citpāvan and Karhād Brahmanas of Maharashtra. The term was apparently a later contracted form of *ghaṭikāsāhasa*[13]. *Ghaṭikāsāhasa*, which is the same as *gahiyasāhasa*, occurs as an epithet of Brahmana donees[14] in inscriptions. It probably implied an association with the *ghaṭikā* of the locality, which was an assembly of learned Brahmanas.

The Karhād Brahmanas of our period appear to have been Śāktas or worshippers of the deified female energy. In an inscription of Bhoja II, the Karahātaka Brahmanas are described as worshippers in the temple of goddess Mahālakṣmī of Kolhapur.[15] The same Mahālakṣmī of Kolhapur continues, to this day, to be the family goddess of the Karhāds.[16] The Karhāds might have associated blood rites with the cult of Mahālakṣmī of Kolhapur, to whom the Rāṣṭrakūṭa King Amoghavarṣa made an offering of one of his fingers in the ninth century. Until recently, the Karhāds allegedly indulged in human sacrifices to the goddess Kālikā; the practice was suppressed by the third Peshwa (1740-61).[17]

Virkar Subcaste

The term Deśastha which denotes an important subdivision of Marathi Brahmanas is not mentioned in early medieval records. But certain groups of emigrant families, which later constituted different septs of this group, appear in the inscriptions of this period. An inscription of the seventh century refers to a group of migrant Brahmana families who received the village Vīra as a freeholding and settled down there.[18] The endowed village Vīra is modern Veer in the Satara district from which the Virkar subcaste of the Deśastha Brahmanas derives its name. It would appear that the Karādis derived their sept name from the place of their origin but the Virkars took the name of their new settlement.

Karnataka Brahmanas

Like the Karhād Brahmanas, the Karnataka Brahmanas, who constitute one of the five subdivisions of Brahmanas known as Pañca Draviḍa, also appear to have emerged during the early medieval centuries. Generic terms like Karnataka Brahmana and Kannāṭa Paṇḍita which seem to identify the Brahmana community of Karanatka as a distinct regional group are mentioned in the records of the Rāṣṭrakūṭa dynasty which ruled Karnataka from the eighth to the tenth century. One of these inscriptional records refers to *mānyakheṭakarṇaṭakapramukhabrāhmaṇa*,[19] meaning the foremost among the Karnataka Brahmanas of the city of Mānyakheṭa. A Karnataka Brahmana who migrated from Badami to Malwa in search of patronage is mentioned in an epigraph of 1022.[20] Obviously, by the close of ninth century, the Brahmanas of Karnataka had crystallized into a regional group like the Gauḍa Brahmanas of north India and the Karhād Brahmanas of Mahārashtra. In a Cola record, found in the Kolar district, mention is made of a Kannāṭa Paṇḍita who was appointed in 1071 by the Śiva Brahmana priests of the temple of Cāmuṇḍeśvarī to perform the *māḍāpattīyam* of the goddess.[21] Interestingly enough, the Śiva Brahmanas who were of Tamil origin and had only recently settled in different parts of the Kolar and Bangalore districts of Karnataka,[22] did not mention the concerned Brahmana by his name; instead they preferred to describe him as a Brahmana of Karnataka, or Kannāṭa Paṇḍita. The expression seems to emphasize the distinction between the Tamil Brahmanas and the Brahmanas of Karnataka.

Despite such consciousness of distinctive regional identities, some social interaction was unavoidable. It may be of interest to note here that the Pannathurars, who are a prominent section of Madhva Karnataka Brahmanas,[23] retain some of the customs of the Tamil Brahmanas. Their marriage badge, for example, is the Tamil *tāli* and not the *bottu.*[24] The contact between Tamil and Karnataka Brahmanas was evidently a consequence of the Cola conquest and occupation of some south Karnataka districts after the battle of Takkolam in 1004.

Konkani Brahmanas

The Sārasvata and Konkani Brahmanas of south Kanara also appear to have developed into a subcaste during the early medieval period although there are no direct references to them in the inscriptions of our period. In the Cochin Census Report of 1909 Konkani Brahmanas are enumerated as a branch of the Sārasvata subdivision of Pañca Gauḍas.[25] Also, the full description of a Konkani Brahmana is Gauḍa Sārasvata Konkanastha.[26] This evidently traces the origin of the Konkani Brahmanas to the Sārasvata section of northern Brahmanas who in the remote past had migrated to Maharashtra. The Chinchani plates of Indra III clearly show that the Pañca Gauḍas or the northern Brahmanas had travelled as far south as Sanjana on the west coast during the tenth century. The Pañca Gauḍīya Mahāparṣat[27] which is mentioned in the Chinchani plates, probably included Sarasvata Brahmanas along with other northern subdivisions. These Brahmanas, who apparently settled along the Maharashtra coast and intermarried with local Brahmanas or women of higher caste were probably the ancestors of the present day Sarasvata and Konkani Brahmanas. The northern origin of the Konkani Brahmanas is also evident from the fact that they are excluded from the Pañca Draviḍa or five subdivisions of southern Brahmanas.

Tradition has it that Paraśurāma brought ten Brahmana families from the north and settled them in and around Gomantaka or modern Goa. The Konkani Brahmanas claim that their original home was Trihotrapura or Tirhut in modern Bihar.

Trihotrapura may be Tirbhukti of the inscriptions, roughly corresponding to the old Tirhut division of Bihar. The region forms part of Mithila, the homeland of the Maithil subdivision of the Pañca Gauḍas. The *Pañji* (family trees) literature of Mithila shows that the Brahmanas of this region had started migrating in different directions from the eighth century. Some of these migrating families may have settled in parts of Konkan or adjacent areas. The Pañca Gauḍas who were inhabiting the city of Sanjan and its neighbouring villages about the first quarter of the tenth century may have been one such group of immigrants from the Tirhut territory. Nine representatives of these Pañca Gauḍas or northern Brahmanas constituted the *pañca-gauḍīya-mahāparṣat* which was managing the affairs of a temple or *maṭhikā* with goddess Daśamī as its presiding deity.

The temple was built at the joint initiative of Annamayya, Reveṇa and Kautuka, who may have been close relations. Of the three, Annamayya was the son of Nārāyaṇa Bhaṭṭa and grandson of Vāsudeva belonging to Bhāradvāja *gotra.* In the inscriptions of Śilāhāra kings, however, the temple is described as a kautuka *maṭhikā.* The Muslim (Tajik) governor, Madhumat (Muhammad) Sugatipa by name, who was administering the whole *sanjana maṇḍala* on behalf of Rāṣṭrakūṭa Indra III (915-28), granted the village Kanaduka as a rent free holding for defraying the expenses of the *maṭhikā.* He also granted half a *dhura* of land in the village Devīhāra, probably for residential purposes. The name Devīhāra would suggest that the village was a settlement of immigrant Brahmana worshippers of Devī or Daśamī.

The Pañca Gauḍīya community of Sanjan and its neighbourhood comprised both householders (*gṛhastha*) and ecclesiastics (*svādhyāyikas*), the latter residing in the *maṭhikā* itself. The *svādhyāyikas* may have included scholars as well as priests. Both groups are frequently cited as trustees of various types of endowment. The management of the temple was entrusted to a council or *mahāparṣat* with nine members who may have represented the householders and priests. The council is also described as *ārya-deśīya-mahāparṣat*, *anagha-parṣat* or just *parṣat* or *mahāparṣat*.

Early in their career, the Pañca Gauḍas of Sanjan picked up a quarrel with the priests (*vārika*) of God Madhusūdana or Bhillamāladeva (so called after Bhillamāla or Bhinmāl near Jodhpur), the patron deity of the Bhinmāl merchants of the city of Sanjan. The dispute surfaced over a plot of land which belonged to the temple of god Madhusūdana, but had been enclosed within the northern boundary of the temple of goddess Daśamī. The former were trying to regain control of the lost possession and the latter were trying to resist it. Each party even tried to pressurize the administration by undertaking fasts unto death. Finally, a decision (*vyavasthā*), said to emanate from god Madhusūdana, bound the priests of the Daśamī temple to pay an annual rent of forty *drammas* to the priests of the Vaiṣṇava god. The amount fell due at the end of the festival of lights (*dīpotsava*) observed every year in the temple of goddess Daśamī. The inscription warns against any pressure tactics either to increase the amount of rent or to defer payment.

In all likehood, there was a good sprinkling of Maithil Brahmanas among the Pañca Gauḍa immigrants of north Konkan. This is suggested by the use of terms *daśamī*, *maṭhikā* and *dhura*. The name Daśamī signifies the ten-day annual worship of goddess Dūrgā or Bhagavatī, which is fairly popular among the *śākta* families of Maithil Brahmanas. Indeed the term Bhagavatī appears as a synonym of goddess Daśamī in one of the inscriptions. Similarly, the term *maṭhikā* or *maṭhiā* frequently denotes a small residential temple in large parts of Gangetic Bihar including Tirhut. The term *dhura* is likewise a frequently used unit of land measurement in both northern and southern Bihar. Although *dhura* is a very small unit of land measure, its size varies from one area to another like any other unit of land measurement. Probably the *dhura* of ancient times was larger and in the sparsely populated Rāṣṭrakūṭa territories the more so to justify its donation as a temple endowment.

Finally, the grant was made at the request of a Bhāradvāja Brahmana, Bhāradvāja being a common *gotra* name of the

Maithili Brahmanas. The annual observance of the festival of lights or *dīpotsava* in the temple of goddess Daśamī would also appear interesting in this connection. In large parts of northern India the festival coincides with the worship of Lakshmī. But in Mithila and Bengal the festival is invariably associated with the worship of Kālī, who represents the fearsome form of goddess Dūrgā or Daśamī.

Modha Brahmanas

The Modhas are an important subdivision of Gujarati Brahmanas who derive the name of their subcaste from Modhera in the Nausari region. The subcaste was formed as the result of the migration of a section of Gujarati Brahmanas from Modhera. Although the first clear mention of Modha Brahmanas is found in the inscriptions of the tenth and eleventh centuries,[28] the beginnings of the process of subcaste formation go back to the sixth century.

An inscription of Mahāśiva Tivara, the Pāṇḍuvaṁśī ruler of south Kosala or the region about Chattisgarh refers to several families of Brahmanas who belonged to different parts of the country receiving the grant of a certain village.[29] Two of the beneficiaries were named Avanti Vikrama Upādhyāy (meaning the valour of Avanti) and Lāṭa Phaliha Svāmin (meaning crystal of the Lāṭa country). Avanti is the region about Gwalior and Lāṭa is identical with Gujarat. It is not known if the Avanti Brahmanas ever formed into a Brahmana subcaste, but Lāṭa or Gujarati Brahmanas constitute an important subdivision of the Pañca Draviḍas. Interestingly, names such as these underline the desire of the immigrants to establish a distinct identity in a new social milieu besides highlighting a distinguished origin. Perhaps the easiest way to do this was to associate the family with the place of its origin.

Going by the epigraphic evidence the history of the Modhas would date back to the middle of the tenth century when a Modha is said to be ruling over Sanjan *maṇḍala* as the subordinate of a Śilāhāra king. The chief, Vijjala by name, styles himself as a sun who caused the lotus bud of Modhakula to blossom forth.

Probably the chief was an enterprising Modha, who along with others pioneered the migration of Modhas and settled down in the Śrīsthāna (Thane) region of north Konkan. Later, he may have found favour with the reigning Śilāhāra king and was appointed governor of the Sanjan *maṇḍal.* Two other Modha chiefs, Cāvuṇḍarāya and Vijja Rāṇaka, who ruled over the same tract, are mentioned in three other Śilāhāra grants dated 1034, 1048 and 1053.

The terms Modhakula, Modhānvaya and Modhavaṁśa are freely mentioned in these records. It cannot, however, be determined whether the Modha family, which is praised in these inscriptions as *Śrī modhānvaya-prasūta-vaṁśa* or the family descended from the illustrious Modha lineage, was of a Brahmana descent. But it seems to be closely associated with the Modha Brahmanas of Śrīsthāna whom Vijja Rāṇaka cites, together with various other officers, assemblies and citizens as witnesses to a *bhojana-akṣhaya-nīvī* or an undecaying free feeding endowment. The purpose of this endowment was to provide food for twenty-five Brahmanas every day. These may well have been Modha Brahmanas, recent migrants without a permanent source of sustenance.

The association of the Modhas with folk elements is hinted by the expression blessed by the goddess Khadiravatī (*Khadiravatī-labdha-prasāda*). Khadiravatī, a goddess of tribal origin,[30] seems to have been the family deity of the Modhas. Non-sanskritic names such as Aigala and Dimaraka (father and grandfather respectively of Vijja Rāṇaka) are also interesting in this connection.

Nāgara Brahmanas

Another important subdivision of the Gujarati Brahmanas was the Ānandanagara or Nāgara Brahmanas. We meet them in the inscriptions of sixth-seventh centuries. The process of their being grouped into a subcaste of a Gujarati Brahmanas must have started about this time. An inscription of the seventh century, for example, mentions the town of Vaṭanagara from which a Brahmana family migrated to the village Koniyanam which it had received as a freeholding. Vaṭanagara, also known as Ānandapura or Nāgara, lay within fifteen miles of the donated village where the Brahmanas took up residence.[31]

In an inscription of the tenth century mention is made of several Brahmanas who migrated from Ānandapura or Vaṭanagara and settled in two villages that had been granted to them as freeholdings. The villages lay in the Mohadavāsak Viṣaya which is identified with Modasa in Prantij taluka of Ahmedabad district. It is interesting to note that the Brahmana donees are described in inscriptions as *Ānandpurīya Nāgarīya*, which clearly shows that the sept name Nāgara had been adopted by a section of migrant Brahmanas by the tenth century.[32]

Ritualistic Subdivisions

The creation of temple-holdings on a large scale does not appear to go beyond the fourth-fifth Christian centuries by which time efforts to popularize the temple-based cults had taken the shape of a powerful religious movement. The social underpinnings of this development can perhaps be understood in terms of a serious undermining of *yajmāni* interests caused by the disintegration of a market economy during the third-fifth centuries. The sources of the period particularly the various Purāṇas of this transitional period would suggest that the development had divided the earlier vedic-educated Brahmanas, who tended the domestic ritual fires and worshipped certain chosen deities, into two rival sections. The dogmatic Śrotriyas were busy consolidating the earlier deity-centric cults in domestic chapels and in publicizing their presumed ritual superiority over all other categories of Brahmanas. The temple priests, on the other hand, were trying to expand public cults centred on permanent structures. The former denounced the latter as irreligious and degraded ones for whom the term *devalaka* is frequently used in a derogatory sense in the puranic chapters on *smṛti* material.[33] Later history, however, shows that the system of public cults in temples became increasingly popular. With it the ranks of the *devalaka* also proliferated, giving rise to new ritualistic and sectarian subdivisions. The Śiva Brahmanas were one of them.

Śiva Brahmanas

The term Śiva Brahmana refers to a group of Brahmanas adept in priestly functions relating to the ritual worship of the deities of Śivaite pantheon.[34] This is confirmed by inscriptions which refer to these Brahmanas as the priests of Śivaite temples and as receiving grants of land[35] and money from various donors for performing ritual worship of Śivaite deities.

In Karnataka the Śiva Brahmanas make their appearance towards the close of the tenth[36] and the beginning of the eleventh century.[37] The formation of Brahmana subcastes as a result of the association of Brahmanas with various temple-based cults and ideologies can be noticed earlier also. The Viṣṇuite Āḷvārs and the Śivaite Nāyanārs did not form into endogamous groups but the Śrīvaiṣṇavas and Māheśvaras who were connected with the ideology of the Āḷvārs and Nāyanārs respectively, did coalesce into two district ritualistic subcastes. The celebrated Tamil saint Sambandar who lived in the seventh century refers to Brahmanas chanting the Veda and Vedāngas as praising Śiva's feet everyday.[38] These Brahmanas may be identified with the caste of Śiva Maraiyor or the Ādi Śaivas mentioned in the story of Pugal Tunai Nāyanār in the *Periya Purāṇa.*[39]

The Tamil origin of the Śiva Brahmanas is evident from records which refer to their activities. First, they appear in inscriptions of the Tamil country from the end of the tenth century. As early as 993-4 a decision (*vyavasthā*) of the *sabhā* of Uttiramerur made the Śiva Brahmanas of the region accountable for the fines imposed on its members. Four years later we get the first inscriptional reference to the movement of Śiva Brahmanas into the border districts of Karnataka. Significantly, most of the records which register gifts to them are found either in the Kolar or in the Bangalore district. It appears that the Śiva Brahmanas who were already a dominant priestly group in Tamil Nadu began to enter Karnataka in the wake of Cola infiltrations into Karnataka which reached a climax with the battle of Takkolam in 1004.

The Tamil origin of Śiva Brahmanas is also evident from the fact that all gifts of land and benefices to this group were made by the Cola kings and all are mentioned in inscriptions engraved in Tamil language and Tamil characters. Even the names of Śiva-Brahmana donees are all Tamil names. The exclusive patronage of Śiva Brahmanas by Cola kings is evident from the fact that whatever donations were given to religious beneficiaries of the conquered Karnataka districts between 997 and 1071 went in favour of the Śiva Brahmanas. The Śiva Brahmanas who constituted a powerful community of Tamil priests and who served as the priestly agents of the Cola dynasty, were evidently called upon to consolidate the social basis of Cola political power in Karnataka. Several Cola inscriptions found in Karnataka would suggest that during the eleventh-twelfth centuries the Śiva Brahmanas brought under their control a number of Śiva temples in those parts of Karnataka where Cola authority was firmly entrenched.

The priestly duties of Śiva Brahmanas were of a varied nature. They managed grants of land revenue on behalf of the temple administration.[40] They were also authorized to distribute among the staff of the temple the prescribed shares of harvested grain. A Kolar inscription of 1071 instructs the Śiva Brahmanas of the temple of Cāmuṇḍeśvarī to set apart 180 *kalams* of paddy for the Kannāṭa Paṇḍita for the performance of the rite of *māḍāpattiyam* in the temple of goddess Cāmuṇḍeśvarī of Kolar.[41] Maintenance of the temple, its images, supervision of the property of the temple, performance of ceremonies were all included among their duties. The rituals performed by these priests were varied and probably innovative in character and for that reason beyond the competence of ordinary local priests. The records show that there was a priest who officiated as Brahmā, another was occupied with the recitation of incantations, a third performed the *nava homā*.[42] Similarly, the proper performance of the sacrificial ritual required the services of a qualified whole-time priest.[43] The sociologists' conception of a situation in which 'performance of rites becomes so technical that there is little room for the activities of lay men' and in 'extreme cases' of which 'the priestly castes may monopolise the cult'[44] proved true of the religious condition of Kolar and its adjoining areas about the tenth-eleventh centuries.

Although most references to Śiva Brahmanas are found in the inscriptions of Kolar district, the influence of the sect was not confined to Kolar. Two Bangalore inscriptions of the twelfth century would suggest that the Śiva Brahmana priests were lorded over several temples in the Hoskote and Dod Ballapur taluks of the district by the Cola occupants of the territory. The Dod Ballapur record, which is dated to the eleventh century mentions a Gāmuṇḍa or headman who entrusted the charge of a temple of Mudisvaram Udaiyar to the Śiva Brahmana priest Penna Beṭṭa (or Bhaṭṭa). The second part of the grant would become significant in the light of the foregoing observations. The record stipulates that worship in the concerned Śivaite temple would be conducted as long the lineages of Gāmuṇḍa and the priest Penna Beṭṭa continue to flourish. It then stipulates that any one who says to Penna Beṭṭa and his descendants 'do not worship the god Mudisvara Udaiyar' would enter the hell.[45] The inscription seems to be anticipating obstruction by local Brahmanas who thought their right to profits from temple-worship was being eroded by outsiders. A Hoskote inscription of an earlier date mentions yet another family of Śiva Brahmana priests who received certain grants for conducting ritual services in a Śivaite temple.[46]

Empowered as they were by their ritualistic authority, the position of the Śiva Brahmanas was further consolidated by the extension of their control over the fiscal affairs of villages in the district of Kolar. This might have entitled them to impose additional levies upon the rural clients including the supply of sheep and goats on appointed days of the week.[47] Fines were to be imposed on those who did not oblige. The rural officers, who were to collect and remit these fines to Śiva Brahmana priests, in addition to supplying their own quota of sacrificial animals and other provisions, were to pay fines in the case of their failure to do so.

The sectarian influence of these priests compares well with the high regard enjoyed by the Śiva Brahmanas of the Tamil country about the same time. An inscription of Vīra Rājendra from the Madhurantakam taluka of Chingleput district refers to three Brahmanas who were appointed to give lectures in Śaiva metaphysics in the Vedic college attached to the temple of

Venkaṭeśa Perumal at Tirumukkadal.[48] Their mention along with the Mahāpāñcarātra, Vaikhānasa, Ṛgvedī, and Yajurvedī teachers indicates that socially they were on par with the Vaiṣṇavas and vedic scholars. The inscription also shows that the Śiva Brahmanas were not mere priests but were also accomplished scholars of Śivaite theology.

At present, the Śiva Brahmanas of Karnataka are, like the Guravas, a poor lot. They are identified with the Stānikas,[49] a class of Kanarese temple servants.[50] Their claim to Brahmanhood is outright rejected by other Brahmanas[51] and they are assigned the duties of collecting flowers, sweeping the premises of the temple, looking after the lamps, cleaning the vessels, ringing the bells and the like.[52] The social invalidation of the Śiva Brahmanas was due, probably, to the machinations of the Mādhva Brahmanas of later times, who, being a more powerful community, dispossessed the former of their authority. Perhaps the Mādhvas found it easier to do in view of the fact that the Śiva Brahmanas were organized not on the basis of kin or heredity but priestly profession. The Mādhvas themselves monopolised the priestly functions and assigned the duties of temple servants to the erstwhile priests in different Śivaite temples. The same treatment was meted out to the Śiva Brahmanas by others of their caste also. For example, the famous temple of Subramaṇya which is said to have been in charge of the Subramanya section of the Stānikas, was wrested from them by the Shivalli or Tulu Brahmanas.[53]

Goravas

The Goravas were, like the Śiva Brahmanas, a class of Śivaite priests, though much less numerous and much less significant than the latter. The word Gorava seems to be derived from the term *guru*.[54] It may also be a vulgarized form of the term *guruvat*,[55] meaning like the *guru* or teacher. Obviously, it was a general term of respect which was applied to the Śivaite priests.

The position of the Gorava approximated to the status of a Brahmana freeholder. Grants of land were made to them for their livelihood and they enjoyed the land as freehold estate on a hereditary basis. Gorava Śivadhārī, who received a plot of land from Govinda III in 803, was evidently a descendant of the Gorava who had received the same plot from Kīrttivarmā II of Badami in 747.[56] In times of necessity the Goravas took up arms to protect the property of the temples. Gorava Kolasudipa is referred to in an inscription as chasing thieves who lifted the cattle of the temple. The Goravas were trustees of the royal charters of benefactions. In case of any change in the terms of donation the Goravas were authorized to implement them. Thus, the Goravas of the Soratur monastery were informed that the king relinquished his right over a cess amounting to 30 *drammas,* which implied that this right now passed on to the temple.[57] Henceforth it was the responsibility of the Goravas to collect the amount. As trustees of religious bodies the Goravas were entitled to oust any member of the establishment for a breach of the code of conduct. A record of Amoghavarṣa I[58] authorized the Goravas to drive away any of the administrators of the temple of the sun god who violated the rule of celibacy.

In the course of time, however, the Goravas lost their position as a class of respectable Śaiva mendicants and priests and were degraded to the position of mere temple servants.[59] This was probably due 'again' to the orthodoxy of Mādhva Brahmanas who being more numerous and powerful dispossessed the Goravas of their privileged status.

Brahmanas by Improvization

Inscriptions generally register grants of land to Brahmanas who are mentioned with their *gotras,* Vedic sections and brahmanical prefixes or suffixes of names such as *bhaṭṭa, upādhyāya, śarmā, svāmī, dīkṣita* and so forth. The names of the beneficiaries are usually names of brahmanical gods and goddesses. Compared to this, we come across inscriptions which refer to Brahmana donees without their *gotra* name or vedic sections, which suggests that the bene-ficiaries did not belong to the traditional Brahmana castes. The non-Sanskritic names of these persons also point to the same conclusion.

A record of Govinda III, issued in 800, registers the gift of a village to thirteen Brahmanas led by Ruddappa Dīkṣita, son of

Govvaika Bhaṭṭa. Of these, three are mentioned without *gotra*. They are Mangappa, Lavvaiya and Vādi, each receiving a share of the gift land. These three persons do not appear to be Brahmanas, notwithstanding their mention along with other Brahmana beneficiaries. They were probably heads of families of agricultural workers who migrated to the new village together with the Brahmanas. This seems to be suggested by their un-Sanskritic names. The compound word Mangappa is formed by *manga* or *manka* and *appa*, a common term of respect.[60] *Manku* or *manka* in Tulu means stupidity[61] while *manka* in Kannada means silliness and stupidity.[62] *Manka* in Kannada also means a monkey[63] while *manku* in Malayalam means blighted ears.[64] Mangappa might, therefore, mean a man with blighted ears or a stupid person. Lavvaiya, which is apparently derived from *la-v* which in the Kolami dialect[65] means fat or from *alavu* which in Kannada[66] means power, strength, force, probably refers to a strongly built person. The third donee was Vādi. Vādi might have originally been a huntsman for *vāda* in Kannada means a ditch or trench for catching elephants.[67] Besides these, the record introduces three fictitious *gotras*, the Kramaitta, the Kutimāsa and the Siguli. None of these is traceable in the Puruṣottama list of *gotras* and *pravaras* of Brough.[68] Kramaitta is a compound formed of *krama* and *ittar*. *Krama* may be the same as *kamuka* (from Sanskrit *kramuka* meaning areca catechu), which in Tamil and Malayalam means a betel-nut tree,[69] while *ittar* or *ittan* in Tulu means 'a man of this place'.[70] The compound word, therefore, may mean 'the betel-nut tree man of this place', suggesting thereby that the family to which Durggappa belonged held the particular plant in totemic esteem. Another *gotra* was Kutimāsa which, again, is a compound of *kuti* and *māsa* or *masu*. *Kutika* or *kutuka* in Telugu and *Kuttige* in Kannada mean throat, neck, voice or tone,[71] while *masu* in Kannada means grey or black and *māsara* means a dusky colour.[72] Evidently, Kutimāsa referred to a man with a dark complexion. The third *gotra*, Siguli, may be a corrupt form of *siggāli* or *siggāri* in Telugu meaning a person who feels ashamed[73] and is derived from the root *siggu* in Kannada meaning shame, bashfulness, timidity, modesty, etc.[74] Siguli *gotra* probably signified a family of modest or low origins.

Another example of improvised Brahmanas can be found in a charter of 742.[75] The grant registers the donation of a village to three Brahmanas, Revāditya Bhaṭṭa of the Bhāradvāja *gotra* who was an *adhvaryu*, and Govisara and Māula. The original residence of all the three was Navasārikā, modern Nausari. The *gotra* of Govisara and Māula is not stated, nor their functions as Brahmanas. Their duties apparently consisted in serving Brahmana beneficiaries as cultivator-cum-managers of donated fields. The personal names also do not admit of their Brahmanhood. *Kovi* in Kannada and *govi* or *grovi* in Telugu stand for *bryonia grandis*, a climbing plant with beautiful red fruit.[76] *Sara* in Malayalam and *sara sara* in Kannada means sound of rustling produced by movement in a shrub.[77] Govisara, therefore, may mean a member of a family whose totem was the plant *bryonia grandis*, suggesting thereby a tribal social origin. The second beneficiary also appears to have had a tribal origin for, *māvuliga*, which may be an enlarged form of *māula*, means in Kannada a man who uses a net to catch deer. This was not a brahmanical occupation.

The Cuttack Museum Charter of the Śailodbhava king Mādhavavaramā refers to the grant of 23 *timpiras* of land to 24 Brahmanas,[78] all of whom have the suffix *svāmī* to their names (though none is mentioned with his *gotra* or the vedic section). No reference to the 'six brahmanical duties' (*ṣaṭkarmanirata*) occurs either. On the contrary some donees bear names which sound not only unbrahmanical but even suggest a low social status. Thus Golasvāmī was the man of the bunch or cluster and Khadirādityasvāmī was a son of the *khadira* plant.[79] The latter probably refers to the head of a family which respected the *khadira* as its totem.

Several persons who received the donation of a village from the Somavaṁśī king Mahāśiva Tivara appear to have claimed Brahmana identity.[80] The charter states that the donees were priests of the Caraka section of the *chāndoga* (Chāndogya) *caraṇa* of the *Sāmaveda* although the Carakas actually belong to the black *Yajurveda*. Besides this incongruity, the donees are named without their *gotras*. Some suffixes like *ghoṣa, datta* and *nāga* to their names. These name-endings constitute at present important surnames of the Kayasthas of Bengal.

Brahmanization of Tribal Priesthood

Several inscriptions of the eastern Cālukya dynasty refer to Boyā Brahmanas who were the priests of the Boyā tribe who received gifts of villages from the kings.

The Brahmana Boyās figure for the first time in a charter of the eastern Cālukya king Viṣṇuvardhana II.[81] The record, dated 668-9, refers to the founding of a colony of Boyā priests at the village Reguru. Some beneficiaries belonged to the Boyā community, as is apparent from the use of the term Boyā as suffix to personal names and place names. Several Boyā donees belonged to one and the same family. For instance, Vinayaśarmā is stated to have belonged to the house of Keśava Boyā and to the Bhāradvāja *gotra*. Two others, Vebaśarmā and Vinayaśarmā, whose *gotra* is not mentioned, are also stated to have belonged to the family of Keśava Boyā. Donaśarmā with Kāśyapa *gotra* and Revaśarmā with no *gotra* are stated to have belonged to the family of Rekādi Boyā. Both received one share each. Jakkiśarmā of the Kauṇḍilya *gotra* and Aruvaśarmā with no *gotra,* are said to have belonged to the house of Penbidi or Banbidi Boyā. They were also granted one share apiece. Similarly, Venniśarmā and Camundiśarmā, both of the Kauṇḍilya *gotra,* are stated to have belonged to the family of Māraṭ Boyā, and each received one share of the land. The *gotra*-wise break-up of the Boyā beneficiaries is also interesting. There were 14 Kāśyapas, 7 Bhāradvājas, 1 Kāṇva and 1 Gautama (no *gotra* is mentioned in the case of 8 donees). In 673 king Sarvalokāśraya, the son of Viṣṇuvardhana II, granted the village[82] Chendarura to 6 Sāmavedīs of the Boyā community. Five of the donees belonged to the Kauṇḍiya or Kauṇḍinya *gotra,* the sixth to the Kālabava. Curiously, no proper names of the donees are mentioned. Indravarmā, the son of Viṣṇuvardhana I, granted to Brahamana Cendiśarmā of the *vājasaneyī caraṇa* a village called Kondanaguru.[83] Cendiśarmā, a Bhāradvāja, was the son of Viṣṇuśarmā and the grandson of Dūrggāśarmā, also called Irralurā Boyā, or Boyā of village Irralura. The beneficiary was the leader of a group of Boyās who received the village as a grant. This is suggested by a clause relating to the division of the village into 64 shares, apparently for the enjoyment of as many donees. The last line of the inscription mentions the grant of one share to an unnamed person and another grant of a third of a share to one Coḍa Bol. Here, again, no *gotra* names of donees are given.

Yet another charter issued by Viṣṇuvardhana II refers to the grant of village Koneki to Viduśarmā of the Parāśara *gotra*, *Taittirīya caraṇa* and *Āpastamba sūtra*.[84] Viduśarmā is the Boyā of village Kanderu and a resident of village Atukuru. The first place-name suggests the place of origin of the family to which the donee belonged, the second place-name indicates that Viduśarmā was residing at the village Atukuru when the grant was made to him. The village was divided into 120 shares and distributed among 15 Brahmanas, whose names end in *śarmā*. Of them 7 are described as Boyās of 7 different villages. Four are referred to merely by their proper names suffixed by the term Boyā and in the case of one of these four the original village name is also mentioned. No *gotra* names of these Brahmanas are mentioned.

Several interesting points emerge from the description of Boyā priests. They received grants of villages just as other Brahmanas did. While in the case of the non-Boyā Brahmanas the number of beneficiaries could be a family or more than one family, the minimum number of Boyā beneficiaries was not less than six. The *gotra* names used by Boyā Brahmanas were generally Kāśyapa and Kauṇḍilya, although a few Bhārdvājas Kauśikas, Kāṇvas and Gautamas are also met with. More striking is the absence of any *gotra* names in the case of a majority of Boyā Brahmanas. For example, of the 16 donees mentioned in the Koneki record[85] only the principal donee is given a *gotra* name, Parāśara. Similarly, of the 70 donees mentioned in the grant of Viṣṇuvardhana II[86], 25 are without *gotra*. Also, the name-ending used by Boyā Brahmanas is invariably *śarmā*. Perhaps the sole exception is Kondaśamī Boyā in which case the surname appears to be *svāmī*. The purpose of land grants made to Boyās was the same as in the case of other Brahmanas. For instance, king Viṣṇuvardhana II granted a village for the sake of strength, victory and freedom from sickness.[87] The same king granted another village for the increase of success, enjoyment, longevity, strength and prosperity.[88] Notably, grants of land to Boyās were made on auspicious occasions as in the case of other Brahmanas. The grant of village Koneki was made on the day of a lunar eclipse in the month of Māgha.[89]

The inscription of Viṣṇuvardhana II which registers the donation of village Reyuru to Boyās refers to Bādiśarmā who was one of the beneficiaries and who belonged to the house of Koyila Boyā.[90] The same grant speaks of Kundiśarmā who belonged to the family of Kavila Boyā, a mistake for Kovil Boyā. *Koyila* or *kovela* in Telugu and *koyil* or *kovil* in Tamil mean temple.[91] Koyila Boyā or Kovil Boyā, therefore, refers to the Boyā of the temple or a Boyā temple priest. Thus, Bādiśarmā and Kundiśarmā belonged to two different families of Boyā priests, and while the former was a Bhāradvāja the latter was a Gautama. The reference to Koyila or Kovil Boyā suggests that the Boyās had their own temples and priests who performed the ritual services in these temples thereby ruling out the necessity of calling in a Brahmana priest from outside. Even today the Myasa Boyās who consider themselves superior to the Uru Boyās and try to prove their superiority by refraining from the consumption of chicken and alcohol (which Uru Boyās freely consume), do not call a Brahmana to officiate for them.[92] The Uru Boyās, however, call a Brahmana for such purposes.

References to the families of Koyila Boyās would suggest that they had their own temples where ritual was conducted along traditional lines. Today the Boyās of the Bellary district enjoy *inām* or rentfree land for propitiating the village goddess by a certain rite called *bhūta bali*, intended to secure the prosperity of the village. The Boyā priest gets himself shaved at midnight and sacrifices a sheep or buffalo, and mixing it with rice, distributes it throughout the village. In the morning, he returns to the temple of the goddess and receives a new cloth from the villagers.[93]

From epigraphic evidence it would appear that the Boyā Brahmanas did not lag behind the traditional Brahmana families in scholarship. The Koneki grant styles the donee Viduśarmā as well-versed in various branches of learning such as the *Brāhmaṇas, Sūtras, Mantras, Tantras* and *Upaniṣads.*[94] His father Mahāsenaśarmā is described as *śrōtriya* who was conversant with the *Vedas* and constantly engaged in *yajan, yājan, adhyayana, adhyāpana, dāna,* and *pratigraha.* Mahāsena is stated to have been renowned as the very Vararuci of the day on account of his erudition in all the *āgamas.*

There are no Brahmanas among the Boyās of today. Neither is their claim of Brahmana origin accepted. Not withstanding this, the Boyās identified themselves during the Census of Mysore as Nisadulu Boyās, descendants of Nisadu who was the son of great Venudu, a direct descendant of Brahmā.[95] Nisadu, who was created by the seven ruling planets from the right thigh of the great Venudu, was repulsively ugly and for that reason deprived of his father's throne and made the lord of the forests.[96] As lord of the forests he begot the Koravas, Chenchus, Yanadis and Boyās. The Boyās were his legitimate children, but others were illegitimate. On the other hand, those Boyās who identified themselves as Vālmikudu characterized themselves as the result of the union of Vālmīki, a Brahmana, and a Boyā girl. Even today Boyā women pour milk into the holes of white ant-hills. These are symbolic of the penance site of their progenitor Vālmīki.

In the present social set-up the above account may appear fictitious and fabricated. Judging, however, from the available data, there is no gainsaying the fact that Boyā Brahmanas were as much a part of brahmanical society as are other Brahmanas at present day. This is also corroborated by the fact that although the Boyā himself has little use for the Brahmana,[97] the latter finds the Boyā indispensable if he wants to perform the *vontigadu*. This is a ceremony by which a Brahmana hopes to induce favourable auspices under which a marriage is to be celebrated. During *vontigadu*, a Boyā is invited and sumptuously fed by the Brahmana at his residence. The feeding, however, takes place in the cow-pen. This contrasts with the north Indian practice according to which the Brahmana alone is entitled to be fed on all auspicious occasions.

The de-brahmanization of the Boyās requires to be explained. Of the four records dealing with land grants to the Boyās, three were issued by Viṣṇuvardhana II and the fourth charter was issued by Indravarmā, son of Viṣṇuvardhana I. All the grants were made during a short period of less than 30 years. The villages granted by Viṣṇuvardhana II lay either in the Nellore or in the Guntur district, while the fourth village granted by Indravarmā was situated in the Visakhapattanam district. Even today the Nellore and Guntur districts which lie in southern Andhra Pradesh have the next largest concentration of Boyās after Kurnool and Cuddappah districts in south-west. No other district of Andhra Pradesh contains any significant number of Boyās.

From these details it would emerge that by granting land to the Boyās, who inhabited the southern portion of the Eastern Cālukya dominions, the kings wanted to create a second line of defence against enemy Pallavas. That the region was vulnerable to Pallava offensive is shown by the invasion of the Pallavas in 736, which resulted in the overthrow of *Pṛithivīvyāghra,* the Niṣāda tribal chief, who was ruling as a feudatory of Viṣṇuvardhana III (709-46).[98] Once, the royal authority was consolidated, however, there was little justification for grants to those people who in spite of their brahmanical *gotras* and academic accomplishments were nothing more than provisional Brahmanas recruited from the indigenous non-brahmanical population. This is evidenced by the fact that during the reign of the Eastern Cālukya king Bhīma I, a brave general, Paṇḍaranga by name, fought and captured 12 Boyā Koṭṭams from one Vaso Boyā. The king, pleased with the feat, granted his general a village and made him a master of the conquered territory. Paṇḍaranga is praised for having made Kandukur, the Boyā stronghold, as beautiful as Bezwada.[99]

The position of the Boyā Brahmanas may be compared to that of the Gorovas and Śiva Brahmanas who also enjoyed grants of land in the early medieval period, and who were as much Brahmanas as the Brahmana priests of today. But they are today degraded into mere temple servants or *stānikas.*

NOTES

1. For details see R.N. Nandi, *Social Roots of Religion in Anceint India,* Calcutta, 1986, Chs. 2 and 3.
2. E. Thurston and K.V. Rangachari, *Castes and Tribes of Southern India,* Madras, 1907, vol. 1.
3. Ibid.
4. Thurston, op. cit., vol. 2, p. 392f.
5. Ibid.
6. *EI,* 18, no. 26, p. 35ff., 1, *Karhād-vinirgata.*
7. *The New Indian Antiquary,* May 1938, p. 145.
8. John Brough, *The Early Brahmanical System of Gotra and Pravara,* Cambridge, 1953, p. 119.
9. *EI,* 22, 28A, ll. 40-1 *Karhād-vāstavya-tat-caturvidya-sāmānya gārgya-gotra-bahvṛcasa-brahmacāriṇah.*

10. *EI*, 23, no. 17 A, p. 101, ll. 10-11.
11. *SII*, 9, pt. 1, no. 162, p. 150.
12. *EI*, 3, no. 29, l. 11, AD 1190.
13. *EI*, 3, p. 108, also see Kielhorn in *EI*, 8, p. 26, n. 1.
14. *EI*, 8, p. 26, n. 1.
15. *EI*, 3, no. 29, p. 216ff.
16. *Census of India*, Hyderabad State, 1921, vol. 21, pt. 1, p. 241.
17. Ibid.
18. *EI*, 19, no. 8. The donated village lay on the north bank of the river Nira in Satimala Bhoga and Palayathāna Viṣaya. The donee was Allaśarmā of Kauṇḍinya *gotra*. Palayathāna is modern Phaltom the chief town of the lower Nira valley.
19. *EI*, 23, no. 17, ll. 10-11.
20. *IA*, 6, p. 53, cited in V. Upadhyaya, *The Socio-Religious Condition of Northern India*, Varanasi, 1964, p. 40.
21. *EC*, 10, Kl. 106, Kl. 108, Kl. 109.
22. See under Śiva Brahmanas.
23. Thurston, op. cit., vol. 1, p. 366
24. Ibid.
25. Cited in Thurston, op. cit., p. 391.
26. Thurston, op. cit., p. 389.
27. *EI*, 32, no. 4, grant of the time of Indra III (915-28). For other references see grant of the time of Kṛṣṇa III (939-67); *EI*, 32, no. 5, AD 1034, grant of Cāvuṇdarāya; *EI*, 32, no. 5, two grants of Vijjala, dated AD 1048 and AD 1053.
28. *EI*, 32, no. 5, grant no. 3, ll. 3-4; also see grant nos. 1 and 2.
29. *EI*, 34, no. 17, p. 122ff.
30. R.N. Nandi, *Religious Institutions and Cults in the Deccan,* Delhi, 1973, Ch. 8.
31. *CII*, 4, no. 14.
32. *EI*, 19, no. 39.
33. This aspect of Brahamana infighting has been discussed in two different sections (IV and V) of my paper 'Client, Ritual and Conflict in Early Medieval Brahmanical Order', *The Indian Historical Review*, vol. 6, nos. 1 and 2.
34. *EC*, 10, Kl. 106 A, AD, 1019; *EC*, 10, Kl. 106 B, AD 1006.
35. Ibid.
36. *EC*, 10, Kl. 106 B, AD 1006.
37. Ibid., Kl. 106 B, AD 1006.
38. C.V.N. Ayyar, *Origin and Early History of Saivism in South India*, Madras, 1936, p. 193.
39. Ibid., p. 314.
40. *EC*, 10, Kl. 107, AD 1054; *EC*, 10, Kl. 106 C, AD 996.
41. Kl., 106 D, AD 1071.
42. *EC*, 10, Kl. 108, AD 1071.
43. Ibid.
44. Joachim Wach, *Sociology of Religion*, Chicago, 1944, p. 366.

45. *EC*, 9, Dod Ballapur 11.
46. *EC*, 9, Hoskote 10, AD 1075.
47. *EC*, 10, Kl. 26, Kl. 25, etc.
48. *EI*, 21, no. 38, p. 220ff.
49. Edgar Thurston, *Castes and Tribes of Southern India*, vol. 6, p. 390.
50. Ibid., p. 402.
51. Ibid.
52. Ibid., p. 403.
53. Ibid., p. 404.
54. M. Monier-Williams, *A Sanskrit-English Dictionary*, s.v. *guru*.
55. Ibid.
56. *IA*, 2, no. 123, l. 12.
57. *IA*, 12, no. 135, p. 256ff., AD 951-2.
58. *KI*, 1, no. 13 of 1939-40, AD 865.
59. *Census of India*, Hyderabad State, 1921, vol. 21, pt. L, p. 225.
60. T. Burrow and M.B. Emeneau, *A Dravidian Etymological Dictionary*, Oxford, 1960, no. 133; for names of donees see *EI*, 23, no. 2, p. 8ff.
61. Ibid., no. 3890.
62. Ibid.
63. Ibid., no. 3777.
64. Ibid., no. 3890.
65. Ibid., no. 248.
66. Ibid.
67. Ibid., no. 883.
68. Brough, op. cit.
69. Burrow, op. cit., no. 1033.
70. Ibid., no. 351.
71. Ibid., no. 1429.
72. Ibid., no. 3918.
73. Ibid., no. 2062.
74. Ibid.
75. *EI*, 25, no. 4, p. 25ff.
76. Burrow, op. cit., no. 1861.
77. Ibid., no. 1946.
78. Ibid., no. 3926.
79. *EI*, 24, no. 21, p. 148ff.
80. *EI*, 34, no. 17, p. 112ff.
81. *IA*, 7, p. 185f.
82. *EI*, 8, no. 24, p. 236ff.
83. *EI*, 18, no. 1, pp. 1-4.
84. *EI*, 31, no. 2, p. 74ff.
85. *EI*, 8, no. 24, p. 236ff.
86. *IA*, 7, p. 189ff.
87. Ibid.
88. *EI*, 31, no. 12, p. 74ff.

89. Ibid.
90. *IA*, 7, p. 185ff.
91. Burrow, op. cit., no. 1810.
92. Thurston, op. cit., vol. 1, p. 184.
93. Ibid., p. 187.
94. *EI*, 31, no. 12, p. 74ff.
95. Thurston, op. cit., pp. 187-8.
96. Thurston, op. cit.
97. Ibid., pp. 196-7.
98. *SII*, 2, no. 74, p. 265; also see *JAHRS*, 12, p. 60.
99. *The Age of Imperial Unity*, op. cit., p. 136

10

The Proliferation of Professional Castes

In the inscriptional sources of the eleventh-thirteenth centuries we come across a large number of professional groups and associations, many of which can be traced today as important trading, artisanal and agricultural castes. A sudden spurt in the number of professional castes seems to be related to the changes which were taking place in different fields of corporate activity about the tenth-eleventh centuries. The inscriptions also refer to inheritance of important offices which again led to the formation of new castes.

The Rise of the Trading Castes: Gavare

Epigraphic records suggest that although the formation of professional castes started during the earlier medieval centuries, it is only during the tenth-twelfth centuries that most of them become identifiable. The more important among these were the mercantile castes like the Gavara and the Gandham, the castes of professional warriors like the Banṭ and the Nāyak, the scribal castes such as Heggaḍe and Karaṇam and the caste of Gauḍa farmers. The term *seṭṭi* which denoted a professional class of traders is widely mentioned in the inscriptions as a caste surname. Although inscriptions give a large number of terms such as *vaṇig*, *vyāpārī*, *śreṣṭhī* and *seṭṭi* for the professional trader, it is only the last mentioned which invariably figures as a name-suffix of professional traders. It would be difficult to find examples in which the other terms are used as name-suffixes. The significance of the term *seṭṭi* as a caste surname would be further evident from inscriptions which refer to the family-tree of certain families of merchants. In such cases all agnates and cognates of the *seṭṭi* householders are also called *seṭṭi*.

The formation of a fairly large number of trading castes may be explained by reference to the revival of large-scale commercial activity from the close of the tenth century. The different categories of merchants described in the inscriptions of the eleventh-twelfth centuries seem to point towards growing markets for different kinds of merchandise which could not any longer be dealt with by the same group of traders. Evidently within the broad framework of a *seṭṭi* trading class there appeared various subdivisions dealing with particular types of commodity. The clustering of merchants on the basis of differentiated professional expertise gave rise to social exclusiveness and a sense of insularity which ultimately ended in the formation of merchant subcastes.

Although most of these subcastes either disappeared or took to occupations other than trade, a few are traceable even today. Two such groups, which figure in early inscriptions, are the Gavara and the Gandiga. Among the indigenous mercantile groups the Gandigas occupy a prominent place. The trade in perfumery goods was already an important mercantile pursuit during the early medieval centuries. But the professional compulsions which helped the growth of an exclusive social identity were obviously not felt before the tenth century from which time the Gandigas began to figure in inscriptions along with other mercantile subgroups. The Gandiga correspond to the modern caste of Gandham, an endogamous sept of the Baliga trading caste. One of the subdivisions of the Gandham subcaste is called Gandhavalli or Gandhapodi which too subsists by selling perfumery goods.

Far more numerous than the Gandham of today is the caste known as Gavara or Gavare, a group of northern merchants who migrated to Andhra Pradesh, Karnataka and Tamil Nadu about the tenth-eleventh centuries. At present they constitute an important caste of agriculturists in the Visakhapatnam district. In other parts of the state, however, they account for an important subdivision of the Komati trading caste. The present day Gavaras speak Telugu and are divided into various endogamous septs.

The records which speak of the migration of the Gavaras come from certain districts of Andhra Pradesh and Tamil Nadu while the epigraphs of Karnataka, which are of a later date, signify the sizeable presence of the Gavara traders in different districts of the state. The records pertaining to the migration of Gavaras suggest that the community was originally settled in the Bareilly and Faizabad districts of present Uttar Pradesh, and that the migration took place between the close of the tenth and the middle of the twelfth century.

The reasons for migration cannot be precisely determined, but certain shreds of information appear to be meaningful. It is of some moment to note that the movement started about the tenth-eleventh centuries, a period which coincides with the revival of commerce and urban life throughout the peninsular region. The inscriptions further show that the immigrants were *seṭṭis*, and that they hailed from important urban settlements such as Hemapura, Ayodhya and Ghazipur. That the Gavaras were professional merchants can be seen from the inscriptions. The commercial fortunes offered by the revival of trade might thus have been a strong inducement to migration to different parts of the south. However, a greater compulsion might have been the frequent obstructions caused by the recurrent Muslim invasions and internal warfare. The role of natural calamities in bringing about the migration is also not ruled out. Studies on post-Gupta society in north India have brought out the constraints of large-scale and well-organized commercial activity.[1] Attention has been drawn to bad roads, and insecure journey conditions. Sources of the period between the eighth and eleventh centuries indicate that plunder of caravans on highways was a recurring feature, and that plunderers included robbers and kings. Coupled with this were frequent disturbances caused by disputed succession and fleecing levies exacted by feudal chiefs.

The Gavaras who form the bulk of the population in the Ankapalli taluka of the Visakhapattnam district[2] are stated to have come in large groups from the Bareilly and Faizabad districts of Uttar Pradesh. An inscription of 1136 records that 1700 families of Gavaras emigrated from Ahicchatra,[3] modern Bareilly region, and took shelter in the eight provinces of the kingdom of the Cālukyas of Kalyani. The migration of Gavaras from Uttar Pradesh is also substantiated by the term *seemā nepālam* applied to the Gavara by the members of other castes to ridicule him.[4] *Seemā nepālam* is apparently reminiscent of the good old days when the ancestors of the Gavaras lived in a particular region whose borders touched Nepal. Probably the limits of Ahicchatra extended in ancient times up to the *terai* of Nepal.

Two more inscriptions[5] found at the Mallesvara temple at Bezwada prove the veractiy of Gavara migration from Uttar Pradesh. The records mention that Gavara Komatis, who are a prominent section of the Telugu speaking merchant community, belonged originally to Hemapura, Ghāzāpur and Ayodhya. The last mentioned corresponds to modern Ayodhya in the Faizabad district of Uttar Pradesh while Ghāzāpur may be identified with Ghazipur in eastern U.P. Two inscriptions from Nelapalli[6] in the Chittoor district also refer to the migration of Mummuḍi Gavare Seṭṭi at the head of 48,000 people without, however, mentioning the place of origin. The records have been assigned to the tenth century on the strength of the contemporaneity of the donor with the Rāṣṭrakūṭa king Kṛṣṇa III.[7]

Some Gavaras also appear to have come from the eastern parts of India, especially Bengal. Thurston thinks that the caste name Gavara is derived from Gaurī,[8] the patron deity of this caste; but Gaurī is also worshipped by other castes.[9] The term *gavara* seems to be the Dravidic form of Gauḍa,[10] meaning the inhabitants of Bengal. The interchangeability of the consonants 'ṛ' and 'ḍ' is permitted by the rules of philology.[11] Therefore, according to the pronounciation in south India *gauḍa* first became *gaura*, then *gavura* and lastly *gavara*.[12] The forms Gavara and Gavaregas also occur in inscriptions.[13] One more argument may be advanced to illustrate the association of Gavaras with ancient Bengal. Gauḍa in former times was also known as Puṇḍravardhana or the land of luxuriant sugarcane growth. This meaning of Puṇḍravardhana is also found in the *Amarakośa*, which refers to *rasāla ikṣus tad bedhaḥ puṇḍra kāntāra kādavaḥ*.[14] Ankapalli taluka, today the principal centre of Gavara population in Andhra Pradesh, is noted for its sugarcane cultivation and manufacture of good quality jaggery.[15] Its principal crop at present is also sugarcane.[16]

The absence of any reference to Gavaras in inscriptions before the tenth century suggests that the first batch of Gavaras emigrated to the south in the tenth century. This is also borne out by the Nelapalli Inscriptions of the first half of tenth century, which record the grant of village Koyaturu in Chittoor district to one Gavara Seṭṭi and his 48,000 followers.[17] Again, the inscription of 1136 which refers to the Gavaras as the overlord of the town Ayyavole or modern Aihole in Bijapur district shows that the Gavaras moved into the northern districts of Karnataka as early as the last quarter of the tenth century. They became the overlords of the locality in the course of a hundred years or so. The period of Gavara movement into the districts of Karnataka and Tamil Nadu may be fixed between the beginning of the tenth century and the beginning of the eleventh century, allowing for a few minor groups which may have entered the region still later.

We have no precise idea of their routes and intermediate halts; probably the Gavaras migrated to the south through two different routes. Those who emerged from the Bareilly and Faizabad regions[18] of Uttar Pradesh apparently crossed the Vindhyas and then catching up the great trade routes along the Western Ghats reached as far south as the Bijapur, Dharwar and Bellary districts of Karnataka. The presence of the Gavaras in these northern and north western districts of Karnataka supports this contention. The Gavaras migrating from eastern India might have passed through Orissa via Midnapore in West Bengal. As an alternative to the latter route, it may be suggested that most Gavaras of the Kanarese districts[19] went to Andhra Pradesh at some later date and settled there as an agricultural community. This suggestion follows from the fact that there are not many references to Gavaras in the inscriptions of the early medieval period from Andhra Pradesh.

It is interesting to observe that although at the time of their migration from north India all the Gauras were merchants, they took to different vocations on resettlement in different parts of south India. For example, in Karnataka, where they figure most frequently in early inscriptional records, the immigrants continued to flourish as a trading community. But in Andhra Pradesh they appear to have taken to agriculture. It is also significant that in Andhra Pradesh the Gavaras constitute a sizeable section of the agriculturists today, but in Karnataka they seem to have disappeared altogether as there is no mention of the Gavaras in the census reports. In the inscriptions of Karnataka, the Gavaras are invariably classified as a trading caste along with the *seṭṭiguṭṭa*, *gandigas* or dealers in perfumes, *seṭṭis*, *balegarum* or bracelet sellers, *bira vaṇigas*, and *gātrigas*.[20] The inclusion of the heads of Gavara families in the merchant syndicate of Vīra Baṇajigas of Sedambal[21] also signifies the importance attached to the immigrant merchants by the ruling families of Karnataka. It seems likely that the Gavara merchants of Karnataka were the principal dealers in agricultural goods and as such were liable to taxation. An inscription of 1150 states that the local Gavaras were to pay 1 *paṇa* annually per sack of goods which they sold, while the Gavaras of other countries were to pay at the rate of 1 *hāga* annually.[22] In contrast, the gold merchants of the locality were asked to pay at the rate of 1 *visa*. The mention of sack in connection with the Gavaras suggests that they were dealers in agricultural commodities.

The immigrant merchants were a powerful social group which exerted considerable influence upon the people among whom they settled. Native traders lost no time in identifying their interests with those of the newcomers. This is evident from their classification together with local merchant groups in the records of the tenth-eleventh centuries. The representation of the heads of Gavara families on the Vīra Baṇanju syndicate of Sedambal[23] shows that they were treated at par with the Vīra Baṇanjus, the great mercantile community of medieval Karnataka. The same inscription also refers to the Gavaras as lords of the city of Ayyavale,[24] which indicates that in certain areas the immigrant merchants ran the administration of important urban settlements. The importance of the Gavaras as a corporate body is also apparent from the fact that they figure in inscriptions as trustees of religious bodies. A record of 1165 refers to 1700 Gavaras along with Vīra Baṇanju merchants and their leaders as the protectors of a Jaina charity.[25]

The Gavaras were also respected on account of their martial

qualities. A record from the Nagamangala taluka of Mysore district, dated in 997, refers to the valour of one Gavara Seṭṭi who died protecting women of the locality from robbers. Another inscription from the Humsur taluka of the same district mentions one Gavara Seṭṭi who set up a memorial stone in honour of his younger brother who had fallen in battle.[26]

Patronage by kings and feudatories enhanced the social prestige of the immigrant merchants. The kings and feudatories could not ignore a community which was powerful on account of its opulence, martial qualities and numerical strength. At certain places, as in the village of Koyaturu in the Chittoor district, the Gavaras even outnumbered the local population. The Nelapalli records[27] illustrate how a Gavara merchant and his followers were patronized by a king of the Noḷamba Pallava dynasty who granted him a village and honoured him with the honorific epithet of Mummuḍi Gavare Pallavāditya Noḷamba Seṭṭi; this in effect elevated the social status of the beneficiary in the eyes of local people.

Some Gavaras today are Vaiṣṇavas, others Śaivas.[28] But at the time of their migration from northern India they were apparently all Śaivas. Their patron deity was Gavareśvara or lord of the Gavaras. Gavareśvara, was evidently a form of Śiva in whose honour the Gavaras erected temples and induced the local people to make donations for upholding the rites of their god. In 1074 we hear of a temple of Gavareśvara at Holal in the Hadagalli taluka of Bellary district;[29] to this temple the Gavaras of Holal along with the 120 *mahājanas*, the *seṭṭis* and the *telligas* made a contribution of some cesses on commercial articles for the service of the god. Another shrine of Gavareśvara was situated in the Shikarpur taluka[30] of Shimoga district; to it the Gavaregas, Gandigas, and Bira Vaṇigas made a grant of certain benefices, for worship as well as repairs. This grant was registered in 1150. Another temple of the same divinity was at Ittagi[31] in the Gadag taluka of Dharwar district; it received the grant of a plot of land in 1178. An inscription from Yewur[32] in the Surapura taluka of Gulbarga district also refers to the existence of a temple of Gavareśvara. It is obvious from the distribution of these temples that the cult was fairly widespread in Karnataka.

Subcastes of Oil-millers: Gānigas

Some evidence for the expansion of the craft of oil milling is furnished by a few Karnataka inscriptions which advert to different families of oilmen which employed different methods for extracting oil from oil-seeds. Some employed stone oil-presses, some wooden mills; some employed bullocks to work their mills while others preferred to operate the mills by hand. Two inscriptions from the Davangere taluka of Chitradurga district refer to two types of oil-mill, one of which was operated manually and the other with the help of bullocks.[33] An inscription of the Hunsur taluka of Hasan district refers to a hand oil-mill or *kaigāna*.[34] In a Belur taluka inscription mention is made of a tread oil-mill[35] while a record from Mysore taluka refers to bullock oil-mill or *ettugāna*.[36] It is likely that such exclusive professional characteristics encouraged the grouping of various oilmen families into endogamous subdivisions differentiated on the basis of the restrictive rules of connubium and commensality. The present position of oilmen castes is not much dissimilar. The term Gāniga mentioned in the inscriptions of the tenth and eleventh centuries today denotes a huge caste of Kanarese oil-millers who are divided into three subcastes none of which interdine or intermarry.[37] The three subdivisions are Heggeniga or those who yoke the oxen to a stone oil-mill, Kirggeniga or those who press oil in wooden oil-mills and Ontiyeddu who yoke only one bullock to their mills. Except the Ontiyeddu Gānigas, who claim to be superior to others and belonging to the right hand (*vadangai*) division of castes, all other castes and subcastes of oil-millers belong to the left hand division (*idangai*).

Castes of Official Origin: Gauḍa and Heggaḍe

In the inscriptions of Karnataka and Andhra Pradesh several terms are used to denote various categories of revenue officers: *kāyastha*, *karaṇa*, *śrīkaraṇam*, *kanakkan* and *heggaḍe*. Of these *heggaḍe* is an important caste name in modern Karnataka. It appears that *heggaḍe* was developing into a caste surname towards the close of our period. There are inscriptions which refer to families in which the office of the revenue officers or *heggaḍe* had become a sort of family inheritance. In a tenth century inscription, mention is made of a hereditary *perggaḍḍe* (*kramāgatada perggaḍḍe*) who ruled a certain territory by ancient right (*abhyantara siddhi*). The term *abhyantara siddhi* signifies that the territory which the official was ruling on a hereditary basis was a family inheritance which could be transferred or disposed of in the same manner as family property is transferred or disposed. The hereditary performance of the *heggaḍe*'s office led, as in the case of Gāvuṇḍa or Nāyaka, to the formation of an endogamous caste which adopted the official designation as a distinctive caste designation. The inscriptional references to expressions like 12 *heggaḍes* and 10 *karaṇams*[38] or 11 *heggaḍes* and 7 *karaṇams*[39] furnish unmistakable proof of the existence of micro-level professional groups which inhabited the same locality and for that reason probably had greater social exchange among themselves than others. This could have easily prompted them to intermarry among themselves and eventually coagulate into an endogamous sub-caste. It is plausible enough to suggest that most of regional subcastes of a larger parent caste had their origin in the regional insularity which gave rise to a sense of ritual superiority and social exclusiveness—the two determining aspects of subcaste formation.

Judging by inscriptions it would appear that the adoption of the official designation furnishes the first signs of the emergence of a new professional caste. In an inscription of 1160 a Heggaḍe family is mentioned prominently. The record shows that the term was used by the father, son and daughter as a prefix to their names. The father was Heggaḍe Dijayya, the son was Heggaḍe Timmane and the daughter is described as Heggaditi Candavve. Inscriptional references to Gāvunḍi, Gānegitti and Mālegitti, which denote women of the families of village headmen, oilmen and florists respectively, would indicate that faminization of official or occupational designation was a common practice in medieval south India and an important stage in the development of a professional group into a caste. Mālegitti Śivālaya is mentioned in an early Cālukya inscription while Gāvunḍi in the sense of wife or daughter of a headman is mentioned in several inscriptions of the tenth-eleventh centuries. In a few inscriptions *heggaḍe* is used as a name suffix also, to wit, Vijayāditya-heggaḍe who built a Śivaite temple and Dekane-heggaḍe, who negotiated a land dispute in 1190.

That the term had crystallized into a caste name of the scribal community can also be seen from the fact that in certain inscriptions the term *heggaḍe* is mentioned as the part of proper name of a revenue officer and also in the sense of the revenue office held by that person. A Shikarpur inscription of the tenth century refers, for example to a person whose name was Perggaḍe Pulimayya and who was a *perggaḍe* (revenue officer) of the Santaliga province. The *perggaḍe* is characterized as having been entrusted with the burden of administration and as holding the rank of a great minister.[40] In another Shikarpur inscription the name of a *perggaḍe* is given as Srimat Perggaḍe Kalimayya.[41]

At present, however, the Heggaḍes are a cultivating caste. In the Madras Census Report of 1901, they have been entered as a caste of Kanarese cultivators. The Heggaḍes of south Kanara are classified as shepherds though the majority of them are cultivators. It is not unlikely that owing to fresh social distribution of administrative role during Muslim rule and also under British administration, the Heggaḍes dropped out of the administrative hierarchy and adopted cultivation as the main basis of their livelihood. This was possible as the Heggaḍes mentioned in early records were hereditary landholders with absolute rights of enjoyment.

The gloss *gāvuṇḍa* or *gauḍa* is, apparently, derived from Sanskrit *grāmakūṭa*[42] just as Marathi *pāṭil* or *paṭel* is derived from Sanskrit *paṭṭakila*.[43] The transformation of *grāmakūṭa* into *gāvuṇḍa* resulted from a corruption of *grāma* into some such forms as *gamvu*, coupled with, in *kuṭa* a disappearance of 'k' and a softening of 'ṭ' into 'ḍ'.[44] The form *gamvu* figures in the Paithan grant.[45] This derivation is also supported by the fact that in colloquial use *gauḍa* is often nasalized as *gaunḍa*.[46] The *Deśīnāmamālā* also gives *gāmaṇḍa* as the Prakrit form of Sanskrit *grāmakūṭa*.[47]

The *gāvuṇḍas* mentioned in inscriptions of the early medieval period correspond with the *gauḍas* who constitute a very large caste of agriculturists. During the early medieval centuries the numerous farming families of Karnataka appear to have developed into a huge endogamous caste with *gāvuṇḍa* as its name. This followed from the frequent association of farming chiefs with the duties of territorial government, particularly the office of a village or district headman.

A large number of instances can be cited to illustrate that as in the case of other official positions, the chiefs of chosen farming families performed the duties of a village headman (*gāvuṇḍa*) and district headman (*nāḍgāvuṇḍa*) on a hereditary basis. The inscriptions frequently refer to important farming families which served their feudal overlord as Gāvuṇḍa, Nāḍgāvuṇḍa and Urgāvuṇḍa on a hereditary basis. A Sorab taluka inscription of 991 mentions the eldest son of a district *nāḍgāvuṇḍa* who was lorded over a certain holdings with chartered governmental rights such as *abhyantara sidhi* and *sadaṇḍa-doṣe.*[48] A Sagar taluka inscription of 1096 refers to four generations of a Gāvuṇḍa's family all of whom served their overlords as trusted officers.[49] All bear names with *gāvuṇḍa*-ending suggesting thereby the adoption of the official designation as a caste name. This seems to be further corroborated by numerous inscriptions which mention the term *gāvuṇḍa* twice in respect of the same person. First it figures as the name-suffix of the official concerned and then as the name of the office which the concerned person was administering.[50] The office of the headman could be bequeathed like a family inheritance and the inheritor could be a son, daughter or wife. One of the early inscriptions mentions the wife of a *nāḍgāvuṇḍa* who succeeded to the office administered by her late husband. The woman, named Jakkiyabbe, is praised in glowing terms as an able administrator who protected her territory well. On the approach of old age, however, she called for her daughter and made over to her the burdens of administration.[51] In this case also the term *gāvuṇḍa* or *gāvuṇḍi* was employed both in the sense of a family surname and an official designation suggesting that the two were fast becoming interchangeable and giving rise to the connotation of a caste surname still used by the huge farming Gauḍa community of Karṇataka.

Even today, the Gauḍas retain an elaborate organization of headmanship. In every village there are two headmen while for every group of 8 or 9 villages there is a superior headman who is called Magana Gauḍa.[52] These headmen no longer function as primary links in the territorial government as they did during the middle ages, but govern the organization of the Gauḍa caste.

The Gāvuṇḍa farmers of early medieval and medieval times appear to have been an indispensable part of the territorial administration, both at the village and at the district level. This is indicated by the appointment of the chosen heads of Gāvuṇḍa families as headmen of villages as well as of districts. Those in charge of villages were known as Gāvuṇḍa or village headmen and those in charge of the district as Nāḍgāvuṇḍa. A person is referred to in a grant of 973 as the Gāvuṇḍa of his village[53] while another is described as the *nāḍprabhū* of the Tuyyala Begur[54] subdivision included in the Nagarakhanda-70. Sometimes a Gāvuṇḍa ruled a bigger administrative unit than the district (*naḍ*), as in the case of Abba Gauḍa[55] who administered Bikkiga-70 and held the rank of *senāpati daṇḍanāyaka.* This almost approximated the position of a feudal lord in terms of rank and size of the territory ruled. One Sovideva who was ruling an area of the same size as the one administered by Abba Gauḍa is described as a *mahāmaṇḍaleśvara.*[56] Till recently, the *gauḍas* ruled the countryside as petty feudal chiefs.[57]

Groups of Gāvuṇḍa householders were sometimes appointed as the headman of the village or district. In one record we come across as many as seven *gāvuṇḍas* who were appointed to jointly administer the village of Nagula.[58] It cannot, however, be determined whether their head-manships continued on a hereditary basis, as in the case of most individual appointments.

The administrative functions of the headman included maintenance of tanks, roads, law and order, defence of the village and management of religious trusts founded in the village. Since the Gāvuṇḍas constituted a dominant section of the medieval farming villages, their cooperation was an absolute necessity for expanding and promoting the irrigational network. Reference may be made to a record of king Polacoradeva which specifically instructs the 106 Gāvuṇḍas of a village to preserve the newly constructed village tank.[59] Frequently, the farmers themselves took initiative in such matters. A record of 907 shows how the Gāvuṇḍa householders of a village transferred 35 *kandugas* of land, lying below the channel of the tank to a merchant who had financed the construction of the channel.[60]

The *gāvuṇḍa* householders who functioned as village headmen shared the management of temple trusts and made grants of land from their own estates as well as from the common village land. In 750, one Dharma Gāvuṇḍa granted 25 *nivartanas* of land to a Jaina temple[61] apparently out of his own estate. In 850, several Gāvuṇḍas who were jointly administering a village granted to the same Jaina temple certain fields.[62] In 937, Kamba Gāvuṇḍa of Kākambāl granted land for a Śaiva temple built by one Goggi.[63] In 973, the headman of the village Kadekeri gave certain plots of land for the benefit of Mahādeva whose temple was situated in the village.[64] Besides the headman, other members of the caste also donated land to the local temples. In 750, several *gāvuṇḍas* sought permission of the governor of the district to give to the Jaina temple some land[65] which, evidently, formed part of the common village land.

The village headman also spent on the construction of new temples and renovation of old ones. In 951, the headman of a village built as many as five temples of Śiva and an equal number of monasteries.[66] In 1021, the Oḍeya of Nugunāḍu caused the ruined temple of Belatur to be reconstructed.[67] Generally, the Gāvuṇḍa may have made land grants and built temples out of purely religious motives. But sometimes personal considerations led them to make such benefactions. In 966, the *nāḍgāvuṇḍa* Ganga Gacci erected a Śiva temple to perpetuate the memory of his eldest son Dadiga, who died prematurely.[68] Some such personal loss appears to have prompted Piṭṭabbe Gāvuṇḍi to set up a Śiva *linga* (phallic emblem) in a temple.[69]

The headman also performed certain duties for religious institutions in his locality. He is frequently referred to as trustee and administrator of religious bodies. According to the Morigere record of 1045, Cikka Gauḍa and his uncle Nema Gauḍa took a decision jointly with the *mahājana* assembly of 60 Brahmana householders to appoint a priest in the Śiva temple.[70]

The defence of a Karnataka village was a collective arrangement to which every able-bodied young man of the village was a party. The headman owed a special responsibility in this matter. He led the rural militia against cattle-raiders as well as the armies of refractory vassals and invading kings. In 950, one Pṛthvī Gāvuṇḍa was killed defending the cattle of the village.[71] In 1010, the son of a headman died in the same manner.[72] Nāḍprabhū Kālagauḍa, the guardian of the limits of Eḍvate circle, is said to have fought bravely against Mahāpradhāna Sangeya Daṇḍanāyaka of the Hoysala kingdom near Honnali.[73] The headman of Bellartha is reported to have perished in saving the cattle of the village.[74] In 1164, Biṭṭeya, the son of the *nāḍprabhū* of Begur, joined the troops led by Mahāmaṇḍaleśvara Sovideva. While the troops were storming the fort of Saliyur, Biṭṭeya scaled up the fort fighting with the enemies, and was killed.[75] The headman's authority as the armed leader of the village is evident from the example of Gariya, the headman of Mangala, who is stated to have revolted against the king.[76] The rebellion was put down by the Pergade Macayya, who was rewarded by the king with the grant of a toll income from twelve villages.

The Caste of Professional Soldiers or Banṭs

In the Tulu language, the term '*banṭ*' or '*bunṭ*' means powerful man or soldier.[77] Old records indicate that in ancient times Banṭs were a numerous caste of warriors who filled the ranks of rural militia. A record of 1072[78] speaks of the Banṭs of the *agrahāra* of Tilivalli in Dharwar district. They numbered a thousand and were under the command of the thousand *mahājanas* who were organized as an administrative body. This is indicated by the reference that the Banṭs were compared to scented elephants of the thousand *mahājanas*. The epigraph also testifies to the martial qualities of the Banṭs by stating that they were the athletes of Oḍagere and possessed unequalled valour. The thousand Banṭs of Tilivalli again figure in a grant of 1126[79] which mentions the death of a Banṭ during a fight with a cattle lifter.

Banṭs were also employed as body-guards or house-guards. An inscription of 965 refers to one Ujjeni Bhujanga, *banṭ* or soldier of the Mahāsāmanta Permmādi.[80] They were also appointed to guard the property of the temples and were maintained on plots of temple land. A record of 1122 found in the Akkalkot taluka of Sholapur district speaks of the appointment of two Banṭs as temple-guards.[81]

The Tilivalli inscription shows that like many other professional groups the Banṭs were also grouping into caste or communal associations about the eleventh century. Whatever earlier references are found relate to individual Banṭ soldiers, not groups or associations. Also, like other professional groups such as traders, artisans and hereditary functionaries of the state, the Banṭs were required to cooperate with the temples and Brahmanas, enriching their coffers by means of contributions which do not appear to have been voluntary. The producer castes were required to pay in both cash and kind, but non-producing groups were asked to pay in cash. The Tilivalli inscription records the decision of the Banṭ assembly of Tilivalli to contribute at the rate of one *paṇa* every Banṭ soldier towards the construction of the stone embankment of the large tank situated in the village. The same meeting decided to grant one *paṇa* per *mattar* of cultivable land within the limits of the village to finance other stone constructions of the tank called Piriyagere. The same assembly also promised to make a *sarvamānya* endowment consisting of house tax and food tax on account of the *bārikā* or watchman of the tank. They also agreed to supply *biṭṭi* or free labour to the headman. The last clause is interesting inasmuch as it indicates the subject status of Banṭ soldiers in Brahmana freeholdings and free peasant holdings. The inscription records a gift of 24 *mattars* of land to two Banṭs who appear to have been chiefs. The lands were apparently service holdings.

In medieval feudal society religious sanctification appears to have been an important basis of status redemption. This might explain the practice of setting up of temples and naming them after individuals and communities. The practice, which has survived to this day is mentioned in several inscriptional records. We have references to the Gavare trading community naming temples built by them as Gavareśvara. The Banṭs of Tilivalli had similarly set up a temple and named it Banteśvara.[82] The inscription registers the provisions made for the ritual service of god Banṭeśvara. The setting up of a Śaiv temple would suggest that the Banṭs of Tilivalli were devout Śaivas. A good number of present day Banṭs also profess Śaivism.[83]

The Banṭs are at present an important land-owning and cultivating group in south Kanara and are, with the exception of Ballavas or toddy drawers, the most numerous caste in the district. Although they have settled down as agriculturists, they retain their independence of character, strong and well-developed physique, and still carry their heads with the same haughty toss as their forefathers did in the stirring fighting days when every warrior constantly carried his sword and shield.[84]

The Scribal Castes: Kāyastha and Karaṇa

The term *kāyastha* means 'situated in the body' which may suggest that the Kāyastha was an embodiment of good qualities. This meaning of the term is given in a record of 1047.[85]

The Kāyasthas were an important class of officers, as is apparent from early literary and epigraphic evidence. The *Viṣṇudharmasūtra*[86] and the *Yājñavalkyasmṛti*[87] refer to Kāyasthas as royal officers. The *Mṛcchakaṭika*[88] refers to a Kāyastha who accompanied a judge to the court; he was perhaps a keeper of court proceedings. Kṣīrasvāmī, commenting on the *Amarakośa*,[89] identifies the Kāyastha as a royal official. Epigraphic evidence also indicates that the Kāyasthas were a class of royal officers. The *prathamakāyastha*[90] of the Damodarapur Inscription was the head of a government department. Nayasena, referred to as a Kāyastha in the Ghugrahati charter[91] of Samācāradeva was also an employee of the king. Kāyastha Śrīpāla who wrote the charter of the Viṣṇukuṇḍin king Mādhavavarmā in 500[92] was a scribe of the writing department of the state. The Kāyasthas developed from a class of officers into a caste. The pattern of development compares with that of other groups discussed above.

The rise of the Kāyastha as a considerable class of professional writers and record-keepers can be fruitfully examined in the light of the growing use of regional scripts and languages in both official and private archives from the fifth century of the Christian era. It is not without significance that the Kāyasthas emerged as an endogamous caste around the eighth century by which time the development of regional scripts was nearly complete. Between the sixth and eighth centuries, we come across as many as seven regional varieties of writing,[93] three in the northern region and four in the southern provinces. Of the three northern scripts, the *Siddhamātṛkā* is met with about the sixth century, the *Nāgarī* about the seventh and the *Śāradā* about the eighth century. Of the four southern regional forms, the *Vaṭṭeluttu* is seen in a developed form about the fourth-fifth centuries, the box-headed Malwa script about the fifth-sixth, Telugu-Kannada characters about the seventh century and the Kalinga script about the eighth century.

Consequent upon the formation of regional scripts the whole bulk of writing work, for both literary and archival purposes, appears to have been done in these scripts and since everyone could not be expected to master the alphabet a hereditary class of professional writers gradually made its appearance; later on such grouping formalized into an endogamous caste. Coupled with the need for scribal expertise in writing was the loss of professional mobility which is so characteristic of the social landscape in early medieval times. The phenomenon can be explained in the conventional manner by a reference to persistent legislative efforts of the Brahmana-dominated elite to consolidate the functional roots of social differentiation in a hierarchically ordered society on the basis of caste-endogamy and hereditary occupation. But this was in fact an effect of a much larger social development relating to the changes at the managerial level of production which seem to have been warranted by the marked scarcity of non-agricultural surplus including money, and the consequent inability of ruling families to sustain a centrally controlled salaried administration. Since salaries were now being paid in land, and land-revenue in kind, any physical movement which might be necessary for a change of occupation was not easily possible. Interchange of professional work at the local level was hardly any more feasible on account of the similar terms of service and specialized nature of various bureaucratic tasks. In fact the very practice of transferring revenue plots to different members of the bureaucracy tended to make the performance of all bureaucratic jobs hereditary, and subsequently, to give rise to bureaucratic castes in different parts of India, the Kāyastha being one of them.

The earliest mention of Kāyasthas in the sense of a caste is found in a Rāṣṭrakūṭa record of 871[94] which refers to a Kāyastha family called Vālabha. A Kāyastha family described pure as water-lilies is referred to in another record of the Rāṣṭrakūṭa period.[95] Khandyama who was holding the office of the private secretary or *rahasya*[96] (which is the same as *rahasyādhikṛta*[97] of other inscriptions) also indicate that Kāyasthas developed as a caste in this period. A Paramāra record of 1059[98] speaks of a Kāyastha family of Valabhī. Another Paramāra grant mentions one Sohika, son of Kāyastha Aiyala, as belonging to the Vālabhya family.[99]

The Karaṇas like the Kāyasthas were originally a class of government officers, but developed later into a caste and were subsequently identified as a section of the Kāyastha community. The word *karaṇa* found in early medieval inscriptions is the contracted form of *adhikaraṇa* meaning a department or office of the state. The holders of these offices were variously known as *karaṇa, karaṇika, adhikṛta* etc. The function of these officers was to keep records. Commenting on the *Amarakośa,* Kṣīrasvāmī refers to *karaṇas* as officials of the state,[100] which is supported by epigraphs. A *karaṇa* called Mendayya appears to be an accountant in a record of 943 from Sira taluka.[101] In another case several *karaṇas,* mentioned along with the Gāvuṇḍas, who together made a grant of land in 751[102] seem to have been accountants. The *jyeṣṭhādhikāraṇika*[103] of Ghugrahati grant was the chief judge of the district court, *adhikaraṇa.* The Irda plates of Nayapāladeva list the *karaṇas* along with the heads of departments or *adhyakṣa,* envoys or *duta,* military generals or *senāpati.*[104] The fact that *karaṇas* appear invariably in connection with the registration of land grants[105] shows that they maintained records of land rights or land revenues.

Transformation of the *karaṇas* from a class of officers into a caste is suggested by the texts of the early centuries of the Christian era. The *Manusmṛti* and the *Yājñavalkyasmṛti*[106] mention the Karana as a caste resulting from the union of a high caste man and a low caste woman.

The identity of Karaṇas and Kāyasthas was the result of similar occupations. Thus, *jyeṣṭhādhikaraṇika* of the Ghugrahati grant was the chief judge[107] of the district while the *dharmādhikaraṇa*[108] Kāyastha Guṇadhavala was a judge. Both the Karaṇa and the Kāyastha got appointments as writers of state departments. Kṣīrasvāmī mentions that the Karaṇa was an officer like the Kāyastha.[109] Identity of Karaṇas with Kāyasthas was so complete that Karaṇa in later times became the caste name of a section of the Kāyasthas in Bengal, Bihar and Orissa. Several families of Kāyastha Prabhūs in the Deccan bear the surname *karaṇika.*[110]

The foregoing illustrates that the occupational factor was instrumental in the origin and development of Kāyasthas and Karaṇas as a caste. Besides occupation, exogamous marriage in the *anuloma* order also explains this development in a large measure.

According to lawgivers, the Karaṇas were the product of the union of a Vaiśya man with a Śūdra woman.[111] The *Ādiparva* states that Yuyutsu was a Karaṇa child of the Kṣatriya Dhṛtarāṣṭra from a Vaiśya woman.[112] A Bengal inscription of the early medieval period also suggests that the Karaṇa was the product of a high caste man and a low caste woman. The maternal great grandfather of king Lokanātha, described as a Brahmana (*dvija varaha*),[113] married a woman of low caste, whose son came to be regarded as a *pārāśava.*[114] Lokanātha's maternal grandfather and his mother were also regarded as *pārāśava.* Lokanātha himself was the son of a *pārāśava* mother and a Brahmana father;[115] but he could not describe himself as either. He is referred to in the inscription as a Karaṇa.[116] Evidently in some cases the Karaṇas, who later came to be treated as Kāyasthas, was the result of an *anuloma* form of marriage.

In our times the place of the Kāyasthas in the *varṇa* scheme has been a controversial issue. According to a judgement of the Calcutta High Court they are Śūdras while according to the verdict of the Patna and Allahabad High Courts they are a twice-born caste.[117] The status of the Kāyastha as a twice-born caste was consequent upon its origin as a result of exogamous union between a high caste man and a low caste woman. Manu allows them the rites prescribed for a twice-born caste.[118] An inscription of the eleventh century found in the Vinukonda taluka of the Guntur district refers to the Kāyastha chieftain Ambadeva as the progeny of some great Kṣatriya warrior, who escaped the extirpation of the Kṣatriya race by Paraśurāma.[119] Evidently this supports the view that Kāyasthas were twice-born. Śrīdharadāsa, a Kāyastha minister of king Nānyadeva of Mithila, who lived about the eleventh century, describes himself as the son of a Kṣatriya family.[120] His descendants are still regarded as *kulīnas* in the Kāyastha community of Mithila. Soddhala, the celebrated author of the *Udayasundarīkathā*, who also lived in the eleventh century, boasts of his descent from Kālāditya, the brother of the Kṣatriya king of Valabhi.[121] All this suggests that Kāyasthas were included in the *varṇa* organization as a twice-born caste. In some cases, however, certain Sūdra families made attempts, through their connections with the king, to raise their status to that of the Kāyasthas. An inscription of 1047 refers to the Kāyastha caste as twice-born,[122] but describes the 'progenitor' of this caste as a *turiya janman*, which, according to Halāyudha (quoted by Bhaṭṭa Lakṣmīdhara,[123]) means a Sūdra.[124] In this case the *turiya janman kāyastha* was probably the issue of a *pratiloma* union between a Kṣatriya mother and a Sūdra father.

Members of the Kāyastha family played an important role in the economic and administrative affairs of the early medieval period. The revenue administration of the districts and villages was entrusted to the Kāyasthas who were popularly known as Karaṇa in the lower Deccan. For all alterations in land settlements reference had to be made to them. The Karaṇa cooperated with others in carrying out the orders regarding land grants.[125] A land grant mentions the chief accountants or Ḳaraṇas besides the *pergaḍe*, the twelve *manneyas*, the *prabhūs* as the witnesses to the donation made by the king.[126] Another epigraph refers to five accountants (*karaṇas*) and a *daṇḍanāyaka* as the protectors of the grant of certain fields.[127] The local influence of the *karaṇa*, who kept all records dealing with land settlements, is obvious from these records.

Some Kāyasthas held important state offices other than that of a record-keeper. In a record of Vajrahasta III, one Dāmodara, the son of Mahākāyastha Māvurayya appears as the great minister for peace and war (*sandhivigrahika*).[128] His father too held the same office. Similarly, Kāyastha Allava is described in a record of Mahābhavagupta as an employee in the office of the great minister for peace and war.[129] Kāyastha Guṇadhavala is stated in a grant of the Rāṣṭrakūta king Amoghavarṣa to hold the dual office of *senābhogika* and *dharmādhikaraṇa*;[130] the first may have been a high military office and the second was the office of a judge.

Because of their connection with the revenue administration and record keeping the Kāyasthas were in a position to interfere, not always unreasonably, with the rights of intermediary land holders and rate-payers, a large majority of whom were Brahmanas. As early as the fourth century, the lawgiver Yājñavalkya enjoins the king to give special protection to his subjects against the machinations and oppressions of Kāyasthas.[131] A hint to this effect seems to be contained in a *Kūrma Purāṇa* verse which refers to the harassment (*tāḍayanti*) of Brahmanas by royal officers who were of Sūdra origin.[132] The passage is relevant in view of the fact that the Brahmanical author and the legal writers considered the Kāyasthas to be of Śūdra origin, and also that the *Purāṇa* is a work of the fifth-sixth centuries and therefore coincidental with a period when the Kāyasthas were emerging as an important caste. Vijñāneśvara a legal writer of the eleventh century, also attests to the growing influence of the Kāyastha and attributes this to their patronage by the kings.[133] All this may partly account for the denunciation of Kāyasthas in orthodox brahmanical writings. Uśanā, who wrote about the eighth-ninth centuries, condemns them as greedy and cunning exploiters.[134]

Kāyasthas are stated to be serving the king in the capacity of physicians and astrologers.[135] The professional duty of the Sūryadhvaja Kāyasthas from very early times has been to describe the effect of the stars.[136] The pseudo-astrologers referred to by Varāhamihira in his *Bṛhatsaṁhitā*[137] probably included some Kāyasthas who tried their hand at astrology. Some inscriptions suggest that in north India people of this caste served as physicians. The Dabok inscription of Dhavalappadeva, issued in 813, refers to Giyaka, as Vaidya Giyaka.[138] The last line of the same charter refers to him as Bhiṣahgiyaka,[139] which confirms that

Vaidya was not a mere honorific title adopted by some Kāyasthas, but the designation of a medical practitioner. Vaidya Yaśodeva, a relative of Vaidya Giyaka, also followed the profession of the physician.[140] According to the *Mitākṣarā* of Vijñāneśvara, the Kāyasthas of the Deccan served their clients both as physicians and as astrologers.[141] At one place the commentator calls the Kāyasthas a *nakṣatratithivaktā* or the reader of the stars and planets.[142]

The present hierarchy of south Indian castes does not know of the Kāyasthas who constitute a considerable endogamous caste in different parts of north India. But there are nevertheless castes which correspond to the Kāyasthas of Bengal, Bihar and Uttar Pradesh and the Karaṇas of Orissa. The origin of these divisions can be traced in the same hereditary ordering of the administrative jobs, as we noticed in the case of the Kāyasthas.

The inscriptions of the early medieval and medieval periods contain terms such as *kanakkan, ur-kanakkan, nagara-kanakkan, śrīkaraṇa, karaṇa, heggaḍe, adhiṣṭhāyaka* and so forth. All these words mean an accountant, but functional differentiation represented by these terms cannot be ignored inasmuch as it explains the origin of different subcastes. Thus the term *ur-kanakkan*[143] referred to the village accountant, *nagara-kanakkan*[144] to the city accountant and *śrīkaraṇa* to the royal accountant. It would appear that the *nagara-kanakkan* was a more prestigious group than the *ur-kanakkan*. Similarly the *śrīkaraṇa* was a higher group in comparison to the *ur-kanakkan*. Descriptions appearing in the inscriptions would also suggest that some families of accountants were superior to others. A Honnali inscription of 1098[145] mentions the *daṇḍanāyaka* Madirāja who is characterized as the *adhiṣṭhāyaka* or manager of the heavy customs duties or the *vaḍḍa-rāvula sunka* of the province of Banavasi-12000. The record then mentions the accountants of various villages as *karaṇagala*, who registered certain remissions on the order of the Adhiṣṭhāyaka Madirāja. Śrīkaraṇa[146] who would approximate the Adhiṣṭhāyaka in terms of powers and position, enjoyed great authority on account of their being in the direct service of the king. The rendering of the term as royal accountant also seems to be strengthened by the expression *arasara-śrīkaraṇa*[147] meaning accountant of the king. There is evidence to show that some Brahamans also served as professional village accountants. Several inscriptions state that land transfers were registered as charters by members of the Brahmana assembly. One inscription shows that the accountant of the Punganur freehold village was a Brahmana.[148] The association with kings and Brahmanas appear to have raised the position of certain accountant families which, when formed into an endogamous subcaste, claimed a status superior to others. This can be noticed in relation to the Śrīkaraṇa itself which is considered to be the highest among the four subdivisions of the Tamil Kanakkan accountant caste.

It would be seen that the gloss *kanakkan* which denotes today a large Tamil accountant caste was used in the inscriptions also as a generic term for accountant families. The term is derived from *kanakku* which means account. Although there is no intermarriage among the four subdivisions of Kanakkans, namely the Śrīkaraṇa, Kaikattu Karaṇams, Sarattus and Solic,[149] all these groups seek approximation to the traditional Brahmana culture by rules of diet, widow marriage and sacred thread. The Śrīkaraṇam and the Karaṇam even claim to be sons of Braḥmā, but this is dismissed by other castes who regard them as the offspring of a Vaiśya father and a Śūdra mother. While the Śrīkaraṇa is regarded as the highest of the four divisions, the Kaikattu Karaṇams, who take a lower position within the hierarchy, might be said to correspond to the large number of village accountants alluded to in the inscriptions.

By and large the Karaṇams continue to perform the same scribal duties which they used to discharge in medieval times. Inscriptions refer to Kanakkans and Karaṇams as maintaining registers of village revenue. In the event of a transfer taking place they were instructed to scrupulously enter the details of change in the concerned registers. In cases of dispute they appeared as official witnesses. Even today it is the duty of the Karaṇams to take care of government survey instructions and, where revenue survey is being carried on, to ensure that village and field boundary marks are correctly made.[150]

NOTES

1. Lallanji Gopal, *The Economic Life of Northern India* (c. AD 700-1200), Delhi, 1965. Some of the sources cited by the author in support of his argument include the *Kuṭṭanīmatam*, the *Upamitibhavaprapañcakathā*, *Tabaquat-i-Nāsiri* and Medhātithi's commentary on the *Manusmṛti*.
2. *JAHRS*, 8, p. 135.
3. *EI*, 19, no. 4, ll. 9-10, *gavaregaḷum ahicchatra vinirggatarumm*.
4. *JAHRS*, 8, p. 135.
5. *SII*, 4, nos. 774 and 796 cited in *JAHRS*, 8, p. 131.
6. Nos. 242 and 243 of the *Epigraphical Report* of 1919 cited in *JAHRS*, 58, p. 129.
7. *JAHRS* 8, p. 129.
8. E. Thurston and K.V. Rangachari, *Castes and Tribes of Southern India*, vol. 2, p. 278f.
9. *JAHRS*, 8, p. 123.
10. Ibid.
11. Ibid.
12. Ibid.
13. *EI*, 19, no. 4, ll. 9-10; *EC*, 7, Sk. 118; *EC*, 4, Ng. 23, AD 977; *EC*, 4, Hs. 32, AD 1045; *SII*, 9, pt. 1, p. 121, AD 1074.
14. *JAHRS*, 8, p. 135.
15. Ibid.
16. Ibid.
17. Ibid.
18. Nos. 242 and 243 of the *Epigraphical Report* of 1919 cited in *JAHRS*, 8, p. 129.
19. *EI*, 19, no. 4
20. *EC*, 7, Sk. 118, AD 1150; *EI*, 19, no. 4, AD 1136.
21. *EI*, 19, no. 4, p. 37.
22. *EC*, 7, Sk. 116.
23. *EI*, 19, no. 4, p. 37.
24. *EI*, 19, no. 4.
25. *MAR*, 1916, p. 46.
26. *EC*, 4, Hs. 32, AD 1045.
27. Nos. 242 and 243 of the *Epigraphical Report*, 1919 cited in *JAHRS*, 8, p. 129.
28. Thurston, op. cit., vol. 2, p. 278.
29. *SII*, 9, pt. 1, no. 139.
30. *EC*, 7, Sk. 118.
31. *EI*, 13, no. 4, lines 94-5.
32. *EI*, 12, no. 37, l. 8.
33. *EC*, 11, Dg. 20, AD 1045 and *EC*, 11, Dg. 133, AD 1071.
34. *EC*, 5, Hn. 54 (Old Series).
35. *EC*, 5, Bl. 114 (Old Series).

36. *EC*, 3, My. 9 (Old Series).
37. Thurston, op. cit., vol. 2
38. *EC*, 10, Kl. 111, AD 1022.
39. *EC*, 10, Kl. 112a, AD 1027.
40. *EC*, 7, Sk. 194.
41. *EC*, 7, Sk. 189.
42. *EI*, 7, no. 25, p. 177ff.
43. Ibid, *Paṭṭakila* is mentioned in the Ujjain records of 975 and 1023, cf. *EI*, 6, p. 51, l. 10; *EI*, 6, p. 53, ll. 7-8
44. *EI*, 7, no. 25.
45. *IA*, 30, p. 517.
46. *EI*, 7, no. 25.
47. *EI*, 5, p. 232
48. *EC*, 8, Sorab 477
49. *EC*, 8, Sagar 80
50. *EC*, 9, Hoskote 142, AD 1043
51. *EC*, 8, Sk. 219, AD 956
52. Thurston, op. cit.
53. *IA*, 12, no. 137, p. 270ff.
54. *KI*, 4, no. 24, AD 1024.
55. *EC*, 11, Bg. 84, AD 1181.
56. *KI*, 4, no. 22.
57. Francis Buchanan, *A Journey from Madras through the Countries of Mysore, Canara and Malabar*, London, 1807, vol. 1, p. 178. Buchanan refers to Kempa Gauḍa, the headman of Magadi, who had a large number of followers and built the fortress of Savana Durga and became a polygar of great distinction.
58. *KI*, 2, no. 5, p. 14ff., AD 859.
59. *SII*, 9, pt. 1, no. 30, p. 16.
60. *EC*, 3, Magadi 14 (Old Series).
61. *KI*, 1, pp. 4-7.
62. Ibid., 2, no. 5, p. 14.
63. *EC*, 11, Cd. 76.
64. *IA*, 12, no. 137.
65. *KI*, 1, pp. 4-7.
66. *Bombay Karnataka Inscriptions*, 1, pt. 1. no. 39.
67. *EC*, 4, Hg. 16.
68. *EC*, 9, Magadi 75.
69. *EC*, 8, Sb. 471.
70. *SII*, 9, pt. 1, no. 86.
71. *EC*, 10, Mulbagal 108.
72. *EC*, 11, Jl. 13.
73. *KI*, 4, no. 43.
74. *EC*, 12, Tiptur 11, AD 930.
75. *KI*, 4, no. 24.
76. *EC*, 4, Ch. 48.

77. Thurston, op. cit., p. 152.
78. *KI*, 2, no. 2, p. 20ff.
79. *KI*, 2, no. 17, p. 71ff.
80. *EC*, 11, Hk. 33.
81. *KI*, 2, no. 16, p. 62ff.
82. *KI*, 2, no. 20, p. 76ff.
83. Thurston, op. cit., p. 151.
84. Thurston, op. cit., p. 149.
85. *EI*, 24, no. 13, v. 34.
86. *Viṣṇudharma*, 7.3 cited in P.V. Kane, *Dharmaśāstra kā Itihāsa*, vol. 1, Lucknow, 1965, p. 128.
87. *Yājñavalkya*, 1. 322 cited in Kane, op. cit.
88. Kane, op. cit.
89. Ibid., p. 127.
90. D.C. Sircar, *Select Inscriptions*, vol. 1, Calcutta, 1965, p. 337.
91. *EI*, 18, no. 11, p. 1, ll. 5-7.
92. *EI*, 27, no. 49, p. 312ff.
93. George Buhler, *Indian Palaeography*, Bombay, 1904.
94. *EI*, 18, no. 26, l. 78, *vālabhya kāyastha vaṁśa jātena*.
95. *IA*, 12, no. 136, p. 263ff.
96. *EI*, 31, no. 24, ll. 27-8.
97. *EI*, 24, p. 145, ll. 15-16; *EI*, 24, no. 43, l. 30.
98. *EI*, 21, no. 9, p. 50.
99. *EI*, 21, no. 26, p. 158.
100. *Amarakośa, Śūdravarga*, 10. 1-2.
101. *EC*, 12, p. 92.
102. *KI*, 1, pp. 4-7.
103. *EI*, 18, no. 11, ll. 5-7.
104. *EI*, 22, no. 25, v. 23.
105. *EC*, 8, Sb. 10, AD 800; *EC*, 11, Dg. 11, AD 1066; *EC*, 11, Dg. 43.
106. *MS*. 10. 41; *Yājñavalkya*, 1. 92 cited in Kane, op. cit., p. 118.
107. Supra.
108. *EI*, 28, no. 28, p. 235ff.
109. Supra.
110. Y.R. Gupte cited in *EI*, 18, p. 224, fn. 1.
111. *Gautama Gr. Sū*. 4.17; *Yājñavalkya*, 1.92 cited in Kane, op. cit., p. 127.
112. *Ādiparva*, 115.43 cited in Kane, op. cit.
113. *EI*, 15, no. 19, v. 6.
114. Ibid., v. 36.
115. Ibid., v. 2.
116. Ibid.
117. Kane, op. cit., p. 128.
118. *MS*. 10. 41 cited in Kane, op. cit., p. 118.
119. *EI*, 25, no. 27, p. 271ff., AD 1290.
120. N.N. Vasu, *Social History of Kāmarūpa*, vol. 3, Calcutta, 1933, *Kṣatravaṁśajabhānu*.

121. Ibid.
122. *EI*, 24, no. 13, v. 34.
123. Kane, op. cit., p. 74.
124. *EI*, 24, no. 13, p. 109, fn. 4.
125. *EC*, 12, p. 92, AD 943.
126. *EC*, 11, Dg. 11, AD 1066.
127. *EC*, 11, Dg. 43, AD 1162.
128. *JAHRS*, 8, p. 145.
129. *EI*, 8, no. 11, p. 138ff.
130. *EI*, 28, no. 28, p. 235ff.
131. *Yājñavalkya*, 1. 322 cited in Vasu, op. cit., vol. 3, p. 153.
132. *Kūrma Purāṇa*, Ch. 29, v. 17, *tāḍayanti dvijendrāṁsca śūdra rājopajīvinaḥ*.
133. Cited in Vasu, op. cit.
134. Uśanā cited in Kane, op. cit., p. 128.
135. Vasu, op. cit., p. 15.
136. Ibid., p. 156.
137. *Br. Sam.*, Ch. 2.
138. *EI*, 20, no. 13, ll. 2-3.
139. Ibid., l. 15, *bhiṣaḥgiyakasūnunā*.
140. Ibid.
141. Cited in Vasu, op. cit., p. 115.
142. Ibid.
143. *EC*, 7, Shikarpur 13 mentions *karaṇams* of various villages, *EC*, 5, T.N. 228 mentions *ur-kanakkan*. For other references to *karaṇam* and *ur-kanakkam* see *EI*, 5, 3B; *EC*, 11, Dg. 11; *EC*, 5 (Old Series).
144. *EC*, 9, Ch. 131.
145. *EC*, 7, Shikarpur 13.
146. For early inscriptional references to Śrīkaraṇa see *EC*, 7, Hn. 47; *EC*, 5, My. 186; *EC*, 2, no. 38; *EC*, 6, Mg. 28.
147. *EC*, 5, Mysore 186.
148. *EC*, 9, Ch. 42 A.
149. Thurston, op. cit., vol. 3.
150. Ibid.

11

Deprivation of Artisans

The Legal View

The dissolution of craft-guilds into occupational castes, which followed widespread decline of craft production in the post-Sātavāhana period encouraged Brahmana lawgivers to socially downgrade different categories of artisans and service castes. In the pre-medieval *gṛhyasūtra* literature there are occasional mild references to the impurity of artisanal workers. But the dimensions which the theories of purity and impurity assumed in later sources can be meaningful only in the context of changing social alignments within the *varṇa* structure. To some extent Brahmanical denunciation of the artisans appears to have been warranted by the emerging pattern of production management which called for perpetual free supply of essential goods and services in Brahmana freeholdings, the temple *devadāna* holdings and Sāmanta service-holdings.

A concerted brahmanical effort to destabilize chosen sections of the working class is first noticed in the *Manusmṛti* which furnishes a fairly long list of *pratiloma* mixed castes. The enumeration covers all those artisanal workers and service castes who enjoyed a distinct position of social and economic advantage in the pre-medieval market economy of commerce. Once the pace was set by Manu, it became customary for all medieval lawgivers to reiterate and even reformulate the theories of social illegitimization. The *Vaikhānasa Smārtasūtra* of the fourth century lists several groups of artisans as fallen ones, ostensibly because of their origin in illegitimate hypergamous marriage or cohabitation. Some of the Śūdra *pratilomas*, smiths, oilmen, fishermen, washermen and saltmen are even declared to be untouchables.

The opinion of brahmanical legal writers hardened with the passage of time. Bhāruci, a sixth-century commentator on the *Manusmṛti* states that artisans were more degraded than Śūdras and followed the occupation of untouchables.[1] The *Bṛhatsaṁhitā*, which is considered to be a southern work, denounces all types of craft work as bad livelihood. The text also foretells the failure of guilds and a bad time for smiths, tailors, bleechers, distillers, painters, etc.[2] Jinasena, a Jain author of the eighth century, refers to two types of craft workers. One group included those who could be touched (*spṛśya kāru śūdra*) and others who could not be touched (*aspṛśya kāru śūdra.*).[3] The list of untouchables furnished by Aparārka, a twelfth-century southern commentator of the *Yājñavalkyasmṛti* includes nearly all the artisanal and service castes.[4]

In downgrading the essential craftsmen to the position of untouchables, the lawgivers were careful to omit those categories whose services could not be accepted without physical contact. As such, the barber who also performed an unclean job, was not classified as an untouchable. Aparārka's comprehensive list of untouchables includes cobbler, huntsman, fisherman, washerman, oilman, butcher, actor and toddy-drawer, but leaves out the smith castes and the barber.[5]

The barber seems to have been an indispensable member of the medieval village community and could not therefore be easily degraded to the position of an untouchable. Land grants often attached families of barbers to Brahmana beneficiaries and apportioned a share of the gift land for their maintenance. The *Ādi Purāṇa* of Jinasena, who lived in Karnataka about the eighth-ninth centuries, refers to the barber as a touchable *kāru śūdra*.[6] The *Skanda Purāna* also includes barbers among the seven best (*uttama*) subdivisions of the artisan caste (*śilpī*).[7] The *Bṛhat Kalpa Bhāṣya* reference to three *nāpita dāsīs*[8] suggests that some women of the barber community were employed as maid-servants. The term *dāsī* does not mean here a slave woman. The barbers often had to pay a professional tax as is indicated by the

Vilavaṭṭi grant of the Pallava king.[9] A Bagali record of 1068 refers to tax payaḅle by barbers.[10]

Disabled as they were by legal writers, the artisan castes were not eligible for political positions. But a few exceptions may not have been altogether impossible. Interesting references are found in Jain sources of the early medieval centuries. For example, the *Yaśastilaka* refers to Pāmarodāra, who, although born in the family of an oilman, held the high office of minister under king Yaśodhara.[11] The king did not dismiss the minister even when he heard of his low origin. Oilmen, who were themselves being reduced to the position of untouchables, could get polluted by the touch of untouchable Cāṇḍālas. The minister Pāmarodāra, who is stated to have been polluted by Cāṇḍālas, rejected the advice of some elderly persons to undergo expiation for this sin. He pleaded that the soul was pure by nature and there was no need for any further purification.[12] This passage in a Jain text might be referring to a conscious attempt to deride the brahmanical notions of untouchability, notwithstanding the fact that the Jain community was as much based on *varna* divisions as brahmanical society itself, and also that the Jains were as much influenced by the notions of pollution[13] and untouchability as the members of brahmanical *varṇa*-society. Secondly, the passage might also reflect the characteristic indifference of a non-twice-born Śūdra to prevalent brahmanical thinking on pollution and untouchability. The *Yaśastilaka* also cites other examples of low-caste men who held high offices under the king. Thus, the king of Kerala appointed a lowly person as the royal priest or *rājaguru*,[14] and the king of Kalinga appointed a barber to the post of a military general.[15]

Artisans in Bond Service

The social illegitimization of artisan and service castes was attended by greater encumbrances in the form of forced unpaid labour and enslavement by Brahmanas and temples. Inscriptions which register grants of lands and revenues to temples also mention certain categories of artisans whose services the temple required on a permanent basis. In some cases the artisans are asked to supply to the temples stipulated quantities of goods produced by them or to pay periodic cash contributions. In a large number of cases, however, the inscriptions register outright transfer of artisan families and workshops to the temples thereby empowering the latter to exact services on a hereditary basis. The Kharepatan grant of 1008 shows that in a coastal town in Maharashtra, a family each of the female attendants (*dārikā-kuṭumbani*), oilmen (*tailikakuṭumbani*), garland-makers (*mālākāra-kuṭumbani*), potters (*kumbhakāra kuṭumbani*) and washermen (*rajaka kuṭumbani*) was transferred to a Śiva temple.[16] A few examples of the transfer of looms to religious establishments are also mentioned. An AD 1087 inscription from the Chitradurga district mentions the transfer of a house of weaving along with two oil-mills to a certain temple.[17]

Since oil was the most sought after commodity, it was the oil-pressing castes which suffered most on account of such transfers. The restrictions were particularly discouraging in view of the fact that the subjections were ordered at a time when the craft was expanding and producing for markets. The subjection of oil-millers was ordered by kings and locality chiefs, village-headmen, district-headmen, Sāmantas, revenue-officers or Brahmanas. An inscription of 947 refers to a village headman who transferred a family of oil-millers to a Śivaite temple.[18] In 1032, another headman transferred as many as six oil-mills to a Śivaite establishment.[19] A record of 975 mentions the transfer of yet another group of six oil-mills to a religious institution.

The practice of enslaving artisanal workers seems to have been fairly widespread during the tenth and eleventh centuries. An early tenth-century inscription describes one Iravi Korttan, the grand merchant of the Ceraman world (Kerala) as having obtained the lordship of the town of Maṇigrāma from king Sthānu Ravi. The king is then stated to have 'given' to the grand merchant five categories of artificers and the oil-makers, who lived in the Maṇigrāma town as slaves.[20] On another occasion, the same Sthānu Ravi made over to the Tarisa church of Kollam one family of carpenters and one family of washerman besides four families of ploughmen 'to do their duty to the god henceforth'.[21]

In Tamil Nadu the enslavement of artisans and service castes by temples appears to have been more or less legitimized by widespread traffic in labour. A Tiruvadandai inscription of Rājarāja I mentions the subjection of as many as twelve families of fishermen to the local Śrī Varāha temple. The subjection was ordered by two officials who served in two different *nāḍu* localities. Each of the twelve subjected families was required to pay three-fourths of a *kalañju* on their incomes from weaving and fishing, besides rendering assistance in the celebration of two annual festivals, one of which was of seven days' duration.[22] The element of compulsion and the hereditary nature of bondage is testified by the stipulation that the *sabhā* and the *ur* of Tiruvadandai undertook to hold the twelve *paṭṭinavar* families and their descendants strictly to their obligations.

It is clear that the slavery to which the artisans and service castes were reduced had to be enforced by coercion as in the above instance. Sometimes the subjected families defied the order of enslavement and, special efforts had to be made to restore the terms of subjection. For instance, some persons purchased by a local temple for employment as slaves and accordingly branded with a trident mark[23] are stated to have taken to mischievous behaviour and defied the chief of the temple or *sthānattar*. The matter was subsequently laid before a general assembly of authorities, the decision of which cannot, however, be read in the damaged inscription.

The enslavement of artisan families and the free appropriation of artisan surpluses was as much prompted by Śivaite temple authorities as by Jain monasteries. A Sorab inscription of 1198 refers to the great minister Mahādeva Daṇḍanāyaka who transferred, in the presence of his Mahāmaṇḍaleśvara and his entire retinue, certain ricelands, a shop and two oil-mills to a Jain temple which he himself had recently constructed.[24] The presence of the overlord and his retinue seem to formalize the transactions. The locality chief also appears to have prevailed upon the community of oil-mongers to make an additional provision of oil for the same Jain temple at the specified rate of one ladle (*sattuga-āya*) to burn lamps in the temple. Another Sorab taluka inscription of 1126 mentions fifty families of oilmillers who were required to supply oil for the lamps in a Jain temple.[25] The temple was also authorized to receive one load of salt per hundred loads and one *hāga* of grain per two hundred loads. The grants in this case were made by a vassal of the western Cālukya king who is variously described as the great minister Madimayya, the *savasi* or keeper of women's quarters, the Kannada minister for peace and war, the general of the army, and the *maneverggaḍe* (chief *perggaḍe*) Bhogayya who was ruling over Banavasi-12000. The grants were made in the presence of *vaḍḍa rāvula* Daṇḍanāyaka and others, which symbolized the formal approval of the king. In yet another Sorab record, dated 1065, the Malaya king Āditya Camūpati, who was dwelling at the lotus feet of his Cālukya overlord, is said to have issued a *śāsana* whereby he commanded the fifty oil milling families of a certain town to provide oil to the local Śivaite temple 'according to their families'.[26] The expression 'according to their families' seems to refer to the number of oil-mills worked by a family or the amount of oil each family could extract every day.

The inscriptions of the tenth-thirteenth centuries show that during this period artisans were forming corporate associations which evidently facilitated greater marketable production of craft goods. In respect of the oil-miller, we come across such expressions as the 'thousand oilmen of such and such towns', 'fifty families of oil-millers', and '*tilligaseṇige*' besides the plural *telliges*. The corporate associations of craftsmen operated from important towns. In towns there was obviously greater possibility of fair earnings, as indeed is seen from regular collection of taxes from groups of oilmen, metal workers, weavers, carpenters, goldsmiths, florists, perfumers and numerous others. But in towns there was also greater possibility of arbitrary exactions and even outright enslavement by temple institutions.

The contributions which were made in both cash and kind evidently ate up much of the surplus which craftsmen produced for the market. Even service castes like barbers and washermen were not spared. A Shikarpur inscription of 1063 ordered the washerman families of a town to pay at the rate of one *hāga* per family to provide for lamp-oil and sandal in the local temple.[27] A Nilgunda inscription of 1079 states that the oilmen (*telligas*), gardeners (*toṭigas*) and sack-makers (*koṇekāras*) of a town were to pay at the stipulated rate of one *pāga* per *ūḷī* and per ladder and one *sotige* of oil per oil-mill to provide for the ritual service of a Śivaite deity.[28] Inscriptional evidence is forthcoming to show that on occasions the artisans applied for remission and a revision of the state's revenue demands. An early fifteenth century inscription from the Kolar district registers remission of taxes in favour of *holeya* weavers, blacksmiths, carpenters and goldsmiths.[29]

Paradoxically, the temple was both a promoter of craft production and an exploiter of craftsmen. The large number of goods requisitioned by the temple could not but stimulate the process of marketization. Articles were either directly purchased by the temple or provided for by devout men as gifts. In certain cases pious men deposited sums of money with the temple the interest on which was utilized for necessary purchases. A Tanjore temple inscription refers to certain deposits of money by pious individuals for the purchase of cardamom seeds to be used to scent the bathing water of the gods.[30]

Within the existing framework of production relations, however, the temple could be least expected to provide any relief to artisanal workers. Instead, it would be more interested in receiving the necessary supplies without having to pay anything on that account. Conditions which could bring about the immunity of craftsmen from arbitrary subjection to private authorities and free supplies of craft-goods could therefore be developed only on the basis of a counter-culture which would challenge the very roots of a temple-based power network.

The Quest for Legitimation

The artisans' quest for social security took on different forms in different regions of south India, even as the basic purpose in every case was to protect the new occupational interests which a particular trade or craft had acquired as a result of revived commodity production. It has been shown that in the Tamil region the process was represented by a polarization of the old Śūdra order into *vaḷangai* cultivating castes and the *idangai* artisan and trading castes. In north-western Karnataka resistence of artisans and traders took the form of a comprehensive religious movement which is known as the Vīraśaiva[31] or Lingayat movement.

Various theories have been developed to explain the origin of the left-hand *idangai* and the right hand *vaḷangai* divisions. But it has not so far been explained why the two mutually hostile but individually co-operative groups should have appeared during the eleventh century, and why artisanal and trading castes should have been grouped together. In our opinion, the development was related to change in the organization of production, the new economic interests which it was projecting from around the close of the tenth century and the different stress-points which surfaced as a result at the lower rungs of the social hierarchy.

It has been observed in the foregoing pages that one of the chief interests of medieval legal writers was to downgrade and socially illegitimize different categories of artisans and service castes, often to the position of untouchables. In respect of the agricultural castes which provided indispensable support to the medieval agrarian order the attitude of Brahmana lawgivers was markedly different. The denunciation of peasant-cultivators or other groups associated with the various agricultural processes to the position of untouchables would be extremely difficult to come by in the brahmanical sources whether it be *smṛti* literature or the pre-eminently religious Puranic texts. On the contrary some agricultural castes are declared to be the result of *anuloma* union, which, in the reckoning of medieval legal writers, meant a status superior to even that of the Śūdra. Even as Śūdras, the cultivating castes would be superior to the artisans whom most of the medieval lawgivers were wont to regard as inferior to Śūdras. Bhāruci in his commentary on the *Manusmṛti* states that the artisans were more degraded than the Śūdras and that their profession was the profession of untouchables.[32] Parāśara, who wrote about the same time as Bhāruci, makes the distinction between cultivating castes and artisans clearer by stating that the food of share-croppers can be eaten by Brahmanas also.[33]

Immunity from social stigma was a significant concession scored by the peasant-cultivators in a social order in which purity of ritual status was the main basis of social recognition and of enjoyment of privileges within the limits of caste hierarchy. In terms of the subjection and exploitation of agricultural and artisanal groups by Brahmana freeholders and Sāmantas there was, however, not much real difference.

During the early medieval centuries, when there seemed little scope for either large-scale commerce or marketable production of craft goods, both the Vaiśya traders and artisanal Śūdras could not but maintain a low social profile. From the beginning of the eleventh century, however, the economic situation began to look up gradually for both trading and artisan castes with the revival of large-scale commercial and artisanal activities. The ascendant pre-eminence of the *vaṇig-seṭṭi* class in the social and economic spheres of life has already been discussed in the previous chapter. Here we would be concerned with some shreds of clinching evidence to illustrate a concerted effort by different artisan castes to group themselves into a large supracaste organization in order to protect their economic interests and enhance their sagging social estimation. Ironical as it may appear, artisan castes claimed higher status on the ground of their association with the Brahmanas who had been quite persistent in denouncing the artisans as despised *pratiloma* and untouchable.

One of the important origin myths of the *idangai* artisan castes, which finds adequate publicity in an early thirteenth century Cola inscription, seems to emphasize this aspect fairly clearly. The record, which comes from the Lalgudi taluka of Tiruchirapalli district, states that the artisans who form the *idangai* division were created from the fire-pit (*agni-kuṇḍa*) of a sacrifice to provide protection to Brahmanas whose sacrifices were constantly disturbed by demons. The artisans are here associated with Kāśyapa, the priest of the divine architect Viśvakarman (lit. maker of the world). The artisans are then stated to have been seated at the back of the chariot in which king Arindama brought the Brahmanas to a newly founded village and where all of them, Brahmanas and artisans, were settled. During the journey the artisans are stated to have taken care of the slippers and umbrellas of their Brahmana mentors.[34] The remaining portion of the inscription is significant inasmuch as it highlights a deepening sense of insecurity on the part of the artisanal order. 'We the 98 subcastes of *idangai* class,' the charter spells out, 'entered a compact in the fortieth year of the king Kulottunga that we shall behave like the sons of the same parents and that whatever good or evil may befall anyone of us shall be shared by all. If anything derogatory happens to the *idangai* class, we shall jointly assert our rights until we establish them.' Comparing the *vaḷangai* charters in which such descriptions do not occur, with *idangai* ones, it would be evident that the quest for social status and occupational security was much greater among the *idangai* castes because of constant threats of forced exactions and enslavement by Brahmanas and temples. The figure 98, which is employed by both the divisions to publicize their numerical strength is, however, conventional.

The terms *idangai* and *vaḷangai* occur in a large number of inscriptions but the process of agglomeration was far from complete. The ranks of *idangai* particularly were being continually reinforced by admitting new local groups. An early thirteenth century inscription from the Vriddhachalam taluka of South Arcot district refers to the *idangai-nāḍus* of eleven different localities meeting in the village of Tiruvalanjuram to grant admission to the *malaiyamākkal* and *nattamākkal* of the said eleven localities, who were henceforth to be treated as the 'eyes and ears of the *idangai* people'.[35]

Notwithstanding such examples of assimilation there still remained a large number of local artisanal groups which could not be incorporated into the *idangai* division. Particularly interesting in this connection is an inscription from the Yelandur taluka of Mysore district which mentions several artisanal castes together with the *idangai* and *vaḷangai* divisions,[36] metal-workers (*taṭṭār*), the weavers (*tāri*) and the washermen (*vannār*) who were freed together with the *vaḷangai* and *idangai* from the payment of taxes (*antarāya*) to the government following the conversion of the village into a *brahmadeya* freeholding. Apparently the *taṭṭār* metal-smiths, the *tāri* weavers and the *vannār* washermen of this remote south Karnataka village had not been included in either of the two divisions which too are mentioned as inhabiting the same village.

The mobilization of artisan castes into a supra-caste organization could not thus cover all craft groups. Those who were not assimilated into the *idangai* order had evidently to find ways to protect their occupational interests and obtain a preferred status in society on a purely local basis. In the Rājāśraya Caturvedīmangalam, mentioned in a Cola inscription of 1118, several groups of artisans who resided in the village submitted a petition to the Brahmana assembly for a consideration of their claim to be classified as Rathakāra.[37] Here the modus of seeking higher status was to conglomerate into a supra-caste division which transcended the inferior statuses of individual castes. This is evident from the fact that the status of Rathakāra was claimed by as many as five different groups, goldsmiths, silversmiths, carpenters, stone-cutters and masons. On receiving the petition the Brahmana residents of the village are stated to have met in full strength and, after going through the opinions expressed by Baudhāyana, Gautama, Kauṭilya and Yājñavalkya, admitted the claim of the petitioners to be described as Rathakāra. The Brahmanas further resolved that the Rathakāra, who, according to the lawgivers, was the offspring of a Māhiṣya father and Karaṇa mother, was entitled by ancient rules to the sacred thread investiture and other ritual rights.[38]

The search for a higher status by the craftsmen of certain localities is further illustrated by an inscription of 1264. The record states that the artisans of the Janaratha Caturvedīmangalam in the Nannilur taluka of Tanjavur district claimed to be the descendants of the ancient Rathakāra caste.[39] The acquisition of a proto-Brahmana status was sought to be reciprocated by raising special contributions for constructing a temple *mandapam* in the concerned village. The fund was to be collected by imposing a special levy called the *inavāri* on the artisans of several named localities. The collection was to be done by the priests of the concerned temple. The signatories to the document included, among others, carpenters and goldsmiths. It is pertinent to mention here that in different localities the stone-mason, carpenter and goldsmith were essential members of the temple's retinue and for that reason lived in familiar access to Brahmana godmen, just as they did in *brahmadeya* and *agrahāra* freeholdings. The prolonged association with Brahmanas and temples eked out for these endemic groups a position of eminence within the existing

Śūdra order. There are subcastes belonging to different Kammalan or Panchala castes which claim for themselves on the ground of their past association with temples, Brahmanas and kings, a superior ritual position and proscription on intermarriage or dining with other subcastes of their parent caste.

In certain localities the problem of redeeming a low social status was solved by means of special mandatory concessions conferred by kings, probably in recognition of special tasks performed by the members of particular artisan castes. The oil-mongers (*telikki*) of Bezwada, for example, describe themselves in several inscriptions as the hereditary servants of eastern Cālukya kings.[40] An inscription of 1084 mentions the Teliga oil-men[41] who obtained from Kulottunga I the right to send bridal couples on horseback to see the king and receive from his hands offerings of betel-leaves. The foregoing discussion would show that in different localities higher status was sought by developing special relationships with the different power groups, the temple, king or Brahmanas.

In Karnataka, the artisans' quest for occupational security and status assumed the form of a powerful religious upsurge known as the Vīraśaiva movement, the chief supporters of which were traders, artisans and peasants led by a few disaffected *smārta* Brahmanas of Karnataka.[42] The sect, which originated in the north-western region of Karnataka about the twelfth century was the product of a social situation in which the revival of commodity production had considerably added to the importance of trading and artisan castes, but whose profits and interests were constantly subjected to infringement by Brahmanas and temples. It is not without some significance that in the Vīraśaiva sect there is no place for traditional Brahmana priesthood or temple-centric cults of brahmanical deities. The anti-brahmanical stance of the sect is also evident from its opposition to the conventional ordering of the social structure on the basis of caste endogamy. The early Vīraśaivas were in fact an undifferentiated fraternal community although later on it became vulnerable to brahmanical norms of social differentiation.

The prominence attached by the sect to certain categories of craftsmen is characteristic of the economic interests which the Vīraśaiva movement represented. The various propaganda stories narrated in early Lingayat hagiologies refer to farmers,[43] weavers and tanners as important characters. Similarly, the list of *vacana* writers includes farmers, goldsmiths, weavers, tailors, tanners, carpenters and minor craftsmen like the palm-sappers, basket makers and rope-workers. Jedara Dāsimayya, who lived a hundred years before Basava and even served as the preceptor of a Cālukya king, was a weaver by profession. Śankara Dāsimayya, whose life was celebrated in the *Śankara Dāsimayya Carita* was a tailor by caste. Siddharāma himself was born in a peasant family.[44]

The relevance of the Vīraśaiva faith to the weaving castes of Karnataka, particularly those of the cotton-producing districts of Belgaum and Bijapur, is evident from the early literature of the sect.[45] In Bijapur the weavers are all Lingayats, while in Belgaum 18 per cent of the total population engaged in crafts chiefly comprise Lingayat weavers. In Dharwar weavers and oil-men constitute 11 per cent of the Lingayat population. The position is not different in other districts, where the weavers and oil-men form the majority of Lingayat craftsmen.

The importance of weaving in Karnataka is attested by foreign chronicles and indigenous records. During the tenth-thirteenth centuries, textile industries developed as a major economic activity in the northern districts of Karnataka, where cotton was produced, as now, on a commercial scale.[46] Significantly, the largest number of weavers' guilds find mention in the inscriptions of Dharwar and Belgaum districts.[47]

The large number of weavers, tailors and dyers, who now occupy the rank of non-*pañcamaśāli* Lingayats, evidently joined the movement in anticipation of greater protection to their craft against oppressive taxation and enslavement by priestly intermediaries and the state. Inscriptions show that taxes were imposed, in both cash and kind, on looms, tailoring houses and dye-mills.[48] The discontent against heavy duties can be seen from the petitions and representations filed by weavers' guilds for remission or revision of existing rates.[49] Equally arbitrary was the transfer of looms and tailoring shops[50] to religious institutions, reducing craftsmen to the position of servile labour without any freedom or mobility of trade. The transfer of cotton land, which formed part of a donated village, to the temple further discouraged the commercial production of cotton since all production on temple lands was directed not towards the market but towards meeting the bare requirements of the temple.

Another important craft which was affected by the growth of Brahmana landlordism was oil-pressing. Though oil-pressing was common in Karnataka, its importance increased during the tenth-thirteenth centuries. Inscriptions of this period refer to the extraction of oil from sesame, castor-seed and coconut.[51] The dumps of linseed fibre, which the Arabs carried to the entrepot of Kish[52] on their way home, may have been a product of the western coast of India. The industry also developed about this time professional subcastes to meet the needs of specialized production of the commodity. For instance, the inscriptions mention different groups of oil-millers who employed different devices for extracting oil.[53] Moreover, the affluence of individual oilmen (*telliga*), who undertook the construction of temples and other public works, would give an indication of the profits which the craft now offered to its members.[54]

The development of the industry, however, suffered on account of the creation of intermediary rights in land and primary crafts, which led to large-scale arbitrary transfer of oil-mills to religious institutions[55] from the eleventh century. Earlier records merely specified the quantity of oil which a mill was required to supply to the temple, but there are no cases of the transfer of entire oil-mills. The mills, which were spared subjection, none the less continued to pay heavy duties to both temple and state. The oil-pressers, whose strength varies between 12 and 20 per cent of the Lingayat population in Dharwar, Bijapur and Belgaum districts, seem to have joined the movement in the hope of providing greater security to the craft and its members. The rejection of temple services by the Vīraśaivas eliminated all scope for the enslavement of craftsmen by religious intermediaries and at the same time lessened the burden of taxation inasmuch as the industry now paid taxes only to the state.

Masons as a Favoured Group

Masonry workers, who appear to have served the special interests of the Brahmana landholding class in the rural society of medieval south India, were evidently spared the ignominy suffered by most other artisans. In the inscriptions of the medieval period masons and stone-cutters are invariably described as *rūpa*,[56] *ruvāri*,[57] *sūtradhārī*[58] and *śilpaka*.[59] *Rūpa* or *ruvāri* is an abbreviated form of *rūpakāra* or *rūpakartṛ*, meaning a maker of forms, a sculptor.[60] *Sūtradhāra* or *sūtradhārī*[61] means the holder of a rule or a thread which implies an architect. The term *śilpaka*[62] is evidently a mistake for *śilpī*, *śilpin*, or *śilpījana* meaning a craftsman.

The use of the Sanskritic and honorific name-endings like *ācāri* and *bhaṭṭa* by these masonry workers probably indicates their increasing social standing. The inscriptions which allude to such name-suffixes of artisans include a grant of 733 issued by Vikramāditya II of Badami. In it the mason Śrīguṇḍa is called Śrīguṇḍācāri. *Ācāri* also figures as a suffix in Ruvāri Gangācāri, mentioned in the Sravana Belgola charter of Mallisena.[63] A grant of Vajrahasta III mentions Nanikañceyemācārin who engraved the inscription of Vajrahasta.[64] A sculptor (*śilpaka*) of Nirgguṇḍa is characterized in a Chamrajanagar record of 1000 as Bhaṭṭācāri.[65] Durggācāri, the engraver of a stone record is mentioned in a charter of Nolamba Pallava king Ayyapadeva.[66] A grant of Pulakesī II speaks of the mason Mahendra Pallavācāri who incised the stone-slab and received 12 *mattars* of land.[67] Inscriptions of a much later date also show that *ācāri* was used as a name by masons. A grant of 1415 mentions stone cutter Yisarācāri who was the son of Maniyācāri.[68] Another record of 1423 refers to Yisarācāri son of Keśavācāri and Māṇiācāri son of Rāmācāri.[69] Some goldsmiths also used *ācāri* as their name-ending. A Gundlupet record of 1030 speaks of the goldsmith Māṇikācāri, son of Rājācāri.[70]

Ācārī was derived from *ācārya*, but the two were not used in the same sense. *Ācārya* does not figure in our records in the sense of a surname; instead, it always occurs as the honorific title of Brahmanas and Jains, and as the name ending of certain Jain monks. On the other hand, *ācāri* figures as the family name of masons in numerous inscriptions,[71] which shows that the honorific title of *ācārya* was not the same thing as the surname *ācāri* used by certain smith castes of south India. *Ācāri* or *ācārin* implies 'one following the established practice'. Masons and goldworkers who observed the rules of their trade could very well describe themselves as *ācāri*, the term being ultimately adopted as a caste name.

The use of the brahmanical *gotra* of Śāṇḍilya by sculptors[72] and masons[73] further emphasizes the degree of social recognition which these groups of workers had secured as a result of their association with temples and temple-centric priesthoods. Śāṇḍilyas or Śāṇḍilas were the descendants of Saṇḍa, who is recognized in the *Taittirīya* and *Vājasaneyī Saṁhitās* as the priest of *asuras* or demons.[74] Their relatively low status is confirmed by their being ranked with the Kāśyapas, who, according to the chapter on *pravara* in the *Baudhāyana Śrauta Sūtra*, were men of questionable origin.[75] Śilpa Kāśyapa is mentioned in the *Bṛhad-āraṇyaka Upaniṣad* as the name of an *ācārya*,[76] presumably of the community of musicians and dancers. The term *śilpa* is explained in the *Kauṣītaki Brāhmaṇa* as meaning fine arts.[77]

The emergence of masonry workers as a status group can also be judged from references to guilds of masons and architects. One such guild, headed by the chief architect Śrīguṇḍācāri, functioned at Kanchipuram. An inscription of 733 issued by the Cālukya conqueror of the Pallava capital mentions that the chief architect Śrīguṇḍācāri, who, along with his fellow-workers, had been excommunicated, were ceremoniously brought to the Cālukya capital of Badami where the chief architect was decorated with the title of *tribhuvanācārya* and rewarded with a fillet of honour. This was followed by the declaration of the Cālukya king that 'there was no caste excommunication (*balligavarte*) of the skilful people (*binmāṇigala*). The fellow workers of the mason, who had been excommunicated for allegedly mixing with the guilty men (*doṣiga*), were also restored to their old position. The cause of excommunication, the sentence of which appears to have been pronounced by the Pallava king, was evidently the offence committed by Śrīguṇḍa and his men in 'mixing with the guilty people'. However, it is not clear who these guilty people were. In all likelihood, the masons were sympathizing with the detractors of the Pallava ruler and ultimately sided with the victorious Cālukya king who invaded and captured Kanchipuram. Some wooing on the part of the Cālukya conqueror, who was wonderstruck at the grandeur of Pallava architecture and was determined to have similar imposing structures at his own capital, is also not ruled out. It is also well known that it was Śrīguṇḍācāri who along with his fellow workers built the majestic Pāpanātha, Virūpākṣa and Mahākuṭeśvara temples at the Cālukya capital which survive today as the earliest specimens of the *besara* or Deccan style of temple architecture.

The importance of masonry-workers is further attested by the fact that the mason and sculptor, who were permanent members of the temple staff, were treated at par with such prestigious functionaries as priests, account officers and theology teachers. Parity was also maintained between the two groups in respect of salary and emoluments. A Kolar record of 1071 specifies that out of the total produce of the temple land 30 *kalams* of paddy was granted as annual subsidy to the mason. This was the same quantity as allotted to the priest, accounts officer and lecturer; but it was double the quantity apportioned for the washerman, potter and parasol bearer of the temple. The higher salary of temple masons is attested in other epigraphic records as well.[78]

The foregoing would suggest that during the early medieval period masons and architects emerged as a status-group while all other groups of craftsmen including smiths, were being denounced as bad Śūdras and even untouchables. The social ascendancy of masons becomes meaningful in view of the new forms of surplus-sharing developed by Brahmanas. The chief area of stone work during the early medieval and medieval periods were the construction of temples and monasteries. In the construction and maintenance of temples where priests collected food and other surpluses from the surrounding countryside, the mason played a key role. This rendered his services indispensable for the new owning class of the temple-based Brahmanas. It would thus appear that masons were inseparably associated with the whole process of accumulating agricultural goods in the rapidly multiplying temple-stores and granaries. The phenomenal rise in the number of temples, brahmanical and Jain, can be seen from the increasing number of land grants to priests between the fifth and the twelfth century. The compilation of architectural literature and the development of the different regional styles of temple architecture during this period also become significant in the above context.

The Rathakāra as a Status Group

The social relevance of a craft in determining the status of the members associated with that craft can also be discussed with reference to the Rathakāra, or chariot maker, apparently a carpenter who was often admitted to the participation of specific Vedic rites. The *Taittirīya Brāhmaṇa* gives certain *mantras* to be recited by the Rathakāra at the *agnyādhāna* sacrifice.[79]

In the *Sūtra* period also Rathakāras maintained their approximation with twice-born castes. They were still entitled to perform the *agnyādhāna* sacrifice.[80] Baudhāyana entitled them to receive the sacrament of initiation or *upanayana*.[81] But it is also in the *Sūtra* period that the decline of the Rathakāras began. For example, Baudhayana himself states that the Rathakāra was a mixed caste descended from a Vaiśya father and a Śūdra mother.[82] In the *Jātaka* literature they are assigned a position lower than that of the Śūdras. Kauṭilya also states that the Rathakāra may become a Śūdra or he may embrace any of the lower castes except the Cāṇḍāla.[83]

Despite the denunciation of the Rathakāra by Brahmana lawgivers, the caste did not altogether lose its earlier ritual authority which entitled them to rank with the Brahmanas. It may also be suggested that the rulings of Brahmana lawgivers were not universally respected. A Śālaṇkāyana inscription registers the grant of a village as *rathakāra agrahāra* to the *Caturvidyā* community of the Rathakāra caste.[84] The grantees are stated to have been capable of cursing and conferring boons. It is further stated that the Brahmanas were engaged in meditation and the study of Vedas prescribed for various *gotras* and *caraṇas* of the Rathakāra caste.[85] Evidently, as late as the fourth century the Rathakāras were considered as respectable as Brahmanas and accordingly were granted villages as freeholds.

In the medieval period also, the Rathakāra was a symbol of high status among the artisan castes. We have cited two examples in which the different artisan castes such as the goldsmith, blacksmith, carpenter, mason and weaver claimed to be regarded as Rathakāra with the right to perform sacraments like the *upanayana*. According to one inscription the claim was admitted by the Brahmana residents of a *caturvedīmangalam*.[86] It appears that during the middle ages when there was a general sinking of all artisanal and service castes, certain artisan groups held fast to the status of the ancient Rathakāra caste. The two examples which we have already discussed illustrate this. The description of the Rathakāra as an *anuloma* mixed caste resulting from the union of a Māhiṣya father and Karaṇa mother further confirms that the caste, however degraded it may be from its ancient position, was still much higher than most artisan castes which were being reduced to the position of untouchables far lower than the position of Śūdras.

To this day there exists in the districts of Krishna, Guntur, West Godavari and East Godavari a class of Viśva Brahmanas who call themselves *rathakāras*[87]; the orthodox among them study *Vedas*, particularly the Black *Yajurveda* and regard themselves as superior even to Brahmanas.[88] They follow the rules of the *Āpastamba Gṛhya Sūtra* in their rituals which are conducted by their own priests. The Rathakāras or Viśva Brahmanas of today include five groups of artisans, the *kaṁsāli, kammāra, kancāra, kase* and *vadrangi* who follow respectively the professions of the goldsmith, silversmith, stone cutter or mason, blacksmith and carpenter. During the closing decades of the last century they fought in the civil courts and quoted the authority of *śruti* literature in support of their claim to brahmanhood.

NOTES

1. *Bhāruci's Commentary on the Manusmṛti*, 10.99, ed. J.D.M. Derrett, Steiner Verlag, Wiesbaden, 1975.
2. See S.K. Maity, *Economic Life in Northern India in the Gupta Period* (revd. edn.), Delhi, 1970, Appendix 1.
3. *Ādipurāṇa*, ed. Pannalal Jain, Ch. 16, vv. 185-6; also p. 342, fn. 9.
4. Infra.
5. Aparārka, 1196 cited in Kane, *Dharamśāstra ka Itihas*, vol. 1, p. 168.
6. *Ādipurāṇa*, Ch. 16, v. 186.
7. *Skanda Purāṇa*, ed. Pausikar, Poona, 1893, Ch. 242, vv. 23-24, 42.
8. *Br. Ka. Bha*., cited in R.S. Sharma, *Sūdras in Ancient India*, p. 229.
9. *SII*, 12, no. 5, p. 5.
10. *SII*, 9, pt. 1, no. 132, p. 114.
11. *Yaśastilakacampū*, Bk. 3, v. 177.
12. Ibid.
13. *Adipurāṇa*, ed. Pannalal Jain, Ch. 16, vv. 185-6.
14. Ibid., p. 285.
15. Ibid.
16. *EI*, 3, no. 40, p. 292ff.
17. *EC*, 11, Cl. 21.
18. *SII*, 9, pt. 1, no. 65.
19. *EC*, 7, Sk. 20 A.
20. V.R.R. Dikshitar, *Selected Malayalam Inscriptions*, University of Madras, G.I. Press, 1952, pp. 11-12.
21. Ibid., pp. 13-14.
22. *Annual Report on Epigraphy*, no. 247 of 1910.
23. K.A.N. Sastri, *The Cholas*, p. 556.
24. *EC*, 8, Sorab 140.
25. *EC*, 8, Sorab 170.
26. *EC*, 8, Sorab 249.
27. *SII*, 3, pt. 1, no. 141.
28. *SII*, 9, pt. I, no. 141.
29. *EC*, 10, Bp. 72, also see *ARSIE*, 1897, no. 118.
30. *SII*, 2, 24.
31. For a detailed discussion see R.N. Nandi, 'Origin of the Vīraśaiva Movement', *The Indian Historical Review*, vol. 2, no. 1.
32. *Bhāruci's Commentary on the Manusmṛti*, op. cit., 10.99.
33. *Parāsara Smṛti* with Monohar Vyākhyā, 21.11.
34. *Annual Report on Epigraphy*, 1913, para 39, Summarized by K.A.N. Sastri, *The Cholas*, pp. 551-2.
35. Cited in Burton Stein, *Peasant, State and Society in Medieval South India, c. 800-1300*, Delhi, Oxford University Press, 1980, p. 183.
36. *EC*, 4, Yl. 98.
37. The term *rathakāra* denoted an important status-group of Vedic society and

consisted of chariot makers. The vedic *rathakāra* was as good as a twice-born with right to perform important vedic sacrifices. The position of the *rathakāra*, however, declined later.

38. *Annual Report on Epigraphy*, 1909, para 45.
39. See Burton Stein, op. cit., p. 197.
40. Ibid.
41. *South Indian Temple Inscriptions*, vol. 3, pt. 2, p. 68 (1954).
42. See R.N. Nandi, 'Origin of the Vīraśaiva Movement', op. cit.
43. Compare the elaborate descriptions of peasant rites and agricultural practices in the *Basavapurāṇa*, *JBBRAS* (1868), pp. 128-30.
44. *Channabasavapurāṇa*, Ch. LIX, *JBBRAS* (1863), p. 210.
45. Compare the importance of weavers in Lingayat hagiologies and the lists of *vacana* writers.
46. In 1908 *The Imperial Gazetteer of India*, vii, viii and xi, reported that in the district of Bijapur cotton was the first major crop grown over 860 square miles; in Dharwar and Belgaum it was the second crop, on the basis of acreage.
47. *EI*, 18, no. 22 E, 196; *BKI*, i(i), no. 97; *EI*, 13, no. 14.
48. For taxes imposed on loom workers, see *EC*, 5, Hn. 119, AD 1173; For taxes realized from dye makers, see *EC*, 9, Cp. 66; *EC*, 5, Hn. 119; for other references, see *EI*, 19, no. 4; *ARSIE*, no. 70 of 1946; *EC*, 7, Sk. 145.
49. *EC*, 10, Bp. 72, AD 1430, refers to remission granted in favour of holeyas, carpenters, blacksmiths and goldsmiths; also see *ARSIE*, no. 118 of 1897.
50. *EC*, 11, Cl. 21, AD 1087, p. 99, mentions transfer of a house for weaving along with two oil-mills.
51. *EC*, *MAR* (1931), no. 20 (for sesame); *EC*, 11, Dg. 85 (castor seeds); *EC*, 5, Bl. 155 (coconuts). *The Imperial Gazetteer of India*, vii, reported in 1908 that sesame, rape-seeds, linseeds and castor were exported in large quantities from the district of Bijapur, where 18 per cent of the Lingayats are oil-millers.
52. *The Itinerary of Benjamin of Tudela*, cited in K.A.N. Sastri, *Foreign Notices of South India*, Madras, 1939.
53. *EC*, 5, Hn. 54, refers to hand oil-mill or *Kaigana*; *EC*, 5, Bl. 114, refers to a tread oil-mill; *EC*, 3, My. 9, refers to a bullock oil-mill or *eṭṭugana*.
54. *EC*, 5, Ak. 110, AD 1142.
55. *EC*, 7, Sk. 20; *EC*, 11, Dg. 20; *KI*, 2, nos. 10, 11, 12, 14, 16; *KI*, 4, nos. 13, 34, 66. Some of the records mention the transfer of as many as six oil-mills at a time. The records cited here were issued between 1000 and 1200.
56. *EI*, 3, no. 2, pp. 6-7, AD 733.
57. *EI*, 3, no. 26, p. 184, AD 1128.
58. *IA*, 10, pp. 164-5, AD 733.
59. *EC*, 4, cf. inscriptions of Chamrajanagar taluka.
60. M. Monier-Williams, *Sanskrit-English Dictionary*, p. 886.
61. M. Monier-Williams, op. cit., p. 226.
62. Ibid., p. 1074.

63. The term *ācāri* and *paṭṭhar* (*bhaṭṭa*) are used as titles by the Kammalans (smith castes) of Tamil Nadu, although these constitute important name-endings of the Brahmanas of south India. Thurston, *Castes and Tribes of Southern India*, vol. 3, p. 118.
64. *EI*, 3, no. 26, l. 223.
65. *EI*, 3, no. 31, ll. 28-9.
66. *EC*, 4, see Chamarajanagar grants.
67. *SII*, 9, pt. 1, no. 21, p. 10.
68. Ibid., no. 46, p. 26.
69. *KI*, 1, no. 40, p. 92.
70. Ibid., no. 46, p. 106.
71. *EC*, 4, Gu. 20.
72. *EI*, 3, no. 2, pp. 6-7.
73. *IA*, 10, p. 165.
74. *Tai. Saṁ.*, 6, 4.10.1; *Vāj. Saṁ.*, 7. 12. 7. 13 cited in Suryakanta, *Vaidik Koś*, (Hindi), pp. 4-5.
75. Cited in Brough, *The Early Brahmanical System of Gotra and Pravara*, p. 204.
76. Suryakanta, op. cit., p. 517.
77. *Kau. Br.*, 29. 5, cited in Suryakanta, op. cit.
78, *EI*, 4, no. 50, p. 355ff.
79. *SBE*, vol. 14, p. 38-9.
80. *Kātyayāna Śrauta Sūtra*, 1.1.9.
81. *Baudhāyana Gṛhya Sūtra*, 2. 5. 12. 9.
82. Ibid, 1. 9. 17. 6.
83. *Arthaśāstra*, 3. 7.
84. *EI*, 31, no. 1, ll. 7-8, *agrahāra rathakāra vidhānena sampāditaḥ*.
85. Ibid., ll. 10-12, *sāpānuggaha samattassa nānā gotta caraṇa topas sajihāya niratassa*.
86. *Annual Report on Epigraphy*, 1909, para 45.
87. *EI*, 31, no. 1, p. 4.
88. Ibid.

12

Women in the Feudal Milieu

Sociological studies of the ethnic survivals would suggest that family in the preliterate society of south India was both matrilocal and matrilineal. The disintegration of the matrilocal family appears to have been caused by the arrival of Brahmana inspired Sanskrit-based culture in the peninsular region about the third-fourth centuries BC. Under the surging influence of a supposedly superior status value of brahmanical culture, the literate classes submitted to the brahmanical norms of social behaviour and adopted the Brahmana patrilocal family as their model. The Sangam literature, which witnessed this process of cultural interaction, however, points towards certain practices which would emphasize the survival of matriarchal traditions in a predominantly patriarchal order. The custom of bride-price, mentioned in several Sangam texts is, for example, alien to brahmanical ideas regarding marriage. The *Tolkāppiyam* evidence relating to the substitution of earlier *kalavu* marriages by brahmanical ritualistic marriages seems to be equally meaningful in this context. The *Padirruppattu* references to the practice of matrilineal inheritance are also relevant.

Mention may be made here of the custom of initiating daughters as *basavis* and *devadāsīs*, noticed among certain groups of the lower order. The *basavi* and *devadāsī* practices are in fact attempts to revert to the *marumakkatthayam* law either temporarily or on a permanent basis. The Kaikkolam weavers, for example, are a caste from which a large number of *devadāsīs* were recruited during the medieval period. Even at the present day the daughter of a sonless Kaikkolan father is dedicated as a *dāsī* which signifies her marriage to a local brahmanical deity. The dedication entitles her to work at the loom just as a male member is permitted to work at the family loom. At the time of her dedication to the temple, which also entitles her to receive favours from Brahmana suitors, it is the maternal uncle or his representative who ties a gold band on the forehead of the girl. As for the actual nuptial, a rich Brahmana or, in his absence, a poorer Brahmana, is invited to the family.[1] Both the temporary reversion to the *marumakkatthayam* law and the importance attached to the maternal uncle are characteristic survivals of a matrilineal ordering of old Dravidian families. Among the Malabar Nayars the family continues to be nucleated round the mother's house and maternal ancestors.

However, the interaction between the Dravidian matrilineal and the brahmanical patrilineal systems was not one-sided. While it was normal practice for all literate classes under brahmanical influence to adopt the patrilocal model, the brahmanical families themselves adopted certain matrilineal traditions of the local population and tried to sanskritize and legitimize these practices.

The Sātavāhana family, which was at once patrilocal and patrilineal, publicized in its official records its maternal descent. The unbrahmanical origin of the family also seems to be confirmed by the ceremonial brahmanization of a Sātavāhana king. Metronymics were also used by the Ikṣvāku rulers of eastern Deccan who were among the earliest dynasties of the peninsular region and proclaimed in their records that they were Kṣatriyas descended from the prestigious solar race,[2] which once again smacks of a suspect origin.

Epigraphic records refer to important feudal houses families of high officers, and even lay Brahmana families as giving publicity to their mother's ancestry in obvious preference to paternal descent. For example, an inscription engraved on a pillar of the gateway at Bharhut refers to a person as Vātsīputra Dhanabhūti who was the son of Gosiputa Aggaraju and the grandson of Gārgīputra Viśvadeva as having constructed the said gateway.[3] On the evidence of brahmanical *gotra* names the persons would appear to be high Brahmanas for whom a description of the paternal ancestry would have been more appropriate.

Another interesting example of a Brahmana family publicizing its maternal descent in preference to paternal ancestry refers to Brahmana Aśvībhūti who was the son of a woman whose *gotra* was Varāha and from whom the Śaka king Usavadāta purchased a field by paying 4000 *kārṣāpaṇas.*[4] Vārāhī is more relevant as a totemic clan-name than as a *gotra.* Other examples of men publicizing their mother's ancestry in preference to their father's pedigree include a Mahārathī who was a Kosikiputra,[5] a Mahābhoja who was a Kautsīputra,[6] a royal physician who was a Vātsīputra and another Mahārathī who was a Gotiputra.[7]

The frequent use of certain recognized Brahmana *gotras* such as Kautsa, Vatsa and Kauśika might give the impression that these families were genuine Brahmana families. However, the practice of publicizing the mother's ancestry as well as the presence of certain tribal clan names unknown to the accepted brahmanical lists of *gotra* and *pravara* seems to suggest that the families were non-brahmanical in origin and that, in the course of their association with Brahmana patriarchal groups, they were lured by the prospects of higher status to employ a Brahmana. For the latter it was customary to lend his clan-name to his valued clients.[8] The tribal matrilocal origin of various literate families becomes clear from a few examples. An Amaravati inscription refers to a Bud-dhist Upāsaka who is described as Goṇḍīputa[9] or the son of a Goṇḍ woman. Guṇḍ or Goṇḍa does not figure in any of the brahmanical *gotra* catalogues; it is fairly likely therefore that the family originated from some matrilocal tribe and in keeping with tribal practice traced its descent from the mother in marked preference to the father who remains obscure in such examples. This is further substantiated by another record which mentions a Buddhist missionary, who was the 'teacher of all the Hīnayāna countries', as Kotiputa and Kasapagota. The patronym Kasapagota shows that the Buddhist monk was the son of a Brahmana father who had married a woman of the tribal Kota family. The Allahabad Pillar Inscription refers to a Kota chieftain who was captured by Samudragupta.[10] That the Kota family was a petty ruling house is evident from its coins found in the vicinity of Delhi and eastern Punjab.[11]

The foregoing would suggest that during the early centuries of the Christian era and also a little before, it was common practice to trace the descent of a family in the maternal line. The examples would further illustrate that the practice, which constitutes a dominant feature of the matrilineal descent system, was fairly popular with all sections of population of both brahmanical and non-brahmanical origin.

The inscriptions of the early medieval period bear out the eagerness of tribal families and petty bureaucrats, who lived in intimate contact with the Sanskrit-educated patriarchal families, to adopt the patrilineal *gotra* and follow brahmanical rituals and observances in an attempt to find a suitable place in the hierarchy of caste society.[12]

The ancestral data of different ruling houses would also confirm the process of cultural interaction between the Dravidian matriarchy and Brahmana patriarchy. For example, the Śālankāyana and Viṣṇukuṇḍin, both of which were important Brahmana dynasties, publicize in their records only their paternal clan-name; but the Sātavāhanas, Kadambas, and Cālukyas, none of whom were Brahmanas, mention their paternal clan-name and maternal ancestry. Some of the later Pallavas also occasionally mentioned their mother's descent even though the paternal clan-name Bhāradvāja is uniformly recorded in all their inscriptions. The Valayur and Velurpalaiyam grants of the family refer to a Pallava ruler as *Cuṭu-Pallava*, meaning thereby that the donor king was born of the marriage of a Cuṭu girl with a Pallava prince.[13] Similarly, the Ganga king Anantavarman, who described himself as a *Coḍaganga*, was publicizing the fact that he was born of the union of Ganga king Devendravarman and Cola princess Rājasundarī.[14]

The vast majority of non-brahmanical families, who could afford to remain indifferent to the patriarchal formulations of Brahmana lawgivers, continued with the matrilineal tradition in a far more systematic manner, some temporarily reverting to matriliny until a male line was obtained and others doing it on a regular basis. Temporary reversion to the rule of descent through the daughter (*marumakkathayam*) is evident from inscriptional references to the dedication of daughters as *basavis*, among whom descent is always in the female line.[15]

In 800, one Aridara Poleyamma of the village Mayile dedicated a virgin to a local temple along with 8 *matters* of land, 1,000 coins and a swing for the use of the deity.[16] In 974, the blacksmith Bidi dedicated two girls to another temple in Hulgund taluk of the Shimoga district.[17] While the donation of property emphasizes the donor's desire to obtain religious esteem and social recognition, the dedication of daughters illustrates the predominant urge to prevent a drain on family-property by way of dowry which the parents would have to give along with the daughter without chance of recompense in the absence of a male heir in the family. The desire to prevent the family property from going to a 'real' outsider often induced a couple to ritually dedicate their daughter to a divine husband, the purpose being to convert her into a *basavi*, who will then be entitled to inherit the family property and stay with her parents even though married to an 'outsider'.

Sometimes the absence of a male heir in the family prompted the couple to convert daughters into *basavis* and procure through her a male heir for the family. Since the daughter is already a *basavi* dedicated to a temple, her marriage to a 'real outsider' would not in any way compel her to leave her parent's house and go over to her husband's family. This seems to be very well illustrated by a Karnataka inscription of the ninth century, in which one Kādacci, who had been dedicated as *basavi* by her father, took a spouse of her own choice and tried to procure a male issue for the family of her father.[18] Unfortunately, she had a daughter named Aycabbe. Ayacabbe, in her turn, renewed the attempt but gave birth to a daughter, Kalingabbe. Kalingabbe's marriage to one Pallaraki again resulted in the birth of a daughter, also named Kalingabbe. The second Kalingabbe ultimately gave birth to a son whose name was Parakayya. The inscription stops with Prakayya, which is meaningful inasmuch as it suggests that Mayadamarasa's lineage was continued by temporarily reverting to the *marumakkathayam* system which resulted in the birth of Parakayya. The inscription does not name any of the husbands or mates of the several women. This is in keeping with the present insignificance of the husband in the *basavi* system. Kalingabbe I's husband is mentioned as a token of gratitude, because it was his daughter who succeeded in procuring a male issue and thereby helped the family to revert back to the system of patrilineal descent (*makkathayam*).

This record, which describes Parakayya as one belonging to lawful descent (*dharma santati*), also anticipates the present position of the children of a *basavi*, who do not suffer social stigma. The practice of dedicating a girl to some deity in the absence of a male heir is prevalent among certain castes in the peninsula. Hutton observes that in Bellary and its neighbourhood, in the absence of a male heir, a daughter is offered to the temple.[19] After her dedication she becomes by established custom the heir of her parents' property and can perform funeral rites as if she were a son. She marries a man of her own choice, of any equal or higher caste, but continues to live in her father's house, and her children take the latter's name and belong to his family, not to their father's.[20] If she has a son, he inherits the property and the question of dedicating a daughter as *basavi* does not arise. But if she has a daughter, again this daughter becomes a *basavi* and renews the attempt to procure a son for the family.[21] The women of the Madiga caste are often made *basavis* or dedicated as *devadāsīs*. In the case of the left hand Kaikkolan caste, which observes temporary reversion to the *marumakkathayam*, the women often belong to the right hand faction.[22]

While the lack of a male heir led some families to temporarily revert to the descent-through-daughter system, other families also practised it. A record of the eighth century refers to a donor, probably a lady, who after saluting her preceptor, her elder brother and blessing her son, announced that 'if the inheritor be without a husband, or having a husband, has all daughters, if they obtain husbands and marry, it is not a violation of this agreement'.[23] Evidently, the inheritor was a lady, a daughter of the benefactress who was probably the wife of one Timmappa Odeya. The statement in the inscription implies that the daughter was to inherit, in preference to the son, the property of her mother. Even if the daughter, after her marriage, gave birth to only daughters, the inherited property was to remain hers. In other words, absence of a male heir would not deprive her of the property. On the other hand, her female offspring were entitled, in their turn, to inherit the property.

The practice of the *aḷiya santāna* law or descent through the sister's son, which is reminiscient of the maternal uncle's influence in a matriarchal family, is also illustrated by the inscriptions of the early medieval period. Earlier, the prevalence of the custom is confirmed by the southern lawgiver Baudhāyana who mentions that a southerner is delighted to take the hand of a maternal cousin.[24] Marriage with the *mātula-kanyā* is also mentioned by the early Tamil classic, *Maṇimekhalai*.[25] Inscriptions show that the *aḷiya santāna* was fairly popular even among the Brahmanas of Karnataka and Andhra. Grants of land or villages originally received from a king, to a sister's son would illustrate that the *aḷiya santāna* law, which was a survival of the Dravidian matriliny, was practised by members of the literate society including some high Brahmanas. Gaṇḍanārāyaṇa, who was a feudatory of the eastern Cālukya king Bādapa and who received a village from the king, regranted it to Candana, the son of his own sister.[26] Two Brahmana brothers, Svāmīyaśas and Viṣṇuyaśas, who received a village from Jayasimhavallabha, also of the eastern Cālukya house, donated a ninth portion to their own sister's son Viṣṇuśarman; Viṣṇuśarman belonged to the Gaviṣṇi *gotra* and was a student of Bahvṛca *śākhā*, and his maternal uncles belonged to the Vatsa *gotra* and were students of the Chāndogya *caraṇa*.[27] The law of *aḷiya santāna* which indicates the survival of matrilineal influence in patrilineal society, became more popular among certain castes in later medieval times.

It falls in line with the above discussion to observe that women, in general, and of princely families in particular, did not remain confined to the domestic forewalls, as were their counterparts in the northern region. They shared in full with their men the regal status and administrative responsibilities. From the palace and the bureaucratic families alike, women were appointed to govern administrative units of varying size; some of the royal families even exercised sovereign authority over the kingdoms of their late husband or minor son.

The practice, which seems to contradict current political theory, may be attributed to the persistent values of Dravidian mother right in a transitional social order undergoing prolonged interaction between two mutually inconsistent descent-systems, one characterized by Brahmana patriliny and the other dominated by matriarchal traditions. The dislike shown by Brahmana theorists in respect of female participation in political affairs can be seen from the *Nītivākyāmṛta* of Somadeva, a tenth-century writer on polity and a distinguished member of the Rāṣṭrakūṭa court at Mānyakheṭa. The text states that the son, brother, step-brother, and uncle of a deceased king can succeed to the throne in that order.[28] If none of them is available, then any male member of the dead king's family or, in his absence, the son of the daughter of the king is entitled to succeed.[29] But if these heirs are wanting then either a suitable person can be elected to the royal office, or a person who usurps the throne can be acknowledged legitimate successor.[30] Notable omissions in this list of successors include all female kin of the deceased king which indicates that they had no right to sit on the royal throne under any circumstances. The list of preferences is clearly dictated by the norms of political behaviour in a regimented patrifocal society, although judging from actual practice, it was not yet the time when laws of Brahmana patriliny would prevail in all spheres of social intercourse.

Notwithstanding the prescriptions of Somadeva, therefore, women of princely families ruled with full authority during the minority of their sons and also when a male successor was not available. Sovereignty of these women rulers is apparent from the fact that they freely disposed of crown property, landed or otherwise. The Sātavāhana queen Nāgaṇikā ruled during the minority of her son Vediśrī.[31] Prabhāvatīgupta of the Vākāṭaka family wielded sovereign power during the minority of her son Divākarasena.[32] The Poona charter issued during her reign compares with another charter issued a hundred years later; the former was issued by the queen without any reference to her minor son, but in the latter inscription the queen-mother made certain grants after specific reference to her son who had assumed power.[33]

In the seventh century, Vijayamahādevī, the widow of Candrāditya of the eastern Cālukya dynasty, succeeded to the throne following the death of her husband.[34] Crowned queen (*mahiṣī*) of the deceased Candrāditya, she is described as

Vijayabhaṭṭārikā, the suffix *bhaṭṭārikā* probably indicating rulership, just as *bhaṭṭāraka* does in the case of sovereign kings. In the fifth year of her reign Vijayamahādevī issued in her own right a charter registering the grant of certain fields to a Brahmana; the donation was made for obtaining religious merit. Divabbarasi, a Kadamba princess, dedicated a village as an *agrahāra* in the sacred memory of her husband.[35] She had succeeded to the throne on the death of her husband and ruled as the sovereign until her minor son came of age. The record adds that the queen mother looked forward to the day when her minor son would get the throne. During her reign she also granted Yelanagar as a freehold estate to the temple of Śiva which she had caused to be built; to this temple she gave a 'sin-destroying bell'.

The practice of elevating the widow of a deceased king to the position of sovereign ruler is evident in the later inscriptions also. For example, Tribhūvana Mahādevī of the Kara dynasty of Orissa is stated to have been requested by the feudatories to accept the sovereignty which had come to her on the death of her husband.[36] To persuade her to accept rulership, they cited the example of Devī Gosvāmini of the same Kara dynasty who had agreed to administer the kingdom under similar circumstances. Thereupon the widowed queen 'ascended the throne like Kātyāyanī'. Daṇḍī Mahādevī[37] and her step-mother Vakula Mahādevī,[38] both of the Kara family, exercised sovereignty on different occasions; the latter granted a village to one Mihadhica. The imperial Kākatīya dynasty of Andhra Pradesh also produced women rulers of note. Widowed queens came to power mostly in emergent situations and prevented the throne from being usurped. In other regions where women were excluded from rulership, the throne was usurped and the state often fell a prey to anarchy.

Women also shared the responsibility of administration with their husbands. An early grant indicates joint rulership of Gautamīputra Sātakarṇi and his queen, who jointly issued an order regarding the gift of a plot of land to some Buddhist monks.[39] In the early medieval period joint rulership assumed two forms. The wives of feudal lords ruled over the entire principality together with their husbands or else were appointed governors of varying territorial units. The first type included the

Kadamba chieftain Harikeśarīdeva, who was a feudatory of the Cālukya king Someśvara I and who ruled over the Banavasi-12,000 province together with his wife Lācchaladevī.[40] Under the second category came Kañcikabbe, the queen of the Ganga king Śrīpuruṣa. According to a record of 767 Śrīpuruṣa himself ruled the kingdom while his queen governed Agali.[41] A Challakere inscription of 815 shows that Parameśvara Pallavādi ruled Noḷambalige-1,000 and Nirgguṇḍanāḍ-300, and his wife Gavagaṇabbe ruled Madarikal.[42] In a grant of 975, Bhujjabbarasi, mother of Butayya the reigning Ganga king, is described as ruling the village Perbal or modern Kebbal.[43] Akkadevī, the sister of the Cālukya king Vikramāditya V, is spoken of in a record of 1010 as the governor of Kisukad-70.[44] Similarly, Ankabbarasi, the wife of Ganga king Mārasiṁha II, is mentioned to in a charter of 971 as administering Pullungur or modern Hulgur.[45] In a Sira taluka inscription of 900 we hear of the four women of a royal family as ruling over four different principalities.[46]

Women who were called upon to administer territories of varying size appear to have been familiar with the tasks of territorial administration. The training may have been part of a formal education, although works on polity prescribe such training for male heirs only. Kadambamahādevī, the queen consort of Pulakeśī II is depicted as a woman versed in political wisdom, *naya*.[47] Lacchaladevī, who is described as adept in all the arts, had, in addition to text-book knowledge, certain qualifications for rulership. Eloquent and discerning, the lady is described as delighting the whole court.[48] Obviously she took a prominent part in discussions with courtiers. An inscription tells us that Jakkiyabbe, who was in charge of the Nagarakhanda-70 subdivision, was skilled in the art of good government and gave adequate protection to the people of her district.[49]

Some women who appear to have been powerful feudatories administered large territories almost independently. They granted state lands to priest and temples, making a nominal reference to the overlord. Akkadevī who acted as the governor of Kisukad-70 granted in 1058 a charter to god Akkeśvara and the thousand members of his temple.[50] Kañcikabbe, another feudatory of the western Cālukya king, granted 5,000 *kammas* for the supply of food to the ascetics of the temple of Suvarṇākṣī.[51] Similarly, the four women who were administering four different areas, made grants of land in their respective territories for the benefit of Jaina temples.[52] One of the four women was Bijjamadevī, the governor of Baragur, who gave 12 *kandugas*; similarly, Paramamahādevī, who was ruling over Dharmmavolal, gave 12 *kandugas*; Akkabbe, who was ruling over Siyavur, gave 8 *kandugas*; and Dombabbe who was administering Tailokvolal, gave 6 *kandugas* of land.

Women made their mark in the sphere of local administration too. Inscriptions refer to them as district heads and village heads. Some even functioned as secretaries in the state departments while others served as advisers to local officers. A record of 902 refers to the wife of one Bittayya as headman of the village Bharangiyur.[53] Another record of 1055 mentions Caṇḍiyabbe as *gāvuṇḍi,* and Jakkiyabbe as her *mantraki* or counsellor.[54] A charter issued by Śrī Rāṇaka Jayavarmadeva refers to Trikalingamahādevī, probably the wife of the king, as registering the deed of donation.[55] Since the composer and the engraver of the charter are separately mentioned, the queen probably served as the secretary of the state department, and as such entered the deed of donation in the records of the government.

Although the male-dominated society discouraged matriarchal institutions it could not altogether eliminate these. This might help us to explain the large degree of difference which existed between a northern woman whose right to property and spheres of social participation were constantly circumscribed in favour of men and a southern woman who inherited, administered and bequeathed the property and public offices alike, notwithstanding the consistent denial of any such rights by Brahmana lawgivers.

Early legal opinion, as expressed by Gautama, Vasiṣṭha and Baudhāyana, denied proprietary rights to women, and regarded them as dependent upon the father in childhood, upon the husband in youth, and upon the son in old age.[56] Manu and Nārada held similar views.[57] Śabara, who came later, however, remarks in his commentary on the *Pūrva Mīmāṁsā Sūtra* of Jaimini that a woman who desires to perform a Vedic sacrifice should set aside the injunctions of the *Smṛti* and possess herself of wealth.[58] The commentator, who wanted to ameliorate the condition of women, prescribed that the wife is the rightful owner of *pariṇaya* or the property received by her at the time of marriage.[59] She is also stated to be the owner of what is acquired by the husband.[60] Śabara's views partly conform to the early juridical thinking on the subject. For, Viṣṇu, Yājñavalkya and Bṛhaspati, the three early *smṛti* writers, recognize the right of a sonless widow to inherit the property of her deceased husband.[61] Later the attitude seems to have become much more rigid. For example, Medhātithi, a ninth century commentator of the *Manusmṛti* takes a hard look at women when he states that whatever the wife acquires belongs to the husband.[62] He adds that the wife is not to inherit the property of her dead husband.[63] In comparison, some southern lawgivers show a much more liberal attitude in allowing property rights to widowed women. The *Mitākṣarā*, an eleventh century commentary on the *Yājñavalkyasmṛti* by a distinguished south Indian lawgiver Vijñāneśvara states that a virtuous widow is entitled to inherit the property of her sonless husband.[64] Notwithstanding small variations, the consensus of legal writers was not in favour of allowing any substantive property-rights either to the wife or to the widow.

Judging from the evidence of inscriptions, which we have already discussed, it would appear that the restrictive rulings of legal writers, most of whom were north Indian Brahmanas, did not find slavish acceptance among south Indian people. On the contrary the permisiveness allowed to women in matters of property rights influenced the thinking of several writers who cared to take particular notice of the south Indian customs. As early as the fifth century BC, Yāska, commenting on the *Nirukta*, states that in the southern countries the widow of a sonless husband was entitled to inherit the entire property of her husband.[65] In the sixth century AD, Varāhamihira advocates the possession of wealth by women.[66] What is more important, inscriptions speak of women who owned property and freely disposed of it.

Women of the princely families also owned and managed property in their own right as is evident from the example of the Sāta-vāhana queen Nāgaṇikā, who spent royal resources on the performance of Vedic rituals.[67] Similarly, Queen Vijayamahādevī of the eastern Cālukya dynasty gave away a few plots of land to a Brahmana.[68] Gifts of villages as freehold estates to priests and temples also indicate the right of princely women to property. Examples of priestly women receiving landed property in donation, either jointly or singly, also point in the same direction. In 688 the village Navatula in the Ganjam district of Orissa was granted jointly to a Brahmana woman Pillikāsavāmini and her brother Pillaśarmā, as a freehold.[69] Similarly, the 12 *nivartanas* of land granted to a Brahmana woman for the performance of the *prājāpātya* rite was as much the property of the priestess as the 25 *nivartanas* donated to priest Āditya of the Kāmika *gotra* for the same purpose.[70]

Cases are also on record to show that public offices and personal estates could be inherited and administered by a wife and a daughter in succession. An inscription of the Shikarpur taluka of Karnataka refers to the wife of a district headman (*nāḍgāvuṇḍī*) who succeeded to the office of her deceased husband and enjoyed the privileges and emoluments the office carried.[71] The incumbent also inherited the estate of her late husband. Later, her daughter succeeded to this office and the estate. Another woman who had lost both her husband and son and was living with the four sons of her widowed younger sister, must have inherited the entire property of her deceased husband, a man of some influence in the government, so as to be able to spend profusely on works of public welfare and religious merit.[72]

At present, the matrilocal and matrilineal family is found among certain tribes and lowly Śūdras who live in peripheral contact with brahmanical society but are seldom recognized as part of it. The present tension between the Brahmana and Śūdra communities of Tamil Nadu, where status-displacement following the introduction of patriarchal institutions was greater than in other parts of the peninsula, can perhaps be related to this historical phenomenon. However, with the progressive alienation of landed property, administrative authority and trade rights to the brahmanical classes, the roots of Brahmana patriliny struck ever deeper.

In the north, priestesses were looked down upon. The

Manusmṛti warns a Brahmana against eating at a sacrifice offered by a village priest (*grāmayājī*) or woman.[73] In peninsular India, however, priestesses received as much regard as priests. They were honoured with grants of land for the performance of specific Vedic rituals like the *prājāpatya*.[74] Some priestesses even received shares of villages as maintenance gifts.[75]

The Jain community of the lower Deccan treated its nuns and priestesses on par with monks and priests. Nuns served as preceptors of householders, both men and women; they were also acknowledged as preceptors by monks. Priestesses managed temple and monastic properties. The widow of the priest Śrutakīrtti was appointed the manager of the estate of a Jain temple at Halsi and a village was granted to her as a freehold. She was entrusted with the arrangement of important festivals of god Jinendra as also the feeding of Jain monks.[76] Huliyabbajjike of the Suraṣṭha Gaṇa monastic order was yet another Jain nun who served as the priestess of a Jain temple. She received the gift of a village in 1071 from Baladevayya, the *herisandhivigrahika* for the upkeep of the temple of which she was the superintending priestess.[77]

NOTES

1. Edgar Thurston and K.V. Rangachari, *The Castes and Tribes of Southern India,* vol. 3.
2. *EI,* 22, cf. Ikṣvāku inscriptions.
3. *Luder's List of Brahmi Inscriptions,* no. 687 cited in *EI,* 22, no. 8, p. 35.
4. *Archaeological Survey of Western India* (henceforth *ASWI*), vol. 2, p. 9a.
5. *ASWI,* vol. 4, p. 8, Kautsī is derived from Kutsa *gotra.*
6. Ibid., p. 83.
7. Ibid., p. 90.
8. The process has been illustrated in two different essays titled 'Gotra and Social Mobility in the Deccan' and Clan-name and Social Mobility in the Deccan', infra.
9. *Luder's List of Brahmi Inscriptions,* no. 1271.
10. *Luder's List of Brahmi Inscriptions,* no. 158.
11. *EI,* 22, no. 8, p. 35.
12. See R.N. Nandi, 'Gotra and Social Mobility in the Deccan', *Proceedings of the 32nd Indian History Congress,* Jabalpur, 1970; also 'Clan-name and Social Mobility in the Deccan', *Proceedings of the 33rd Indian History Congress,* Muzaffarpur, 1971, pp. 111-18. Boasts of genuine noble ancestry are also more frequent in southern epigraphic records.

13. *JRASB*, 8, p. 3.
14. Ibid., 12, p. 112.
15. See J.H. Hutton, *Caste in India*, p. 162.
16. *EC*, 8, Sb. 9.
17. *EC*, 7, Hl. 64.
18. *EC*, 11, Dg. 17.
19. J.H. Hutton, op. cit., p. 162f.
20. Ibid.
21. Ibid.
22. J.H. Hutton, op. cit., p. 162f.
23. . . . many . . . *Tamal illa ture Devesapana padana nama gurubhaṭṭar-aryan padane namme Timmap odeyar padana namma anna Devodeyara padane namma maga Devanamane gand tandu maduvemada dane yi vak anige tappal illa gou-brammarige tapida hage kote yastaka munde nadevī sava* . . . *Devesa*, etc., *EC*, 11, Dg. 17.
24. *Baudhāyana Dharma Sūtra*, I, 19-26 cited in P.V. Kane, *Dharmaśāstra ka Itihas*, vol. 1, p. 28.
25. *Maṇimekhalai*, book XXII.
26. *EI*, 19, no. 24, p. 137f.
27. *EI*, 31, no. 20B, p. 133f.
28. P.V. Kane, *Dharmaśāstra ka Itihas*, vol. 2, p. 596.
29. Ibid.
30. Ibid.
31. *B.C. Law Volume*, ed. D.R. Bhandarker, Calcutta, 1945, pt. 1, p. 159.
32. *EI*, 15, p. 41, cited in *EI*, 22, no. 17, p. 98ff.
33. *JRASB*, vol. 20, p. 58, cited in *EI*, 22, no. 17, p. 98ff.
34. *IA*, no. 53, p. 163ff.
35. *EC*, 10, *Mulbagal* 38, p. 78, AD 890.
36. *EI*, 22, no. 17, p. 93ff.
37. *JBORS*, vol. 2, p. 422f, cited in *EI*, 22, p. 98ff.
38. *EI*, 36, no. 38, p. 307ff.
39. *EI*, 22, no. 17, p. 98ff.
40. *EI*, 13, no. 14, p. 168ff, AD 1055.
41. *EC*, 10, *Mulbagal* 80, p. 97.
42. *EC*, 11, Cl. 33, p. 100.
43. *EI*, 4, no. 50, p. 350ff, AD 975.
44. *EI*, 15, no. 6, p. 76.
45. *EI*, 24, no. 12, p. 51ff, AD 971.
46. *EC*, 12, Sira 24.
47. *A.P. Government Museum Copper Plate Inscription*, vol. 1, p. 11ff.
48. *EI*, 13, no. 14, ll. 20-3.
49. *EC*, 7, Sk. 219, p. 130f., cited in Saletore, *Medieval Jainism*, p. 155.
50. Cf. *EI*, 15, no. 6, p. 76, AD 1010 and *KI*, 15, no. 6 (2), p. 83, AD 1058.
51. *EI*, 16, no. 1, ll. 43-6.
52. *EC*, 12, Sira 24.
53. *Mysore Archaeological Report*, p. 38 (1911).

54. *EC*, 11, Cg. 30, pp. 172-3, cited in Saletore, op. cit., p. 158.
55. *EI*, 23, no. 42 D, pp. 267-9.
56. P.V. Kane, op. cit., p. 6.
57. *Manusmṛti*, 9.127; *Nāradasmṛti*, 24-6, cited in Kane, op. cit., pp. 900-7.
58. *B.C. Law Vol.*, op. cit., p. 160.
59. Ibid.
60. Ibid.
61. Kane, op. cit., p. 329.
62. Ibid., p. 906ff.
63. Ibid., p. 908.
64. Ibid.
65. Kane, op. cit., vol. 1, p. 329.
66. Ibid., p. 327.
67. *B.C. Law Volume*, op. cit., p. 159.
68. *IA*, 7, no. 53, p. 163ff.
69. *IHQ*, 20, p. 232, AD 688.
70. *IA*, p. 88.
71. *EC*, 7, Sk. 219, p. 130f.
72. *EC*, 8, Nr. 35.
73. *Manusmṛti*, 4.204, cited in *B.C. Law Volume*, op. cit., p. 159ff.
74. *IA*, 6, p. 88.
75. *IHQ*, 20, p. 88.
76. *IA*, 6, no. 22, l. 16, p. 12.
77. *Bombay Karnataka Inscriptions*, vol. 1, pt. 1, no. 111.

Bibliography

1. *Sanskrit and other Texts*

Ādi Purāṇa of Jinasena, ed. Pannalal Jain, Kasi, 1963.

Amarakośa (Kosha or Dictionary of the Sanskrit Language by Amara Singh), Tr. H.T. Colebrook, 1st pub. 1807, Indian Reprint, Delhi, 1990.

Arthśāstra of Kauṭilya, ed. R. Shamasastry, Mysore, 1919; *Kautalya*, T. Ganapati Sastri, Trivandrum, 1924-5; R.P. Kangle, Bombay, 1965.

Bauddha Gān-o-Doha, ed. H.P. Sastri, Vangiya Sahitya Parishad.

Bhāruci's Commentary on the Manusmaṛti, ed. J.D.M. Derrett, Steiner Verleg, Wiesbaden, 1975.

Bhoja-Prabandha, The Velvedere Press, Sanskrit Series, no. 5.

Brahmāṇḍa Purāṇa, text and Bengali trans. by Panchanana Tarkaratna, 4th edn., BEM Press (Bangavasi Electro Machine Press), Calcutta, Bengali Year 1315.

Bṛhannāradīya Purāṇa, text and Bengali tr. by Panchanana Tarkaratna, BEM Press (Bangavasi Electro Machine Press), 2nd edn., Calcutta, Bengali Year 1316.

Bṛahaspati Smṛti, tr. J. Jolly, Sacred Books of the East, vol. 33, Oxford, 1889.

Bṛahaspati Smṛti, G.O.S. (Gaekwad Oriental Series), 1941.

Bṛhatsaṁhitā of Varāhamihira, ed. H. Kern, B.I. (Bibliotheca Indica) Calcutta, 1965.

Caraka Saṁhitā, ed. and trans. in Hindi, Gujarati and English by Gulab Kunverba, Ayurvedic Society, Jam Nagar, 1949.

Caturvargacintāmaṇi of Hemādri (Prāyaścitta Khaṇḍa), Asiatic Society of Bengal, Calcutta, 1921.

Cannabasava Purāṇa of Virupākṣa, ed. S.S. Basavana, Linagayat Education Association, Dharwar, 1934.

Daśakumāracarita of Daṇḍin, ed. M.R. Kale, Delhi, 1966.

Deśī-nāma-mālā of Hemachandra, ed. R. Pischel, 2nd edn., Bombay Sanskrit Series, no. XVII, 1938.

Dāyabhāga of Jīmutavāhana, 2nd edn., Sidhesvara Press, Calcutta, 1893.

Dohākośa of Siddha Sarahapāda, ed. P.C. Bagchi, University of Calcutta, 1935.

Dohākośa, ed. and tr. by Rahula Sankrtyayana, Bihar Rashtrabhasa Parishad, Patna, 1957.

Garūḍa Purāṇa, Venkateswar Press, Bombay, 1963.

Gāthāsaptaśatī of Hala, ed. Sadashiva Atmaram Jogalekar, Poona, 1956; text and trans. in Bengali by R.G. Basak, Calcutta, Bengali Year 1962.

Harṣacarita of Bāṇabhaṭṭa, tr. into English by E.B. Cowell and F.W. Thomas, London, 1897.

Kāmasūtra of Vātsyāyana, Nirnayasagar Press, Bombay, 1900; tr. K.R. Iyangar, Lahore, 1921.

Karpūramañjarī of Rājaśekhara, ed. Sten Konow, Harvard, 1901.

Kūrma Purāṇa, Bibliotheca Indica, Asiatic Society of Bengal, 1890.

Lekhapaddhati, Gaekwad Oriental Series, 1925.

Mahābhārata, ed. with commentary of Nīlakaṇṭha, Poona, 1929-33; Critical edn., Poona, 1927ff; tr. M.N. Dutt, Calcutta, 1895-1905.

Mālatīmādhava of Bhavabhūti, with commentary of Jagaddhara, M.R. Kale, Delhi, 1967.

Mānasāra, ed. P.K. Acharya, Oxford University, 1933.

Mānasollāsa, 2 vols., G.O.S., 1926 and 1939.

Manimekhalai of Sittalai Sattanar, tr. into English by S.K. Ayyanagar, London, 1928.

Manusmṛti, tr. into English by W. Jones, Calcutta, 1794; also tr. by G. Buhler, SBE, vol. 25.

Manusmṛti with commentary of Medhātithi, ed. G.N. Jha, Asiatic Society of Bengal, 1932, tr. G.N. Jha, Calcutta, 1922-23.

Manusmṛti with commentary of Kulluka, Haridas Sanskrit Granthamala, no. 114, Banaras, 1935.

Mārkaṇḍeya Purāṇa, ed. by K.M. Banerjee, BI, Calcutta, 1862.

Matsya Purāṇa, Bombay, Śaka Samvat 1845, text and Bengali tr. by Panchanana Tarkaratna, BEM Press, Bengali Year 1315.

Mayamata, ed. T. Ganapati Sastri, Trivandrum Sanskrit Series, 1919.

Mitākṣarā of Vijñāneśvara, N.S.P., Bombay, 1909; S.B.H. (Sacred Book of the Hindus) Series, Allahabad, 1918.

Nāradasmṛti, tr. J. Jolly, Sacred Books of the East, vol. 33, Oxford, 1889.

Navasāhasāṅkacarita of Padmagupta, Bombay Sanskrit Series, no. 53, 1895.

Nītivākyāmṛta of Somadeva, Manikachandra Digambara Jaina Granthamala, Bombay, 1887-8.

Pālkuriki Somanātha Kavi, ed. Baudara Tammayya, Secundrabad, 1948.

Parāśarasmṛti with the Commentary of Manohar, Banaras Sanskrit Series, Varanasi, 1907.

Pariśiṣṭa Parvan of Hemachandra, ed. H. Jacobi, Calcutta, 1883.

Paṭṭupāṭṭu, ed. and tr. by J.V. Chelliah, Madras, 1962.

Pavana Dūta of Dhoyī, Sanskrit Sahitya Parishad Granthamala, no. 13, Calcutta, 1926.

Periyapurāṇam of Sekkilar, ed. by T. Chentivelu Mudaliar, Madras, 1903.

Prabandha-Cintāmaṇi of Merutunga, ed. H.P. Dvivedi, S.T.G., no. 3, 1940; tr. Tawney, Calcutta, 1901.

Prabhūlingalīleya Saṁgraha of Cāmarasa, ed. by M.S. Basavalingayya and M.R. Srinivasamurti, Mysore, 1940.

Prabodhacandrodaya of Kṛṣṇa Miśra, Trivandrum, 1936.

Rājatarangini of Kalhana, tr. by M.A. Stein, Westminster, 1900.

Rāmacarita of Sandhyākara Naṇdin, ed. by H.P. Sastri, Calcutta, 1901.

Ratnakaraṇḍa Śrāvakācāra of Samantabhadra, ed. by Champat Rai Jain, Arrah, 1917.

Sāgāra Dharmāmṛta of Āśādhara, Manik Chandra Digambara Jain Granthmala, no. 2, Bombay, 1917.

Samarāiccakahā of Haribhadrasūri, ed. H. Jacobi, Calcutta, 1926.

Śilappadikāram of Ilango Aḍigal, tr. into English by V.R.R. Dikshitar, London, 1939.

Skanda Purāṇa, ed. Pausikar, Poona, 1893.

Smṛticandrikā of Devaṇṇa Bhaṭṭa, ed. by L. Srinivasacharya, Mysore, 1914.

Upamiti-Bhava-Prapañca-Kathā, ed. by P. Peterson, Calcutta, 1899.

Uttarapurāṇa of Guṇabhadra, Kasi, 1954.

Vacanaśāstrasāra, ed. by P.G. Halakatti, Bijapur, 1923-38.

Vāmana Purāṇa, text and Bengali tr. by Panchanana Tarkaratna, BEM Press, Calcutta, Bengali Year 1314.

Varāngacarita of Jatāsiṁhanandi, ed. by A.N. Upadhye, Bombay, 1938.

Viṣṇu, Purāṇa, text with Hindi tr. by Muni Lal Gupta, 3rd edn., Geeta Press, Gorakhpur, Vikram Samvat 2009.

Viṣṇusmṛti, with extracts from the commentary of Nanda Paṇḍita, ed. J. Jolly, BI, Calcutta, 1881; tr. J. Jolly, SBE, vol. 8, Oxford, 1880.

Yājñavalkyasmṛti with the commentary of Aparārka, Anandashrama Sanskrit Series, no. 46, pt. 2; Poona, 1904.

Yājñavalkyasmṛti, with the Mitākṣarā commentary of Vijñāneśvara, English tr. with notes, explanations, etc. by J.R. Gharpure, 1st edn., Bombay, 1920.

Yaśastilakacampu of Somadeva, ed. Sundarlal Sastri, Varanasi, 1960.

Yoga Śāstra of Hemachandra (Bibliotheca Indica, no. 172), Calcutta, 1907.

2. Epigraphical Sources

ANDHRA PRADESH GOVERNMENT ARCHAEOLOGICAL SERIES

Copper Plate Inscriptions of Andhra Pradesh Govt. Museum, vol. 1, ed. N. Ramesan, Hyderabad, 1962.

Kannada Inscriptions of Andhra Pradesh, eds. P. Sreenivasachar and P.B. Desai, Hyderabad, 1961.

Selected Malayalam Inscriptions, ed. V.R.R. Dikshitar, University of Madras, 1952.

Select Stone Inscriptions of Andhra Pradesh, ed. P.B. Desai, Hyderabad, 1962.

ANDHRA PRADESH GOVERNMENT EPIGRAPHY SERIES

Epigraphia Andhrica, vol. I, ed. N. Venkataramanayya, Hyderabad, 1971.

Epigraphia Andhrica, vol. III, ed. N. Venkataramanayya, Hyderabad, 1974.

Epigraphia Andhrica, vol. IV, ed. P. Parabrahma Sastri, Hyderabad, 1975.

Inscriptions of Andhra Pradesh: Warangal District, ed. N. Venkataramanayya, Hyderabad, 1974.

Inscriptions of Andhra Pradesh: Cuddapah District, vol. I, 1977, vols. II and III, 1981.

Inscriptions of Andhra Pradesh: Karimanagar District, ed. P. Parabrahma Sastri, 1974.

Annual Report on (South Indian) Epigraphy, for the years 1887-1944/45, Madras, 1887-1995 (Govt. Pub).

Annual Report of the Mysore Archaeological Department, Bangalore, 1935.

ARCHAEOLOGICAL SURVEY OF INDIA

Epigraphia Indica, 42 vols., Calcutta/Delhi, 1892 onwards (Govt. Pub).

ARCHAEOLOGICAL SURVEY OF SOUTHERN INDIA

Vol. IV, *Tamil and Sanskrit Inscriptions*, by Jas Burgess with tr. by S.M. Natesa Sastri, Madras, 1886.

HYDERABAD ARCHAEOLOGICAL SERIES
(BY THE NIZAM'S GOVT.)

No. 18, *A corpus of Inscriptions in the Kannada Districts of Hyderabad State*, ed. P.B. Desai, Hyderabad, 1958.

No. 19, *A Corpus of Inscriptions in the Telingana Districts in Andhra Pradesh*, ed. P. Sreenivasachar, pt. 3 (Text and introductory notes), Hyderabad, 1956.

Indian Antiquary, Bombay, 1872-1923.

Karnataka Inscriptions (Pub. Kannada Research Institute, Dharwar).

Vol. I, ed. R.S. Panchamukhi, Dharwar, 1941.
Vol. II, ed. R.S. Panchamukhi, Dharwar, 1952.
Vol. III, pt. I, ed. R.S. Panchamukhi, Dharwar, 1953.
Vol. IV, ed. A.M. Annigeri, Dharwar, 1961.
Vol. V, ed. B.R. Gopal, Dharwar, 1969.

MYSORE ARCHAEOLOGICAL SERIES

Epigraphia Carnatica

Vol. I, *Coorg Inscriptions*, ed. B.L. Rice, Bangalore, 1886.
Vol. II, *Inscriptions at Sravana Belgola*, ed. B.L. Rice, Bangalore, 1889; revd. edn. by R. Narsimhachar, Bangalore, 1923.
Vol. III, *Inscriptions in the Mysore District*, pt. I, ed. B.L. Rice, Bangalore, 1894.
Vol. IV, *Inscriptions in the Mysore District*, pt. II, ed. B.L. Rice, Bangalore, 1898.
Vol. V, *Inscriptions in the Hassan District*, ed. B.L. Rice, Bangalore, 1902.
Vol. VI, *Inscriptions in the Kadur District*, ed. B.L. Rice, Bangalore, 1902.
Vol. VII, *Inscriptions in the Shimoga District*, pt. I, ed. B.L. Rice, Bangalore, 1902.
Vol. VIII, *Inscriptions in the Shimoga District*, pt. II, ed. B.L. Rice, Bangalore, 1904.
Vol. IX, *Inscriptions in the Bangalore District*, ed. B.L. Rice, Bangalore, 1905.
Vol. X, *Inscriptions in the Kolar District*, ed. B.L. Rice, Section I, Bangalore, 1905.
Vol. XI, *Inscriptions in the Chitra Doorg District*, ed. B.L. Rice, Bangalore, 1905.
Vol. XII, *Inscriptions in the Tumkur District*, ed. B.L. Rice, Bangalore, 1906.
Vol. XIII, *General Index*, pt. I, M.H. Krishna, Bangalore, 1934.
Vol. XIV, *Supplementary Inscriptions in the Mysore and Mandya Districts*, ed. H.M. Krishna, Mysore, 1943.
Vol. XV, *Supplementary Inscriptions in the Hassan District*, ed. M.H. Krishna, Mysore, 1943.
Vol. XVI, *Supplementary Inscriptions in the Tumkur District*, ed. K.A. Nilakanta Sastri, Mysore, 1945.

SOUTH INDIAN INSCRIPTIONS
(PUB. ARCHAEOLOGICAL SURVEY OF INDIA)

Vol. I, *Tamil and Sanskrit from Stone and Copper-Plate Edicts at*

Mamallapuram, Kanchipuram in the North Arcot Dist. and other Parts of the Madras Presidency, Chiefly collected in 1886-87, ed. and tr. E. Hultzch, Madras, 1890.

Vol. II, *Tamil Inscriptions of Rajaraja, Rajendra-Chola and others in the Rajarajesvara Temple at Tanjavur*, pt. I, ed. and tr. E. Hultzch, Madras, 1891; pt. II, ed. and tr. E. Hultzch, Madras, 1892; pt. III, ed. and tr. E. Hultzch, Madras, 1895; pt. IV, ed. and tr. V. Venkayya, Madras, 1913; pt. V, *Pallava Copper-Plate Grants From Velur Palayam and Tandnatottam*, ed. and tr. H. Krishna Sastri, Madras, 1919.

Vol. III, *Miscellaneous Inscriptions from Tamil Country*, pt. I, ed. and tr. H. Hultzch, Madras, 1899; pt. II, ed. and tr. H. Hultzch, Madras, 1903; pt. III, ed. and tr. H. Krishna Sastri, Madras, 1920; pt. IV, ed. and tr. H. Krishna Sastri, Madras, 1929.

Vol. XI, *Bombay-Karnataka Inscriptions*, vol. I, pt. I, ed. C.R. Krishnamacharlu, Madras, 1940; pt. II, ed. N. Lakshminarayan Rao, Madras, 1953.

Vol. XII, *The Pallavas*, ed. V. Venkatasubba Ayyar, Madras, 1943.

Vol. XV, *Bombay-Karnataka Inscriptions*, vol. II, ed. P.B. Desai, Delhi, 1964.

Vol. XX, *Bombay-Karnataka Inscriptions*, vol. IV, ed. G.S. Gai, Delhi, 1965.

TIRUMALAI-TIRUPATI DEVASTHANAM EPIGRAPHICAL SERIES

Vol. I, *Early Inscriptions*, ed. and tr. S. Subrahmanya, Madras, 1931.

Vol. VI, pt. II, *Epigraphical Glossary on Tirupati Devasthanam Inscriptions* by V. Vijayaraghavacharya, Madras, 1938.

TRAVANCORE ARCHAEOLOGICAL SERIES

Vol. I, ed. T.A. Gopinatha Rao, Madras, 1910-13.

Vol. II, *Tamil and Vatteluttu Inscriptions on Stone and Copper Plates*, 3 pts., ed. T.A. Gopinatha Rao, Trivandrum, 1922-3.

Vol. III, *Stone and Copper Plate Inscriptions of Travancore*, 2 pts., ed. K.V. Subrahmanya Aiyer, Trivandrum, 1922-3.

Vol. IV, *Stone and Copper Plate Inscriptions of Travancore*, 2 pts., ed. K.V. Subrahmanya Aiyer, Trivandrum, 1924.

3. Excavation Reports

Deo, S.B. and Gupta, R.S., *Excavations at Bhokardan* (1973), Nagpur, 1974.

Hanumantha Rao, M., *Excavations at Hemmige*, Mysore, 1974.

Mahalingam, T.V., *Excavations in the Lower Kaveri Valley*, 1962-64, Madras, 1970.

Sankalia, H.D., *Report on Excavations at Maheshwar and Navdatoli*, Poona, 1958.

———, *Excavations at Brahmapuri (Kolhapur)*, Poona, 1952.

Sharma, Y.D., 'Exploration of Historical Sites', *Ancient India*, no. 9.

Shesadri, M., *Excavations at T. Narsipur*, Bangalore, 1971.

Wheeler, R.E.M. *et al.*, 'Arikamedu: An Indo-Roman Trading Station on the Eastern Coast', *Ancient India*, no. 2.

———, 'Brahmagiri and Chandravalli (1947)', *Ancient India*, no. 4.

4. Journals And Periodicals

Annals of Bhandarkar Oriental Research Institute, Poona.

Bulletin of Deccan College Research Institute, Poona.

Bulletin of the School of Oriental and African Studies, London.

Indian Antiquary, Bombay.

Indian Archaeology—A Review, Delhi.

Indian Culture, Calcutta.

Indian Historical Quarterly, Calcutta.

Jaina Antiquary, Arrah.

Jaina Siddhanta Bhaskara, in Hindi, Arrah.

Journal of the American Oriental Society, Baltimore.

Journal of the Andhra Historical Research Society, Rajahmundry.

Journal of the Asiatic Society of Bengal, Calcutta.

Journal of Bihar and Orissa Research Society, Patna.

Journal of the Bombay Branch of Royal Asiatic Society, Poona.

Journal of the Department of Letters, Calcutta.

Journal of the Economic and Social History of the Orient, Leiden.

Journal of Indian History, Trivandrum.

Journal of the Kannada Research Institute, Dharwar.

Journal of the Karnataka University, Social Sciences, Dharwar.

Journal of Oriental Research, Madras.

Journal of Peasant Studies, London.

New Left Review, London.

Journal of the University of Bombay, Bombay.

Memoirs of the Archaeological Survey of India, Delhi.

New Indian Antiquary, Bombay.

Proceedings of the Indian History Congress.

Proceedings and Transactions of All India Oriental Conference.

Sāradīyā Ānanda Bāzār Patrikā, Bengali Magazine (Annual Puja Issue), Bengali Year 1372 (AD 1965).

Social Scientist, Delhi.

Studies in History, New Delhi.

5. Foreign Accounts

Adler, M.N., *The Itinerary of Benjamin of Tudela*, London, 1970.

Gibb, H.A.R., *Ibn Battuta, Travels in Asia and Africa, 1425-1354*, London, 1929.

Giles, H.A., tr. *The Travels of Fa-hien*, Cambridge, 1923; rpt. Delhi, 1972.

Legge, J.H., *Fa-hien's Record of Buddhistic Kingdoms*, Oxford, 1886.

McCrindle, J.W., *Ancient India as described in Classical Literature*, Westminster, 1901.

Prasad, Mahesh, *Suleman Saudagar*, Kasi, Vikram Samvat 1978.

Sachau, E.C., *Alberuni's India*, London, 1914.

Spies, Otto, *An Arab Account of India in the fourteenth century*, Stuttgart, 1936.

Takakusu, J., *A Record of the Buddhist Religion (A.D. 671-695)* by I-tsing, Oxford, 1896.

Watters, T.W., *On Yuan Chwang's Travels in India (629-645 A.D.)*, London, 1904-5.

Yule, Henry, *The Book of Ser Marco Polo*, revd. 3rd edn., London, 1904-5.

6. Secondary Works

Abraham, M., *Two Medieval Merchant Guilds of South India*, New Delhi, 1988.

Alavi, S.M. Ziauddin, *Arab Geography in the Ninth and Tenth Centuries*, Aligarh, 1965.

Allchin, B. and Allchin, R., *The Rise of Civilization in India and Pakistan*, New Delhi, 1983.

Alayev, L.B., 'Soviet Historians on Indian Feudalism', *Proceedings of the Seminar on Problems of Social and Economic History*, Aligarh Muslim University, Mimeograph, 1968.

———, 'The Systems of Agricultural Production, South India', in Tapan Roy Chaudhury and Irfan Habib, eds., *The Cambridge Economic History of India*, vol. 1 (1st edn., Cambridge, 1982), rpt. Delhi, 1984.

Ali, S.M., *Geography of the Puranas*, New Delhi, 1965.

Altekar, A.S., *Rāṣṭrakūṭas and their Times*, Poona, 1934.

Althuser, L., *For Marx*, Vintage Books, New York, 1969.

Anderson, P., *Passages from Antiquity to Feudalism*, London, 1974.

———, *Lineages of the Absolutist State*, London, 1977.

———, *In the Tracks of Historical Materialism*, London, 1984.

Appadorai, A., *Economic Conditions in Southern India* (1000 AD-1500 AD), 2 vols., Madras, 1936.

Ayyangar, S.K., *Some Contributions of South India to Indian Culture*, Calcutta, 1923.

———, *Manimekalai in its Historical Setting*, London, 1928.

Ayyar, C.V.N., *Origin and Early History of Saivism in South India*, Madras, 1936.

Ayyar, K.G. Shesha, *Some Vaisnava Saints of South India*, rpt. from Sir Asutosh Memorial Volume, 1927.

Baden Powell, B.H., *The Indian Village Community*, London, 1896.

———, *The Land Systems of British India*, 3 vols., London and New York, 1892.

Bailey, A.M. and Lobera R., *The Asiatic Mode of Production* (An Annotated Bibliography, pts. 1 and 2), 1974-5.

———, 'Karl A. Wittfogel and the Asiatic Mode of Production: A. Reappraisal', *Sociological Review*, vol. 27, no. 3, 1979.

Banaji, J., 'The Peasantry in the Feudal Mode of Production: Towards an Economic Model', in *Journal of Peasant Studies*, vol. 3, no. 3, 1976.

Banerjee, J.N., *Development of Hindu Iconography*, Calcutta, 1941.

Barker, E., The *Politics of Aristotle*, Oxford, 1946.

Barth, A., *Religion of India* (English tr. by J. Wood), London, 1882.

Basham, A.L., *Studies in Indian History and Culture*, Calcutta, 1964.

Benton, T., *The Rise and Fall of Structural Marxism: Althusser and his Influence*, London, 1984.

Bernal, J.D., *Science in History*, 4 vols., Penguin, 1954.

Beteille, A., *Caste, Class and Power*, London, 1971.

———, *Studies in Agrarian Social Structure*, London, 1974.

Bhandarkar, D.R. (ed.), *B.C. Law Volume*, pt. 1, Calcutta, 1945.

Bhandarkar, R.G., *Early History of the Deccan*, Bombay, 1896; rpt. Calcutta, 1957.

Bhardwaj, H.C., *Aspects of Ancient Indian Technology*, Delhi, 1979.

Bloch, Marc, *Feudal Society*, London, 1961.

———, *Slavery and Serfdom in Middle Ages*, London, 1975.

Bongard-Levin, G.M., 'On the Problem of Land Ownership in Ancient India', in *Soviet Anthropology and Archaeology*, XIII, 1974-5.

Brenner, R., 'On the Origin of Capitalist Development: A Critique of Neo-Smithian Marxism', in *New Left Review*, no. 104, July-August, 1977.

Brough, John., *The Early Brahminical System of Gotra and Pravara*, Cambridge, 1953.

Brown, C.P., 'Essays on Creeds, Customs and Literature of Jangamas', *Journal of Science and Literature*, Madras, 1940.

Brown, Percy, *Indian Architecture* (Hindu and Buddhist), 4th edn., Bombay, 1959.

Brown, R., *The Origins of English Feudalism*, London, 1973.

———, *English Castles*, London, 1976.

Buchanan, Francis, *A Journey from Madras through the countries of Mysore, Canara and Malabar*, London, 1807.

Buhler, George, *Indian Palaeography*, Bombay, 1904.

Carr, R.C., *Lingayats*, Madras, 1906.

Champaklakshmi, R., 'Growth of Urban Centres in South India: Kudamukku and Palaiyarai, the Twin City of the Cholas', *Studies in History*, vol. 1, no. 1, New Delhi.

———, *Trade Ideology and Urbanization in South India (300 BC to AD 1300)*, Delhi, 1996.

Chanana, D.R., *Slavery in Ancient India*, Delhi, 1960.

Chattopadhyay, B.D., *Coins and Currency Systems in South India*, New Delhi, 1976.

———, 'Irrigation in Early Medieval Rajasthan', *Journal of the Economic and Social History of the Orient*, vol. XVI, pts. 2-3.

———, *The Making of Early Medieval India*, New Delhi, 1994.

Chelliah, J.V., *Perumpanattrupadai*, 200-10, in *Paṭṭupāṭṭu*, Madras, 1962.

Claessen, H.J.M., *The Early State*, Mouton, The Hague, 1978.

Coomarswamy, A.K., *History of Indian and Indonesian Art*, London, 1927.

Coulborn, R. (ed.), *Feudalism in History*, Princeton, 1956.

Cornforth, M., *Dialectical Materialism*, 3 vols., London, 1952-4.

Cousens, Henry, *The Chalukyan Architecture of Kanarese Districts*, 1926.

Currie, K., 'The Asiatic Mode of Production: Problems of Conceptualising State and Economy', in *Dialectical Anthropology*, 8, 1984.

Das, S.K., *The Economic History of Ancient India*, Calcutta, 1944.

Decaens, J., 'Residence Seigneuriale', *Archaeologie Medievale*, vol. 2, pp. 167-201, 1981.

Desai, P.B., *Jainism in South India and Some Jain Epigraphs*, Sholapur, 1957.

———, *Basavesvara and His Times*, Kannada Research Institute, Dharwar, 1968.

Dikshitar, V.R.R., *Selected Malayalam Inscriptions*, University of Madras, 1952.

Dobb, Maurice, *Studies in the Development of Capitalism*, (1st pub. 1946), 6th impression, London, 1954.

Drekmaier, C., *Kinship and Community in Early India*, Stanford University Press, Stanford, 1962.

Duby, Georges, *The Early Growth of European Economy*, London, 1974.

Dumont, L., *Homo Hierarchicus*, London, 1970.

Dutta, B.N., *Studies in Indian Social Polity*, Calcutta, 1944.

Dutt, N.K., *Origin and Growth of Castes in India*, Calcutta, 1968.

Elliot, H.M., *History of India as Told by its Own Historians*, 8 vols., London, 1867-77.

Finley, M., *The Ancient Economy*, London, 1973.

Freeman, E., *The History of the Norman Conquest*, Oxford, Clarendon Press, 1877-9.

Gailey, C.W., 'The State of the States in Anthropology', *Dialectical Anthropology*, 9, 1985.

Ganguly, D.C., *Eastern Chalukyas*, Banaras, 1937.

Gangoly, O.C., *The Art of the Rastrakutas*, Calcutta, 1958.

Ganshoff, F., *Quest-Ceauela Feodalite*, Brussels, Neuchatel, 1944.

Ghosal, U.N., *A History of Indian Political Ideas*, London, 1959.

Ghurye, G.S., *Caste and Class in India*, Bombay, 1950.

Giddens, A., *A Contemporary Critique of Historical Materialism*, Macmillan, London, 1981.

Gledhill, J., Bender, B. and M.T. Larsen, *State and Society*, London, 1988.

Gluckman, Max., *Politics, Law and Ritual in Tribal Society*, Oxford, 1977.

Gode, P.K., *Studies in Indian Culture*, vol. 1, Hoshiarpur, 1961.

Godelier, M., 'The Concept of the Asiatic Mode of Production and Marxist Model of Social Development', *Soviet Anthropology and Archaeology*, IV, no. 2, 1965a.

———, 'Infrastructures Societies and History', *New Left Review*, 112, November-December, 1978a.

Goody, Jack (ed.), *The Character of Kinship*, Cambridge, 1973.

Gopal, Lallanji, *Economic Life of Northern India (c. AD 700-1200)*, Delhi, 1965.

———, *Aspects of the History of Agriculture in Ancient India*, Varanasi, 1980.

Gopalachari, K., *The Early History of the Andhra Country*, Madras, 1941.

Gopalan, R., *History of the Pallavas of Kanchi*, ed. S.K. Aiyangar, 1928.

Gramsci, A., *Selections from the Prison Notebook*, Lawrence and Wishart, London, 1971.

Gunawardana, R.A.H.L., 'The Analysis of Pre-Colonial Social Formations in Asia in the Writings of Karl Marx', *The Indian Historical Review*, vol. 2, no. 2, January 1976.

Gurukkal, Rajan, 'Characterizing Ancient Society: The Case of South India', *Presidential Address* (Ancient India Section), 59th Indian History Congress, Patiala, 1998.

———, *The Kerala Temple and Early Medieval Agrarian System*, Kottayam, 1992.

Habib, I., 'An Examination of Wittfogel's Theory of Oriental Despotism', *Enquiry*, 6, 1962.

———, 'Distribution of Landed Property in Pre-British India', in R.S. Sharma and V. Jha, ed., *Indian Society: Historical Probings*, Delhi, 1974.

———, 'The Peasant in Indian History', *Presidential Address*, Indian History Congress, 43rd Session, Kurukshetra, 1982.

Hall, K.R., *Trade and Statecraft in the Cola kingdom*, Delhi, 1980.

Handiqui, K.K., *Yaśastilaka and Indian Culture*, Sholapur, 1949.

Harfield, C.G., 'Control of resources in the Medieval Period', in J. Gledhill, B. Bender and M.T. Larsen, eds., *State and Society*, London, 1988.

Hazra, R.C., *Studies in the Puranic Records on Hindu Rites and Customs*, 2nd edn., Delhi, 1975.

Hegel, G.W.F., *The Philosophy of History,* tr. J. Sibree, Dover, New York, 1956.

Heitzman, J., 'State formation in South India, 850-1280', *Indian Economic and Social History Review,* vol. 24, 1985.

———, *Gift of Power Lordship in an Early Indian State,* Delhi, 1997.

Hilton, R. (ed.), *The Transition from Feudalism to Capitalism,* London, 1978.

Hirst, P. and Hindess, B., *Pre-Capitalist Modes of Production,* London, Macmillan, 1975.

Hobsbawm, E.J. (ed.), *Pre-Capitalist Economic Formations,* London, 1964.

Hooper, J.S.M., *The Hymns of the Alvars,* Calcutta, 1929.

Hunashal, S.M., *The Lingayat Movement,* Dharwar, 1947.

Hutton, J.H., *Caste in India,* Oxford, 1963.

Ishwaran, K., *Religion and Society of the Lingayats of South India,* Delhi, 1983.

Jaiswal, Suvira, 'Caste in the Socio-Economic Frame-work of Early India', *Presidential Address,* Section I, Indian History Congress, 38th Session, Bhubaneshwar, 1977.

Jha, D.N., *Revenue System in the Post-Maurya and Gupta Times,* Calcutta, 1969.

———, 'Early Indian Feudalism - A Historiographical Critique', *Presidential Address,* Section I, Indian History Congress, 40th Session, Waltair, 1979.

Kane, P.V., *Dharmaśāstra ka Ithihas,* vol. 1, Lucknow, 1965.

Kangle, R.P., *Kauṭliya Arthaśāstra - A Study,* Bombay, 1965.

Karashima, Noboru, *South Indian History and Society,* Delhi, 1984.

Kesavan, V., *The Political Structure of Early Medieval South India,* Delhi, 1993.

Kher, N.N., *Agrarian and Fiscal Economy in the Mauryan and Post Mauryan Age,* Delhi, 1973.

Kingsbury, F., *The Hymns of the Tamil Saivite Saints,* London, 1921.

Kittel, Rev. F., 'The Lingayat Literature', *Indian Antiquary,* vol. 4, 1875.

Kosambi, D.D., '*An Introduction to the Study of Indian History,* Bombay, 1956.

———, 'Social and Economic Aspects of Bhagavad Gītā', *Journal of Economic and Social History of the Orient,* vol. 4, pt. 2, 1961.

Krader, L., *Formation of the State,* London, 1968.

Krishnaswamy, S.Y., 'Major Irrigation Systems of Ancient Tamilnadu', *Proceedings of the 1st International Conference Seminar of Tamil Studies,* vol. 1, Kualalumpur, 1968.

Krishnamoorty, Vaidehi, *Social and Economic Conditions of Eastern Deccan,* Hyderabad, 1970.

Kulke, H., *Kings and State Formation and Legitimation in India and Southeast Asia,* New Delhi, 1977.

———, (ed.), *The State in India 1000-1700*, Delhi, 1995.

Law, B.C., *Tribes in Ancient India*, Poona, 1943.

Levi-Strauss, Claude, *Structural Anthropology*, Penguin, 1972.

Liceria, Sister M., 'Social and Economic History of Karnataka', unpublished Ph.D. thesis, Patna University, 1970.

Lorenzen, David, *The Kapalikas and Kalamukhas*, Delhi, 1972.

Mahalingam, T.V., *Administration and Social Life under Vijayanagar*, Madras, 1940.

———, *Kanchipuram in Early Indian History*, Bombay, 1969.

Maity, S.K., *Economic Life of Northern India in the Gupta Period (A.D. 300-500)*, Delhi, 1970.

Majumdar, R.C., *Corporate Life in Ancient India*, Calcutta, 1922.

———, (ed.), *The Age of Imperial Unity*, Bombay, 1951.

Majumdar, R.C. (ed.), *The Classical Age*, Bombay, 1962.

———, *The Age of Imperial Kanauj*, Bombay, 1964.

Majumdar, D.N., *Races and Cultures of India*, Calcutta, 1965.

Majumdar, G.P., *Vanaspati* (The Griffith Memorial Prize Essay For 1925), Calcutta, 1927.

Marx, K. and Engels, F., *Selected Works*, 2 vols., Progress Publishers, Moscow, 1951.

Mazumdar, B.P., *The Socio-Economic History of Northern India* (11th and 12th Centuries), Calcutta, 1960.

———, 'Collective Landgrants in Early Medieval Inscriptions (*c.* 606-1206 AD)', *Journal of the Asiatic Society of Bengal*, vol. 10, 1968.

Minakshi, C., *Administration and Social Life under the Pallavas*, Madras, 1938.

Mitchell, P. William, 'The Hydraulic Hypothesis—A Reappraisal', *Current Anthropology*, XIV, December, 1973.

Moraes, G.M., *The Kadamba Kula*, Bombay, 1931.

Mukhia, Harbans, 'Was There Feudalism in Indian History?', *Presidential Address* (Section II, Medieval India), 40th Indian History Congress, Waltair, 1979.

Nandi, R.N., *Religious Institutions and Cults in the Deccan*, Delhi, 1973.

———, 'Origin and Nature of Saivite Monasticism', in R.S. Sharma and V. Jha, ed., *Indian Society: Historical Probings*, New Delhi, 1974.

———, 'Gotra and Social Mobility in the Deccan', *Proceedings of the 32nd Indian History Congress*, Jabalpur, 1970.

———, 'Clan-name and Social Mobility in the Deccan', *Proceedings of the 33rd Indian History Congress*, Muzaffarpur, 1971.

———, 'Origin of the Virasaiva Movement', *The Indian Historical Review*, vol. 2, no. 1.

———, 'Some Social Aspects of the Nālayira Prabandham', *Proceedings of the Indian History Congress*, 37th Indian History Congress, Calicut, 1976.

———, 'Client, Ritual and Conflict in Early Brahmanical Order', *The Indian Historical Review,* vol. 6, nos. 1 and 2.

———, 'Feudalization of the State in Medieval South India', *Social Science Probings,* vol. 1, no. 1, March 1984.

———, *Social Roots of Religion in Ancient India,* Calcutta, 1986.

Nandimath, S.C., *A Handbook of Virasaivism,* Dharwar, 1942.

Narayanan, M.G.S., *Foundations of South Indian Society and Culture,* Delhi, 1994.

Needham, J., 'Review of Oriental Despotism', *Science and Society,* 23, 1959.

O' Leary, Brendon, *The Asiatic Mode of Production,* London, 1989.

Patterson, T.C. and C.W. Gailey, 'State Formation and Uneven Development', in John Gledhill, Barbara Bendar and Mogens Trolle Larsen, (eds.), *State and Society,* London, 1988.

Pillay, K.K., *A Social History of the Tamils,* vol. 1, 2nd edn., Madras, 1975.

Pirenne, Henry, *Economic and Social History of Medieval Europe,* London, 1937.

Prakash, Om, *Food and Drinks in Ancient India,* Delhi, 1961.

Prasad, Awadh Kishore, 'Devadasis: A Study of Temple Dancing girls in South India', Ph.D. thesis, Patna University, 1982.

Prasad, Beny, *The State in Ancient India,* The Indian Press, Allahabad, 1928.

Prasad, Bisheshwar, ed., *Ideas in History,* Bombay, 1968.

Prasad, Kameshwar, *Cities, Crafts and Commerce under the Kusanas,* Delhi, 1983

Prasad, Om Prakash, 'Towns in Early Medieval Karnataka', Ph.D. thesis, Patna University, 1980.

Parasher, A., 'Nature of Society and Civilization in Early Deccan', *The Indian Economic and Social History Review,* vol. 29, no. 4; 1992.

Premi, N.R., *Jain Sahitay Aura Itihasa,* Bombay, 1956.

Rai, Jaimal, *The Rural-Urban Economy and Social Changes in Ancient India,* Varanasi, 1974.

Rai, G.K., 'Forced Labour in Ancient India', *The Indian Historical Review,* vol. 3, no. 1.

———, *Involuntary Labour in Ancient India,* Allahabad, 1981.

Ramakrishanyya, K., *Studies in the Dravidian Philology,* Madras, 1935.

Rama Rao, M., *Eastern Chalukyan Temples of Andhra Desa,* Hyderabad, 1964.

Ramaswami, Vijaya, 'Some Enquiries into the Conditions of Weavers in Medieval South India', *The Indian Historical Review,* vol. 6, nos. 1 and 2.

Randhawa, M.S., *A History of Agriculture in India,* 2 vols., New Delhi, 1980.

Rangaswamy, M.A. Dorai, *The Religion and Philosophy of Tevaram,* University of Madras, 1958.

Rao, S.R., 'Excavations at Kanheri', in S.N. Ritti and B.R. Gopal, eds., *Studies in Indian History and Culture,* Dharwar, 1971.

Rao, Sheshagiri B., *Studies in South Indian Jainism*, Madras, 1922.

Rawlinson, H.G., *Intercourse Between Indian and The Western World*, Cambridge, 1916.

Raychaudhuri, T. and I. Habib, *Cambridge Economic History of India*, vol. 1, Cambridge University Press, Cambridge, 1982.

Ray, Nihar Ranjan, 'The Medieval Factor in Indian History', Presidential Address, *Proceedings of the Indian History Congress*, 29th Session, Patiala, 1967.

———, 'The Rural-Urban Dichotomy in Indian Tradition and History', *Presidential Address*, Bhandarkar Oriental Research Institution on the Occasion of the Institute's anniversary on 29 August 1976.

Risley, H., *The people of India*, 2nd edn. by W. Crooke, Calcutta, 1915.

Round , J., *Feudal England: Historical Studies on the Eleventh and Twelfth Centuries*, London, 1895.

Saletore, B.A., *Medieval Jainism*, Bombay, 1938.

Sastri, A.M., *India as seen in the Bṛhat-Samhita of Varahamihira*, Delhi, 1969.

Satyanarayana, K., *A Study of the History and Culture of the Andhra People*, New Delhi, 1975.

Schraeder, F. Otto, *Introduction to the Pāñcarātra and the Ahirbudhnya Samhitas*, Madras, 1916.

Settar, S. and Gunther D. Sontheimer, eds., *Memorial Stones*, Dharwar, 1982.

Sewell, Robert, *A Forgotten Empire*, 1st Indian edn., Delhi, 1962.

Sharma, B.N., *Social Life in Northern India*, Delhi, 1966.

Sharma, R.S., *Indian Feudalism (A.D. 300-1200)*, Calcutta, 1965.

———, *Social Changes in Early Medieval India (c.AD 500-1200)*, Delhi, 1969.

———, 'Dacay of Gangetic Towns', *Proceedings of the Indian History Congress*, 33rd Session, Muzaffarpur, 1972.

———, 'Problem of Transition From Ancient to Medieval in Indian History', *The Indian Historical Review*, vol. 1, March 1975.

———, 'The Kali Age: A Period of Social Crisis', in S.N. Mukherjee, ed., *History and Society*, (Essays in Honour of Professor A.L. Basham), Calcutta, 1982.

———, *Perspectives in the Social and Economic History of Early India*, Delhi, 1983.

———, 'How Feudal was Indian Feudalism?', *Social Scientist*, vol. 13, no. 2, Feb. 1984.

Sharma, S.R., *Jainism and Karnataka Culture*, Dharwar, 1940.

Sharma, Y.D., 'Exploration of Historical Sites', *Ancient India*, vol. 9.

Shastri, K.A.N., *The Colas*, 2 Vols., Madras, 1935.

———, *Foreign Notices of South India*, Madras, 1939.

———, *A History of South India*. 2nd edn., London, 1958.

———, *Cholavaṁśa* (Hindi), Delhi, 1979.

Sircar, D.C., *Land System and Feudalism in Ancient India,* Calcutta, 1964.

———, *Landlordism and Tenancy in Ancient and Medieval India as Revealed by Epigraphical Records,* Lucknow, 1969.

Sjoberg Gideon, *The Preindustrial City: Past and Present,* New York, 1960.

Slater, Gilbert, *The Dravidian Element in Indian Culture,* London, 1924.

Smith, V.A., *Early History of India,* Oxford, 1924.

Spencer, George W, 'Religious Networks and Royal Influence in the Eleventh Century South India', *Journal of the Economic and Social History of the Orient,* vol. 13, no. 1, 1969.

Srinivas, M.N., *Caste in Modern India and Other Essays,* Bombay, 1962.

Srinivasan , T.M., *Irrigation and Water Supply in South India, 200 B.C.-1600 A.D.*, Madras, 1991.

Stein, B., 'The State and the Agrarian Order in Medieval South India: A Historiographical Critique', in B. Stein, ed., *Essays in South India,* University Press of Hawaii, Honolulu, 1975.

———, *Peasant, State and Society in Medieval South India c. 800-1300,* Delhi, Oxford University Press, 1980.

———, 'Politics and Peasants and Deconstruction of Feudalism in Medieval India', *Journal of Peasant Studies,* 12, 2-3, 1985.

———, 'The Segmentary State: Interim Reflections', in Hermann Kulke, ed., *The State in India 1000-1700,* Delhi, 1995.

Subbarayalu, Y., The State in Medieval South India (600-1350 A.D.)', Ph.D. thesis, Madurai University, 1976.

———, 'Mandalam as a Politico-Geographical Unit in South India', *Proceedings of the 39th Indian History Congress,* Hyderabad, 1978.

Sundram, K., *Studies in the Economic and Social Conditions of Medieval Andhra,* Madras, 1968.

Swamy, B.G.L., 'Sources for a History of Plant Sciences in India', *Journal of the History of Science in India,* vol. 8, no. 18, 1973.

Tambiah, S.J., 'From Varna to Caste through Mixed Unions', in Jack Goody, ed., *The Character of Kinship,* Cambridge, 1973.

Thakur, V.K., *Urbanization in Ancient India,* Delhi, 1982.

Thapar, Romila, *Ancient Indian Social History,* Delhi, 1978.

———, *Presidential Address,* 44th Indian History Congress, Burdwan, 1983.

Thapar, Romila (ed.), *Recent Perspectives of Early Indian History,* Bombay, 1995.

Thorner, D., 'Marx, India and the Asiatic Mode of Production', *Contribution to Indian Sociology,* IX, December 1966.

Thurston, Edgar and Rangchari, K.V., *Castes and Tribes of Southern India,* 7 vols., Madras, 1907.

Tirumalai, R., *Land Grants and Agrarian Reactions in Chola and Pandya Times,* Madras, 1987.

Upadhyaya, B.S., *India in Kalidasa,* Allahabad, 1947.

Upadhyaya, V., *The Socio-Religious Condition of Northern India,* Varanasi, 1964.

Vasu, N.N., *Social History of Kāmarūpa,* in 3 vols., Calcutta, 1922, 1926, 1933.

Wach, Joachim, *Sociology of Religion,* Chicago, 1944.

Warmington, E.H., *The Commerce between the Roman Empire and India,* Cambridge, 1928.

Weber, Max, *The Religion of India,* Illinois, 1958.

———, *Sociology of Religion,* London, 1963.

Whitehead, Bishop, *The Village Gods of South India,* Calcutta, 1921.

Wickham, C., 'The other Transition: From Ancient World to Feudalism', *Past and Present,* vol. 103, 1984.

Williams, R., *Jaina Yoga,* London, 1963.

Wiser, H.H., *The Hindu Jajmani System,* Lucknow, 1936.

Winternitz, M., *History of Indian Literature,* vol. 3, pt.1, tr. into English by Subhadra Jha, Delhi, 1963.

Wittfogel, K.A., *Oriental Despotism: A Comparative Study of Total Power,* Vintage Books, New York, rpt. of 1957 edn. published by Yale University Press, 1981.

Wurth, Rev. G., 'The life of Cennabasava', *JBBRAS,* 1868.

———, 'The Life of Basava', *JBBRAS,* 1868.

Yadava, B.N.S., 'The Accounts of Kali Age and the Social Transition from Antiquity to the Middle Ages', *The Indian Historical Review,* vol. 5, nos. 1 and 2.

———, *Society and Culture in Northern India in the Twelfth Century,* Allahabad, 1973.

———, 'The Problem of the Emergence of Feudal Relations in Early India', *Presidential Address* (Section 1), 41st Indian History Congress, Bombay, 1980.

Yazdani, G., *Early History of the Deccan,* London, 1960.

7. *Dictionaries*

Burrow, T. and Emeneau, M.B., *A Dravidian Etymological Dictionary,* O.U.P., London, 1960.

Kittel, F. Rev., *A Kannad-English Dictionary* (1st pub. 1894), New Delhi, 1982.

Monier-Williams, M., *A Sanskrit-English Dictionary* (1st Oxford edn., 1899), 1st Indian edn., Delhi, 1970.

Suryakanta, *Vaidik Kos* (in Hindi), Varanasi, 1963.

Watt, George, *Dictionary of the Economic Products of India,* vol. 6 (1st Published 1892), 2nd rpt., Cosmo Publications, Delhi, 1972.

Index